Working For Yourself

The Daily Telegraph

GUIDE TO SELF-EMPLOYMENT

Working
For Yourself

FIFTEENTH EDITION

Godfrey Golzen

KOGAN
PAGE

First published in 1975
Fourteenth edition 1993
Fifteenth edition 1994

Kogan Page Limited
120 Pentonville Road
London N1 9JN

© Godfrey Golzen, contributors and Kogan Page Ltd 1994

British Library Cataloguing in Publication Data

A CIP record for this book is available from the
British Library.

ISBN 0-7494-1272-0

Typeset by DP Photosetting, Aylesbury, Bucks
Printed in England by Clays Ltd, St Ives plc

Acknowledgements

We should like to thank the many experts who have provided information for this book and the freelance and self-employed people who have contributed to Parts 2 and 3, particularly those who have answered questionnaires and allowed us to reproduce their comments.

We should be grateful for readers' comments and suggestions. There are as many ways of running small businesses as there are proprietors, and any advice on methods other than those we have indicated will be considered for inclusion in future editions of the book.

Contents

IF YOU'RE LOOKING FOR BUSINESS, IT'S THE BUSINESS.

The last time you needed a decorator or a plumber, where did you look? Exactly. So where better than Yellow Pages to advertise your own company?

It's used more than 100 million times a month* when people want to find a supplier. That supplier could be you.

Find out how to advertise in Yellow Pages by ringing 0753 550079 for Southern directories and 021 455 7930 for Northern directories.

It's the business.

*Source: N.O.P. Corporate and Financial © British Telecommunications Plc 1992.

WHAT EVERY BUSINESS NEEDS, GOOD CONTACTS.

How does a chippie from Carpenter's Park get hold of a wood-turner in Laytham? Business Pages, of course.

There are three Directories covering London, The Midlands and The North West. They are classified business to business directories. Which means they only contain classifications relevant to you, the businessman.

There are over 7,500 classified advertisers in Business Pages and 345,000 business to business companies.*

Simply ring Business Pages on 0772 701899 to get your copy.

It could be the best contact you've ever made.

Preface

The recession has shown that businesses which depend heavily on financial support from the banks and which are based on optimistic cash flow forecasts are very vulnerable. Those that survive best are either service businesses with low overheads, those that have genuinely spotted a gap in the market (but are flexible about moving into other opportunities the moment they sense their business sector going off the boil) or those that have managed to plug into an enduring, recession-proof niche.

The scope of the book

Those who become self-employed, whether full-time or part-time, are joining a trend which, despite the state of the UK economy, remains on an upward curve. The Department of Employment estimates that the total number of self-employed people is around 3 million – over 10 per cent of the workforce.

They are, however, a diverse group and not all will flourish equally or consistently. They include: sales and distribution, specialist consultancy, catering and tourism, technology and cleaning services, skilled crafts and techniques (especially where one person can offer more than one skill), and the professions. In this book the last-named group have been excluded because although there are certain sections of it that they would find helpful, there are nevertheless crucial differences between running a professional practice like that of an architect, doctor or lawyer, and an ordinary business. Otherwise we have identified the self-employed as falling into the following broad categories.

☐ People working part-time, often from home, in addition to a main job, perhaps as an interim stage to setting up a full-time business of their own.

- Freelances who provide a service and work full-time for several different principals.
- Those who provide goods and services as sole traders or partners, usually from premises other than their own home.
- Shareholders in small private companies who are also working directors. They are not strictly speaking self-employed, being employees of the companies they control, but in every practical sense the lessons of this book apply to them.

For any enterprise Part 1, which covers the problems of raising capital, making financial projections and understanding commercial and employment law, will be useful. But it is particularly valuable as a crash course in basic business principles for those starting a small business. Yet the person (designer, typist, teacher, etc) who is simply supplementing his or her income by some freelance work will also find something of value in Part 1: how to assess yourself for tax purposes, the importance of proper invoicing, the part played by professional advisers, and the need to plan workload and meet schedules.

Though the reader should be aware of the several 'audiences' at which the book is aimed and should pay closest attention to the section which is of most direct concern, profit may also be gained from the other sections. And, who knows, today's freelance book designer may tomorrow have his own art studio, with staff to manage, creditors to satisfy and clients to cultivate. The section on business management will at least make you aware of the problems and pressures of expanding the scope of any business, and of the pleasures that come with success.

The second part of this book looks at some specific self-employment opportunities which are divided broadly between those that require capital investment – if on a small scale – and those where the level of investment is minimal or even non-existent. The range of activities described is obviously not comprehensive, but it covers, if briefly, some of the areas in which people thinking of self-employment have been found to be most interested. Certainly the principles that emerge are those that can be applied to any type of enterprise one cares to look at.

- Consider the drawbacks
- Be realistic about the risk you are taking
- Be aware of the competition to what you offer
- Be certain that your enterprise is financially sound
- Know and act within the law as it applies to you
- Use professional advice where necessary
- Fulfil commissions accurately and on time
- Commit yourself totally to a project.

These principles apply to the man or woman with a medium-sized business as much as to the retailer or restaurateur, the part-time editor, typist or translator. If a service is required and completion is guaranteed to a satisfactory standard, people are prepared to pay for it – a reputation is established and customers return. An established group of clients provide a basis on which to expand and perhaps diversify, and, if this is achieved without standards falling, the process will be repeated. Whatever your area of interest and size of operation, we hope that our advice aids that process and enables you to avoid the pitfalls and enjoy the profits of self-employment.

The text of this book was correct at the time of going to press. It incorporates the two 1993 Finance Budgets, but readers should note the tendency to bring in further fiscal measures between Finance Acts.

PART 1:
Running Your Own
Business

CHAPTER 1.1

Going it Alone

Between 1979 and 1993 the percentage of self-employed people in the total UK workforce rose from 7.4 to 12.5 per cent. That was a bigger jump than in any other European Union country, though it does no more than bring the UK up to around the European average.

The important place of self-employment in the economy reflects the changing pattern of employment generally. Big employers in all sectors are cutting down their payrolls and buying in services from outside as and when they need them – as Tom Peters has remarked, there is almost nothing going on in any organisation that cannot be subcontracted. Increasingly that may be true for some goods as well. A logical consequence of just-in-time manufacturing is that components as well as raw materials are sourced from the outside.

But the growth in self-employment is being driven by social as well as economic factors. Self-employment is sometimes seen as an alternative to unemployment. Certainly, this is true in some cases but the evidence is that more people choose self-employment than are forced into it for lack of an alternative. A lot of people simply prefer it to working for someone else, particularly since the concept of a safe job no longer has any place in this age of mergers, acquisitions and rationalisations.

They are being encouraged in this course by the government, even though its policy on interest rates has come in for a lot of stick during the recession. Nevertheless the underlying mood is favourable and the encouragement of small business formation through Local Enterprise Agencies and Training and Enterprise Councils (Local Enterprise Companies in Scotland) continues to gather pace. The enterprise culture is not simply a phenomenon of the Thatcher years. The self-employed sector is now too large, and self-employment has shown itself to be too popular an option for too many people to be a prey to changes of political fortune. Indeed, it could be argued that the self-employed have not made enough use of their political muscle in areas where they have been subject to bureaucratic harassment.

18

From £499 our prices are as
beautifully
proportioned as the
400*ex* series.

Who are the self-employed?

Research by the Institute of Manpower Studies (*Self-Employment in the United Kingdom* by Nigel Meager) has come up with some interesting conclusions:

- Men are more likely to be self-employed than women though the numbers of self-employed females has been going up rapidly.
- More older people are self-employed, which may be a reflection of the fact that the self-employed do not have to retire.
- More married than single people are self-employed, which points to the importance of the spouse (possibly as unpaid help?) in self-employment.
- More highly qualified women than men are self-employed, which may be a reflection of the difficulties women continue to experience in getting to senior positions in a great many firms.
- Self-employed people work considerably longer hours than their counterparts in the employed sector.

What self-employed people do

As might be expected, self-employment is stronger in the service sector than in manufacturing. The arts, building trades and management services feature prominently. Over the past decade entry into self-employment has been disproportionately high in financial, business and personal services such as catering and cleaning.

This also points to the nature of the market for self-employment. It is mistaken romanticism to think that we can go back to a society of individual craftsmen without an unacceptable drop in our standard of living. But maybe, it has been argued, we should leave to machines what machines do best and get human beings to cater to the individual taste, the quirky needs, the one-off problems and the sudden emergencies and breakdowns that machines cannot handle.

This is certainly where the opportunities for the self-employed lie, and one of the objects of this preamble is to make an important practical point. The game the giants play has its limitations, but do not take them on direct. If, for instance, you are a skilled cabinet-maker, do not get into mass-produced furniture: you simply will not be able to get your prices down far enough to make a living, nor will you be able to handle distribution on the scale that mass production implies. Do something the giants do not do, such as making things to individual specification. If you have always wanted to own a grocery shop, do not do the same thing as the supermarket round the corner. Bake your own bread or make your delicatessen stay open round the clock – do something you can do better or differently.

London Society of Chartered Accountants

BOTHERED? CONFUSED? Feeling in need of practical advice and assistance in starting a business, with VAT or talking to the bank manager or the tax inspector?

The London Society of Chartered Accountants Enquiry Service can help to put you in touch with a chartered accountant in your area who can provide help and advice. Please contact:

London Society of Chartered Accountants
52 Tabernacle Street, London EC2A 4NB
Telephone: 071-490 4390

How well prepared are you?

Having a sound idea is only part of the story. How prepared you are to take it further depends on the extent of your experience; not that it is absolutely essential at the 'thinking about it' stage to have all-round direct experience of the sort of self-employment opportunity you want to exploit. But you have to be aware of what you know and do not know about it. You may be a manager who is also a keen gardener and you want to set up a market gardening business. In that case you probably have a rather better knowledge of management essentials than that of a hypothetical competitor who is currently employed by a market gardener and wants to set up on his or her own. But on the finer points of growing techniques and hazards, and where to sell the products, your competitor is going to be much better equipped than you.

The first step, therefore, is to make a list of all the aspects you can think of about running the business: show it to someone who is already in the field to make sure nothing of importance has been missed out, and tick off the ones you think you can handle and consider how you are going to deal with the areas where your experience is limited. The best way may well be to gain practical first-hand experience. If you are

21

Working From Home

Much has been written recently about the increase of 'teleworking' – people working from home either as employees of large firms, connected to their firm via phone, fax and PC, or as a self-employed person running their business from a converted room in their house. Big businesses see teleworking as offering a number of benefits: increased productivity and employee satisfaction; more effective use of office space leading to reduced overheads; and a change from fixed to variable costs ot match fluctuating business cycles.

Of those who are running their business from an office at home, many are using Mercury for their telecommunications services. Over half a million people in the UK have already joined Mercury's Residential Service and are continuing to do so at the rate of 25,000 a month. In the ten years the company has been operating, Mercury has invested £2.5 billion in its network which now covers over 90% of the UK population.

The initial attraction to move away from BT lies in the cost savings. For long distance calls Mercury guarantees minimum savings of 20%* over BT on weekday evenings and 10%* in the daytime and at weekends. For international calls Mercury guarantees a minimum saving of 10%* at all times.

There are a number of other advantages in joining Mercury. Calls are measured to the nearest second and charged to the nearest tenth of a penny. BT charges you for each unit used, always rounding up to the next whole unit.

All customers receive fully itemised bills monthly or quarterly, depending on their preference. This allows them to see exactly how their phone bill breaks down. Mercury also offers the option of cost centre codes so that charges can be allocated out to different people sharing the same phone or as a way of separating out personal calls from business calls. Mercury Customer Services are available 24 hours a day, 365 days a year.

Approximately 50,000 of Mercury's residential customers are registered as working from home. Last year the decision was taken to treat these people as a distinct group of customers with their own special needs. They now receive their own quarterly customer newsletter, "Business Dialogue", which offers advice on subjects such as home insurance, tax and business training. These customers are also offered a number of different call management reports in order to analyse trends in their telecoms spend.

In addition, there is a scheme called 'YourCall' where customers can nominate their 5 most frequently called long distance numbers (one of which may be abroad) and qualify for a further 5% discount on calls made to these numbers. Research shows that on average 5 numbers make up between 50-60% of a customer's bill.

Who should become a Mercury Customer? Call patterns vary but a simple benchmark is that if someone's BT bill is £75 per quarter and they regularly make calls outside their local calling area, they are very likely to save money by joining Mercury.

To become a Mercury customer just phone Mercury FreeCall 0500 500 194 and you can join over the phone (subject to status). Annual charge is just £10 (excluding VAT). Nothing changes when you join Mercury. You do not need a new line or phone number. You will remain in the phone book and you can still call anyone anywhere.

*Guaranteed savings compared to current BT basic rates before any special promotions or discounts are applied. (Correct at time of going to print 04/94)

"I say, are you aware that you can **GUARANTEE SAVINGS** on long distance and overseas calls with Mercury, which **IS PARTICULARLY** useful if you run your **BUSINESS FROM HOME?**

?

FreeCall **0500 500 400** <u>or</u> fill in the coupon

Mercury offer <u>guaranteed</u> savings on long distance and international calls (compared to current BT basic prices before any promotions or discounts are applied).

Annual charge £11.75 (inc VAT at 17.5%). Service available to 90% of homes, subject to status. Details and prices correct at 12.4.94.

Please send me a free brochure describing the benefits of Mercury's Service at home. Post to Mercury Communications Ltd, Residential Sales Enquiries, FREEPOST MR 9564, PO BOX 49, Wythenshawe, Manchester M22 5GJ.

Name: (Mr/Mrs/Miss/Ms)

Address:

Postcode:_____Tel (STD Code):_____Number:_____

My last quarterly phone bill came to roughly £

A CABLE & WIRELESS COMPANY

Mercury
COMMUNICATIONS

Pottery Portraits
...and now Nova Chrome

Ian Howley and his wife Yvonne have spent the last 13 years as directors of Pottery Portraits Ltd, a company manufacturing and supplying photo-glazing machines.

With one of these, photographs can be glazed onto plates and other specially designed ceramics within minutes, giving the opportunity for an entrepreneur to produce personalised giftware and promotional items. There is endless potential and the finished products can be sold through a variety of retail outlets or via mail order, party plan and so forth.

Low capital outlay and high profit margins make this an ideal home-based business with plenty of scope. No special skills are required and each machine is sold complete with a starter kit and video tape illustrating the whole operating procedure as well as with written instructions.

Ian's knowledge of the gift and promotional markets convinced him that there was an opportunity to expand into 'sublimation printing'. This simple and easy method, using a combination of heat and pressure, transfers the dyes from a sublimation print onto various metal, ceramic or fabric items. He decided to launch a business called Nova Chrome UK to run alongside Pottery Portraits. Although they are now entirely different processes, they complement each other very successfully.

Nova Chrome UK supplies the Nova V. Zoom and a range of presses, such as the flatbed press, cap press and mug press, as well as a selection of consumables.

The Nova V. Zoom sublimation copier is the nucleus of the business. With it the operator can produce sublimation transfers, possibly taken from the customer's own business card or logo, in up to seven different colours. The transfers can then be put onto a variety of gift or promotional items using one of the presses that Nova Chrome supply. T-shirts, baseball caps, metal clocks, coasters, plaques, badges, sweatshirts and other items can all be personalised using the customer's own artwork.

With the flick of a switch, the Nova V. Zoom converts to a normal office copier thus adding a bonus to the business at no extra cost. It also uses ordinary copy paper, keeping costs lower for the user.

A video system is also available from Nova Chrome UK. With this, a sublimation photo is taken through a video camera and the image can then be transferred onto a mug or even a baseball cap.

Initially Ian and Yvonne have been selling the sublimation systems to existing businesses, already involved with printing or creating trophies. However, they are confident that their process can be successfully operated from home by anyone with a little imagination and flair. The Nova is no bigger than a normal office copier and the various presses are compact enough to fit into a small room.

The couple get great satisfaction knowing that their customers are operating successful home businesses. Although they do not stipulate that consumable items must be purchased from them, they get steady, repeat orders for materials to use with both Pottery Portraits and Nova Chrome, from plates and glaze to dyes and papers.

An initial information pack on either business is available from Ian or Yvonne.

Ian and Yvonne Howley, Heulfre, Caergeiliog,
Anglesey LI 65 3YL   Tel: 0407 742020

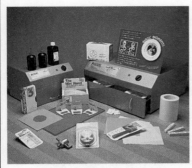

thinking of buying a shop, for instance, working in one for a few weeks will teach you an amazing amount about the public's tastes – what sells and what does not – and you may save yourself hundreds of pounds in making the right buying decisions later on. As far as management principles are concerned, your library will provide you with lists for further reading.

You should also take advice from your local Training and Enterprise Council or TEC (Local Enterprise Company in Scotland). They fund the various Local Enterprise Agencies and are the prime source of information on training and other forms of support for local business. Information is free and counselling incurs only a modest charge. You should also ask about the business start-up courses that are being offered by business schools such as Cranfield School of Management. These courses are heavily subsidised by the government and are very good value for the modest fees they charge. By all accounts, attending such a course will dramatically increase your chances of small business success. The addresses of the regional centres are given in Appendix 1. In Scotland the service is operated through Scottish Enterprise; in Wales by the Welsh Development Agency. In Northern Ireland the Department of Commerce provides an information service. A special service for established rural industries in England is provided by the Rural Development Commission.

Such national services are now being increasingly augmented by business advice given by Training and Enterprise Councils and Local Enterprise Agencies at local level and related to local conditions. They tend to be funded by a mixture of local authority grants and finance from businesses in the area and are often very knowledgeable about local business opportunities. The larger ones run courses, provide guidance on grant and loan schemes, operate professional advice panels and even issue registers of suitable vacant properties. They are run in many cases by experienced businessmen who have been seconded by their firms to help neighbouring industries – a recognition of the fact, perhaps, that no business is an island and that the health of larger firms depends also on the prosperity of smaller ones. A *Directory of Enterprise Agencies and Community Action Programmes* is available from Business in the Community.★

The small business boom is attracting publishers in droves and it is already possible to spend quite a lot of money on books of advice of varying quality. It is worth mentioning, therefore, that several of the clearing banks have got into the act and are producing free books and pamphlets, some of which are very good. Ask your bank manager for any such material.

The importance of planning

If you are going to borrow money to get your firm off the ground, the lender (if he has any sense!) will want to know how you plan to use his money and if the operation you have in mind is going to give him an adequate return on his investment. This means that you must have a clear idea of how your business is going to develop, at least for the next year, where you see work coming from and whether you are going to have the future resources, human and financial, to handle it (see Chapter 1.7 on the importance of cash flow and financial forecasting).

Even if you do not need to borrow money, planning is vital. Landing a big contract or assignment for a new business is a heartening beginning, but well before work on it is completed you should be looking around for the next job. The completion dates you have given should take this into account, unless the amount of money you are going to get from it is so much that you will have plenty of time to look for more work after this first job is done. But that, too, is a matter of planning.

★ Addresses of this and other bodies referred to in the text are given in Appendix 1.

Is self-employment right for you?

Let us leave aside Samuel Smiles-like homilies about having to be your own hardest taskmaster. We will take it for granted that you are not considering working for yourself as a soft option. But apart from the question of whether your health can stand the fairly demanding regime that full-time self-employment implies, there are also other questions you have to ask yourself about your aptitude – as opposed to a mere hankering – for going it alone. First of all, there are severely practical considerations: whether you have enough money or the means of raising it. And remember you will need money not only to finance your business or practice, but also for your own personal needs, including sickness and holiday periods.

Self-employment may mean a drop in your standard of living, possibly a permanent one, if things do not go as planned. Are you prepared for that? Is your family going to like it? Have you seriously considered the full price to be paid for independence? Is your wife (or husband) able and willing to lend a hand?

Insecurity, a necessary condition of self-employment, is not everyone's cup of tea. Neither are some of the implications of being your own master. One of the most important of them is the ability to make decisions and if you very much dislike doing this, self-employment is probably not the right channel for your abilities. You are constantly going to be called on to make decisions, some of them rather trivial, where it does not matter greatly what you do decide so long as you decide *something*; but some of them will be fundamental policy decisions that could make or break your business.

You are also going to be called on to make decisions about people, and these are often the hardest of all. It is extremely difficult to sack someone with whom you have worked in the intimacy of a small office, but sooner or later that kind of situation will land in your lap. So another quality that is called for is toughness. This does not mean overbearing nastiness, but it does mean the readiness, for instance, to part company with a supplier, even if he is a personal friend, if his service starts to fall consistently below standard.

We have touched on the question of your aptitude for self-employment as such, but there remains the matter of your aptitude for the sphere of activity you have chosen. A management consultant friend of the writer's uses a basic precept in advising companies on personnel problems: staff are best employed doing what they are best at. The same applies to self-employment and most people go into it with that in mind. The problem with self-employment, however, is that at least at the outset you cannot absolutely avoid all the aspects of the work, such as bookkeeping, that in a bigger organisation you might have delegated or passed on to another department because you yourself do not much enjoy doing them. What you have to do is to maximise the number of tasks you are good at and minimise the others. This may mean taking a partner to complement your skills or employing an outside agency to handle some things for you: selling, for instance, if you are good at making things but not so good at negotiating or dealing with people. That means less money for you, but at the risk of sounding moralistic, you are unlikely to succeed if making money is the only thing you have in mind and overrides considerations such as job satisfaction.

At the same time, the costs of doing anything in business must always be taken into account. For example, if you take a partner, is there going to be enough money coming in to make a living for both of you? Unless you constantly quantify your business decisions in this way, you are unlikely to stay in business very long. In fact, you should not even start on your career as a self-employed person without investigating very carefully whether there is a big and lasting enough demand for the product or service you are proposing to offer, and whether it can be sold at a competitive price that will enable you to earn a living after meeting all the expenses of running a business.

It is said, of course, that business is a gamble and that there comes the point where you must take the plunge. However, there are certain times when the odds are better than at others. For instance, the closing down of a factory with heavy lay-offs would affect local business conditions, though it may also create opportunities if the demand for what the factory has been producing still continues. You have to weigh up such factors in arriving at the conclusion that your chances of success are better than 50:50. Unless you are reasonably sure you can beat those odds with whatever it is you are setting out to do, you ought to think again or get further advice on how you can either improve your chances or minimise your financial risk.

In conclusion

If you have faced the issues we have touched on in the last paragraphs and feel confident about dealing with them, your chances of success in self-employment, whether full-time or part-time, are good. As for the opportunities, they are legion and later we examine what is involved in some areas. The list obviously cannot be comprehensive (though it should serve as a stimulus to looking in other directions as well) and neither can the coverage of basic management techniques in Part 1. But one of the essentials of effective management is to pick out no more from any topic than you need to know to accomplish the task in hand. We hope that these chapters give you the kind of technical information that you will be concerned with at this early stage of your career as a self-employed person.

Checklist: going it alone

1. Can you measure the demand for your product or service in terms of money?
2. Who are your competitors and what can you offer that they cannot?
3. Is the market local or national and how can you reach it? Can you measure the cost of doing so in financial terms?
4. How much capital do you have and how easy is it to realise?
5. How much money do you need for start-up costs and if it is more than your capital, how can you make up the difference?
6. How long is it likely to be before your income meets your outgoings and how do you propose to manage until then?
7. Do you have any established contacts who can give you business?
8. Is your proposed activity a one-off opportunity or a line for which there is a continuing demand?
9. What aspects of your proposed activity do you have first-hand experience in and how do you propose to fill in the gaps?
10. How good is your health?
11. What are you best at/worst at in your present job and how does this relate to your area of self-employment?
12. Is there any way you can combine your present job with self-employment for an experimental period while you see how it goes?
13. Have you made a realistic appraisal of your aptitude for going it alone, both generally and in the context of the line of work you have chosen?
14. Should you join up with someone else and, if so, is the net income you anticipate going to provide a livelihood for all the people involved?
15. Can you work from home or do you have to be in an office or other rented premises?

Starting a Business

Before you start talking to bank managers, solicitors, accountants or tax inspectors you will have to start thinking about what sort of legal entity the business you are going to operate is to be. The kind of advice you seek from them will depend on this decision, and you have three choices. You can operate as a sole trader (ie a one-man business – it does not necessarily have to be a 'trade'), a partnership, or as a private limited company. Let us see what each of these options implies.

Sole trader

There is nothing – or at least very little – to stop you from starting a business under your own name, operating from a back room of your own house.* But if the place you live in is owned by someone else, you should get the landlord's permission. If the business you are starting in your home is one that involves a change of use of the premises, you will have to get planning permission from the local authority's planning officer. In that case you may also find that you are re-rated on a commercial basis. If you own your house, you should also check that there are no restrictive covenants in the deeds governing its use. On the whole, a business conducted unobtrusively from a private residence is unlikely to attract attention from the local authority but, to be perfectly safe, it is as well to have a word with the authority's planning department since any change of use, even of part of your residence, requires planning permission.

---

* If your business is likely to disturb neighbours or cause a nuisance (noise, smells, clients taking up parking space) or if it necessitates your building an extension, converting an attic, etc, you must apply for planning permission. Your property may then be given a higher, commercial rateable value.

ROYAL MAIL CONNECT

THE FREE PROGRAMME THAT SHOWS HOW ROYAL MAIL CAN HELP SMALL BUSINESSES.

WORKING ON YOUR OWN? MAKE THE RIGHT CONNECTIONS.

If you're working for yourself, you'll be looking to stay one step ahead of your competitors. Royal Mail Connect aims to help you do just that.

A comprehensive guide to all Royal Mail services, it can help every part of your business.

For instance, from advising how to put together a direct mail package, to giving advice about hurrying-up late-paying clients.

It'll even show how to save on expensive couriers, by using fast, but inexpensive Royal Mail services instead.

To find out more, simply write to us at **Royal Mail Connect, FREEPOST (SN 1952), MELKSHAM SN12 7SZ.**

And see how knowing Royal Mail can help your business.

The next step is to inform your local tax inspector or to get your accountant to do so (see Chapter 1.4 on choosing professional advisers). This is always advisable if the nature of your earnings is changing and imperative if you are moving from employee to full-time self-employed status, because it changes the basis on which you pay tax. The inspector will give you some indication of allowable business expenses to be set off against your earnings for tax purposes. These will not include entertainment of potential customers (unless they are overseas buyers) but will cover items 'wholly and exclusively incurred for the purposes of business'. These are spelt out in more detail in Chapter 1.12. Some things, of course, are used partly for private and partly for business purposes – your car or your telephone, for instance. In these cases only that proportion of expenditure that can definitely be attributed to business use is chargeable against tax. Careful records of such use must, therefore, be kept, and its extent must also be credible. If you are not exporting anything in the way of a product or service, you may be unable to convince the inspector that a weekend in Paris was in the course of business! But if you are, he is unlikely to quibble about a modest hotel bill, even if the business part of your visit only took a couple of hours.

The principal cautionary point to bear in mind about operating as a sole trader is that you are personally liable for the debts of your business. If you go bankrupt your creditors are entitled to seize and sell your *personal* possessions, not just equipment, cars and other items directly related to your business.

Partnerships

Most of the above points are also true if you are setting up in partnership with other people. Once again, there are very few restrictions against setting up in partnership with someone to carry on a business, but because all the members of a partnership are personally liable for its debts, even if these are incurred by a piece of mismanagement by one partner which was not known to his colleagues, the choice of partners is a step that requires very careful thought. So should you have a partner at all? Certainly it is not advisable to do so just for the sake of having company, because unless the partner can really contribute something to the business, you are giving away a part of what could in time be a very valuable asset to little purpose. A partner should be able to make an important contribution to running the business in an area which you are unable to take care of. He may have some range of specialised expertise that is vital to the business; or he may have a range of contacts to bring in work; or the work may be of such a nature that the executive tasks and decisions cannot be handled by one person. He may even be a 'sleeping

partner' who is doing little else apart from putting up some money in return for a share of the eventual profits.

But whatever the reason for establishing a partnership as opposed to going it alone and owning the whole business may be, you should be sure that your partner (of course, there may be more than one, but for the sake of simplicity we will assume that only one person is involved) is someone you know well in a business, not just a social, capacity. Because of this, before formally establishing a partnership it may be advisable to tackle, as an informal joint venture, one or two jobs with the person you are thinking of setting up with, carrying at the end of the day an agreed share of the costs and profits. That way you will learn about each other's strengths and weaknesses, and indeed whether you can work together harmoniously at all. It may turn out, for instance, that your prospective partner's expertise or contacts, while useful, do not justify giving him a share of the business and that in fact a consultancy fee is the right way of remunerating him.

Even if all goes well and you find that you can cooperate, it is vital that a formal partnership agreement should be drawn up by a solicitor. This is true even of husband-and-wife partnerships. The agreement should cover such points as the following:

1. Who is responsible for what aspects of the operation (eg production, marketing, etc)?
2. What constitutes a policy decision (eg whether or not to take on a contract) and how is it taken? By a majority vote, if there is an uneven number of partners? By the partner concerned with that aspect of things? Only if all partners agree?
3. How are the profits to be divided? According to the amount of capital put in? According to the amount of work done by each partner? Over the whole business done by the partnership over a year? On a job-by-job basis? How much money can be drawn, on what basis, and how often in the way of remuneration?
4. What items, such as cars, not exclusively used for business can be

Budgeting for Business

Leon Hopkins

All businesses need to plan ahead. Acquiring the skills and discipline of budgeting enables business owners to check how well their companies are doing at any given point, and to take remedial action in good time.

In *Budgeting for Business* you will find the tools you need to:

- *Devise budgets tailored to your business*
- *Use budgets to analyse cash flow, capital spending and profits*
- *Rate the effectiveness of your budgeting*
- *Make the best use of scarce resources.*

£6.99 Paperback 1994 Ref KS042 86 pages (p & p £1.00)
Published by Kogan Page, 120 Pentonville Road, London N1 9JN;
Hotline 071 278 0433

KOGAN PAGE

charged to the partnership? And is there any limitation to the amount of money involved?

5. If one of the partners retires or withdraws how is his share of the business to be valued?
6. If work is done in office hours, outside the framework of the partnership, to whom does the income accrue?
7. What arbitration arrangements are there, in case of irreconcilable differences?
8. If one of the partners dies, what provisions should the other make for his dependants?

There are obviously many kinds of eventualities that have to be provided for, depending on the kind of business that is going to be carried on. Some professional partnerships, for instance, may consist of little more than an agreement to pool office expenses such as the services of typists and telephonists, with each partner drawing his own fees quite independently of the rest. The best way to prepare the ground for a solicitor to draw up an agreement is for each partner to make a list of possible points of dispute and to leave it to the legal adviser to produce a form of words to cover these and any other points he may come up with himself.

37

Private limited companies

Legislation over recent years has made it less attractive to start out trading as a limited company unless you are in a form of business that might leave you at risk as a debtor – as might be the case, for instance, if you were a graphic designer commissioning processing on behalf of a client. The reason for this is that, in law, a limited company has an identity distinct from that of the shareholders who are its owners. Consequently, if a limited company goes bankrupt, the claims of the creditors are limited to the assets of the company. This includes any capital issued to shareholders which they have *either paid for in full or in part*. We shall return to the question of share capital in a moment, but the principle at work here is that when shares are issued the shareholders need not necessarily pay for them in full, though they have a legal obligation to do so if the company goes bankrupt. Shareholders are not, however, liable as individuals, and their private assets outside the company may not be touched unless their company has been trading fraudulently. On the other hand, if creditors ask for personal guarantees, directors of limited companies are not protected and *personal* assets to the amount of the guarantee as well as business assets are at risk in the event of bankruptcy.

There is also another important area where the principle of limited liability does not apply. Company directors are liable, in law, for employees' National Insurance contributions. This is a personal liability which is being enforced by the DSS in the same way as bank guarantees. There have even been cases of non-executive directors of insolvent companies being pursued for non-payment of NI contributions by companies with which they were involved, though the Social Security Act of 1975 states that the directors are only responsible in such circumstances if they 'knew or reasonably could have known' that these were not being paid.

Company directors can also be held guilty of 'wrongful trading', which essentially means trading while they know their company is insolvent. In that case they may be obliged to contribute personally to the compensating of creditors.

Under EC legislation, a limited company can be formed by a single shareholder who must be a director. It must also have a company secretary, who can be an outside person such as your solicitor or accountant. Apart from this, the main requirements relate to documentation. Like sole traders or partnerships, a limited company must prepare a set of accounts annually for the inspector of taxes and it must make an annual return to the Registrar of Companies, showing all the shareholders and directors, any changes of ownership that have taken place, a profit and loss account over the year and a balance sheet.

Apart from the more exacting requirements regarding documentation, a significant disadvantage of setting up a limited company as compared to a partnership or sole trader is that tax has to be paid on actual year basis, both in the form of corporation tax on the company and PAYE which has to be paid on directors' remuneration. A further significant advantage enjoyed by sole traders and partnerships is that any losses they incur in the first four years' trading can be set off retrospectively against the owners' income tax on earnings in the three preceding years. This may enable you to recover tax already paid in earlier years of ordinary employment. This concession does not, however, apply to investment in your own limited company, or to investments made in such a company by those closely connected with the shareholders. If it makes losses, those losses can only be set off against the *company's* corporation tax in other years when it makes a profit. If it fails altogether, then the loss of your investment is a *capital* loss which can only be set off against other capital gains you make – not against other earned income. Therefore, if the nature of your business is a service which does not involve exposure to liabilities that you need to protect – for instance, if you are a consultant, rather than a shopkeeper or a manufacturer incurring liabilities to suppliers – there may be a distinct advantage in opting for partnership or sole trader status rather than establishing a limited company; but see the recommendation to seek professional advice below. There may, for instance, be factors other than trading risks which need to be protected by limited liability. Highly profitable ventures can also benefit from limited company status because their profits are taxed at corporation tax rates rather than the much higher personal income tax ones.

The cost of forming a company, including the capital duty which is based on the issued capital (we shall come to the distinction between this and nominal capital shortly), is likely to be around £200, depending on what method you use to go about it. The cheapest way is to buy a ready-made ('off the shelf') company from one of the registration agents who advertise their services in specialist financial journals. Such a company will not actually have been trading, but will be properly registered by the agents. All that has to be done is for the existing 'shareholders' (who are probably the agent's nominees) to resign and for the purchasers to become the new shareholders and to appoint directors. Full details of the procedures are available from Companies House.

Alternatively you can start your own company from scratch, but whichever course you choose professional advice is vital at this stage. The technicalities are trickier than they sound, though simple enough to those versed in such transactions.

Ultimately, the decision on whether or not to form a limited company depends on your long-term objectives. If you are planning to become an entrepreneur, and to build a business for significant capital growth, a limited company structure and the creation of shares has to be considered at an early stage. It will, for instance, be essential if you want to raise serious amounts of money from outside investors, as we will show in the next chapter. But if you are thinking about what is essentially a salaried income replacement venture, a sole trader or partnership structure would usually be the better and simpler option.

Registration of business names

One problem you may encounter with an 'off the shelf' company is when it has a name that does not relate meaningfully to the activity you are proposing to carry on. In that case you can apply to the Registrar of Companies (Companies Registration Office, Crown Way, Maindy, Cardiff CF4 3UZ) to change the name. A fee of £50 will be charged for this.

The other option is to trade under a name which is different from the company's official one; for instance, your company may be called 'Period Investments Ltd', but you trade as 'Regency Antiques'. Until 1982 you had to register your business name with the Registrar of Business Names but that office has since been abolished. Instead, if you trade under any name other than your own – in the case of a sole trader or partnership – or that of the name of the company carrying on the business in the case of a company, you have to disclose the name of the owner or owners and, for each owner, a business or other address within the UK.

The rules of disclosure are quite far-reaching and failure to comply with them is a criminal offence. You must show the information about owners and their addresses on all business letters, written orders for the supply of goods or services, invoices and receipts issued in the course of business and written demands for payment of business debts. Furthermore, you have to display this information prominently and readably in any premises where the business is carried on and to which customers and suppliers have access.

It is worth giving a good deal of thought to the choice of a business name. Clever names are all very well, but if they do not clearly establish the nature of the business you are in, prospective customers leafing through a telephone or business directory may have trouble in finding you; or, if they do find you, they may not readily match your name to their needs. For instance, if you are a furniture repairer, it is far better to describe yourself as such in your business name than to call yourself something like 'Chippendale Restorations'. On the other hand, if you already have a big reputation in some specialised sector, stick with it.

Legislation makes it possible to protect a trading name by registering it with the Trade Marks Registry at the Patent Office. The advantage of that is that you can prevent other traders from using your name – or something very similar – and cashing in on your goodwill. You can also register a trade mark – the sign or logo that identifies your business on letterheads, packaging and so forth. The activities for which marks can be registered include service industries as well as manufacturing ones.

The rules governing the use of business names are like those for company names, except that the Registrar is less concerned about the fact that a similar trading name may already be in existence. Obviously, however, it is advisable in both cases to wait until the name you have put forward is accepted before having any stationery printed. There are, it should be said, certain words that the Registrar of Companies has proved likely to object to: those that could mislead the public by suggesting that an enterprise is larger or has a more prestigious status than circumstances indicate. Cases in point are the use of words such as Trust, University, Group. National adjectives ('British') are also unpopular. When you get to this stage the names of the proprietors (or, in the case of a limited company, the directors) have to be shown not only on letterheads, but also on catalogues and trade literature.

Limited companies, in addition, have to show their registration number and the address of their registered office on such stationery. This address may not necessarily be the same as the one at which business is normally transacted. Some firms use their accountant's or solicitor's premises as their registered office. You will probably see quite a number of registration certificates hanging in their office (they are required by law to be so displayed) when you go there. This is because it is to that address that all legal and official documents are sent. If you have placed complete responsibility for dealing with such matters in the hands of professional advisers, it is obviously convenient that the related correspondence should also be directed there. Bear in mind, though, that this does involve a certain loss of control on your part. Unless you see these documents yourself, you will have no idea, for instance, whether the important ones are being handled with due dispatch.

Limited company documents

When you set up a limited company, your solicitor or accountant will be involved in drafting certain papers and documents which govern its structure and the way it is to be run. When this process has been completed you will receive copies of the company's Memorandum and Articles of Association, some share transfer forms, a minute book, the company seal and the Certificate of Incorporation. Let us explain briefly what these mean.

The Memorandum
This document sets out the main objects for which the company is

formed and what it is allowed to do. There are standard clauses for this and your professional adviser will use these in drafting the document. The main thing to watch out for is that he should not be too specific in setting out the limits of the proposed operation, because if you change tack somewhere along the line – for instance, if you move from mail order to making goods for the customers you have built up – you may lose the protection of your limited liability unless the Memorandum provides for this. There are, however, catch-all clauses which allow you to trade in pretty much anything or any manner you like. Furthermore, the 'objects' clauses can be changed by a special resolution, passed by 75 per cent of the shareholders.

The Memorandum also sets out the company's nominal or authorised share capital and the par value per share. This is a point about which many newcomers to this aspect of business get very confused. The thing to remember is that in this context the value of share capital is a purely *nominal* value. You can have a company operating with thousands of pounds' worth of nominal share capital. This sounds very impressive, but what counts is the *issued* share capital, because this represents what the shareholders have actually put into the business or pledged themselves so to do. It is quite possible to have a company with a nominal capital of £1000, but with, say, only two issued shares of £1 each to the two shareholders that are required by law.

The issued share capital also determines the ownership of a company. In the case we have just quoted, the two shareholders would own the company jointly. But if they then issue a third £1 share to another person without issuing any more to themselves they would now own only two-thirds of the company. This is a vital point to remember when raising capital by means of selling shares.

Apart from determining proportions of ownership, issued share capital also signifies how much of their own money the shareholders have put into the company or are prepared to accept liability for. Therefore, in raising money from a bank or finance house, the manager there will look closely at the issued share capital. To the extent that he is not satisfied that the liability for the amount he is being asked to put up is adequately backed by issued share capital, he is likely to ask the shareholders to guarantee a loan or overdraft with their own personal assets – for instance, by depositing shares they privately hold in a public quoted company or unit trust – as security. In the case of a new company without a track record this would, in fact, be the usual procedure.

The nominal share capital of a new small-scale business is usually £100. It can be increased later, as business grows, on application to the Registrar of Companies. The point of such a move would be to increase the *issued* share capital, for instance, if a new shareholder were to put money into the company. But, once again, it should be borne in mind that if the issued share capital was increased from £100 to £1000, and a

backer were to buy £900-worth of shares at par value, the original shareholders would only own one-tenth of the business; the fact that they got the whole thing going is quite beside the point.

One last question about issued share capital which sometimes puzzles people. Must you actually hand over money for the shares when you start your own company, as is the case when you buy shares on the stock market, and what happens to it? The answer is yes. You pay it into the company's bank account because, remember, it has a separate legal identity from the shareholders who own it. However, you need not pay for your shares in full. You can, for instance, pay 50p per share for a hundred £1 shares. The balance of £50 represents your liability if the company goes bankrupt, and you actually have to hand over the money only if that happens or if a majority at a shareholders' meeting requires you to do so. The fact that you have not paid in full for shares issued to you does not, however, diminish your entitlement to share in the profits, these being distributed as dividends according to the proportion of share capital issued. The same applies to outside shareholders, so if you are raising money by selling shares to people outside the firm, you should normally ensure that they pay in full for any capital that is issued to them.

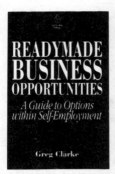

The Articles of Association

These are coupled together with the Memorandum, and set out the rules under which the company is run. They govern matters such as issue of the share capital, appointment and powers of directors and proceedings at general meetings. As in the case of the Memorandum the clauses are largely standard ones, but those relating to the issue of shares should be read carefully. It is most important that there should be a proviso under which any new shares that are issued should be offered first of all to the existing shareholders in the proportion in which they already hold shares. This is particularly so when three or more shareholders are involved, or when you are buying into a company; otherwise the other shareholders can vote to water down your holding in the company whenever they see fit by issuing further shares. For the same reason, there should be a clause under which any shareholder who wants to transfer shares should offer them first of all to the existing shareholders. The Articles of Association also state how the value of the shares is to be determined, the point here being that if the company is successful and makes large profits, the true value of the shares will be much greater than their par value of £1, 50p or whatever. It should be noted, though, that the market valuation of the shares does not increase the liability of shareholders accordingly. In other words, if your £1 par shares are actually valued at, say, £50, your liability still remains at £1.

Table A of the Companies Act of 1948, which can be purchased at any HMSO branch, sets out a specimen Memorandum and Articles.

The minute book

Company law requires that a record be kept of the proceedings at both shareholders' and directors' meetings. These proceedings are recorded in the minute book, which is held at the company's registered office. Decisions made at company meetings are signed by the chairman and are legally binding on the directors if they are agreed by a majority. Therefore, any points of procedure that are not covered by the Memorandum and Articles of Association can be written into the minutes and have the force of law, provided that they do not conflict with the former two documents. Thus, the various responsibilities of the directors can be defined and minuted at the first company meeting; so can important matters such as who signs the cheques. It is generally a good idea for these to carry two signatures to be valid.

The common seal

This used to be a stamp affixed with the authority of the directors, but nowadays documents can be executed by the signatures of two directors. That has the same legal effect as the seal used to have, but it may still be used in some special circumstances.

46

"How to cut your mortgage payments in half (or even more!)"

Written by an insider who's been helping clients for years to dramatically reduce their mortgage bills. A MUST read!

Which is easiest - to earn more money, or to pay less out?

This Kogan Page/Daily Express book is jam-packed full of exciting new businesses that you can start NOW to make more money, full time or part time. But have you ever thought, I mean REALLY thought, about WHY you want to earn more money?

A great chunk of most people's monthly income goes on paying off a mortgage. It's the largest debt most of us ever take on, and certainly leaves many running simply to keep up with the outgoings. But what if there were ways to dramatically reduce that burden and make the whole thing much more manageable?

Fortunately there are ways - lots of them - but only a few are known or seriously considered by those taking out a mortgage. Some consultants know these "tricks of the trade" and help their clients to structure their mortgages in the most effective way. One such has written a blockbuster of a new book on how to go about reducing YOUR monthly outgoings - "How To Cut Your Mortgage Payments In Half (Or Even More!)."

Even after starting with a mortgage it is still possible to arrange things to your benefit. All you need is "the knowledge" of what to do. This book will give you that - and more!

What about both?

"How To Cut Your Mortgage Payments In Half (Or Even More!)" is available EXCLUSIVELY from agents for **Breakout!** , the publishing initiative from The Marketing Network. Other titles available within **Breakout!** cover a wide range of subjects, each of them vital to achieving success today.

Content, layout, illustration and presentation are always of the highest possible quality, making these books that people like to buy AND sell! You can be involved NOW and in at the start of what look set to be record sales. For FREE details please fill in the slip and send off to our FREEPOST address. We'll return your action pack the same day.

YES, I want to stay ahead and obtain full details NOW!

Tell me about Breakout! and the opportunity as soon as possible.

Name ....
Address ....
....
....
Postcode ....
Tel. No: ....

Please cut out, or copy, and send to:-

**The Marketing Network
(11013KP)
FREEPOST 600
Ramsgate
Kent
CT11 8BR**

The Certificate of Incorporation

When the wording of the Memorandum and Articles of Association has been agreed and the names of the directors and the size of the nominal capital have been settled, your professional adviser will send the documents concerned to the Registrar of Companies. He will issue a Certificate of Incorporation which is, as it were, the birth certificate of your company.

Company directors

When your Certificate of Incorporation arrives you and your fellow shareholders are the owners of a fully fledged private limited company. You will almost certainly also be the directors. This title in fact means very little. A director is merely an employee of the company, who is entrusted by the shareholders with the running of it. He need not himself be a shareholder at all, and he can be removed by a vote of the shareholders which, since each share normally carries one vote, is a good reason for not losing control of your company by issuing a majority shareholding to outsiders.

Another good reason is that since the ownership of the company is in proportion to the issued share capital, so also is the allocation of profits, when you come to make them. If you let control pass to an outsider for the sake of raising a few hundred pounds now – there are other means of raising capital than the sale of shares, as we shall show in Chapter 1.3 – you will have had all the problems of getting things going, while only receiving a small part of the rewards. Remember, furthermore, that without control you are only an employee, even if you are called 'managing director'.

Checklist: setting up in business

Sole trader

1. Do you need planning permission to operate from your own home?
2. Does your lease allow you to carry on a trade from the premises you intend to use?
3. If you own the premises, whether or not they are your home as well, are there any restrictive covenants which might prevent you from using them for the purpose intended?
4. Have you notified your tax inspector that the nature of your earnings is changing?

SCODIE DEYONG
CHARTERED ACCOUNTANTS

071-935-0163   0642-250609

UNITED HOUSE, 23 DORSET STREET, LONDON W1H 3FT AND: 39 WILSON STREET, MIDDLESBROUGH, TS1 1SA We are a four partner practice, specialising in small and medium size businesses and personal taxation. We provide an in depth business start-up service including all statutory registrations, cashflow projections, budgeting and system implementation. Registered Auditors.

---

5. Are you aware of the implications of being a sole trader if your business fails?
6. Have you taken steps to register a business name?

Partnerships

1. Points 1 to 6 above also apply to partnerships. Have you taken care of them?
2. How well do you know your partners – personally and as people to work with?
3. If you do not know them well, what evidence do you have of their personal and business qualities?
4. What skills, contacts or other assets (such as capital) can they bring into the business?
5. Have you asked your solicitor to draw up a deed of partnership and does it cover all the eventualities you can think of?
6. Have you talked to anybody who is in, or has tried, partnership in the same line of business, to see what the snags are?

Private limited companies

1. Do you have the requisite minimum number of shareholders (two)?
2. Do you have a competent company secretary, who can carry out the legal duties required under the Companies Acts?
3. Are you yourself reasonably conversant with those duties?
4. Have you registered, if this is required, a company name and a business name?
5. Has permission been granted to use the names chosen?
6. Have the necessary documents been deposited with the Registrar of Companies? (Memorandum and Articles of Association, a statutory declaration of compliance with registration requirements, a statement of nominal share capital.)

7. Have you read and understood the Memorandum and Articles? Do they enable you to carry out all present and any possible future objects for which the company is formed?
8. Do your stationery, catalogues, letterheads, etc show all the details required by the Companies Acts?
9. Is the Registration Certificate displayed in the company's registered office, as required by law?
10. Do you understand the wide range of benefits – company cars, other business expenses, limited liability, self-administered pension schemes, etc – enjoyed by limited companies?
11. Clauses 1 to 3 of the 'Sole trader' checklist may also apply to you. If so, have you taken care of them?

CHAPTER 1.3

Raising Capital

There are many methods of raising money. Some of these are direct forms of borrowing or obtaining loans; others are ways in which you can spin out your cash resources. But for most small businesses, and many large ones, bank borrowing is the one most widely used.

Approaching your bank

Banks make money by using the funds deposited with them to lend out at rates of interest which vary according to government policy. During periods of economic expansion that rate will be lower – and money easier to get – than during the 'stop' parts of the 'stop and go cycle' which has characterised the British economy since the war. But banks, like everybody else, have to continue to trade even through less prosperous times. You will find, therefore, that the bank manager will be willing to discuss making money available to you, because potentially you are a source of income to him. How much that will be depends somewhat on the size of the branch you are approaching. This is an argument in favour of going to a large branch if you need a sizeable sum; on the other hand, in a smaller community, where personal contacts still matter, your professional adviser may well have a shrewd idea of what the bank manager's lending limits are.

Whether you can convince him that your business is a good risk depends on how well you have thought out your approach. To some extent he will go on personal impressions and on what he can gather of your previous business experience. If you have already been running your own firm for a year or two he will have some hard evidence to go on in the shape of your profit and loss account and your balance sheet. He will look at the financial position of your firm, particularly the relationship of current assets to current liabilities and of debtors to

creditors (see Chapter 1.5). He will want to be satisfied that you are valuing your stock realistically and he will want to know how much money you (and your partners, if you have any) have put into the business from your own resources. In the case of a limited company he will want to know what the issued share capital is. Proposals for lending to a new business will need to be fully worked out and have realistic and thorough cash flow projection.

The bank will be looking to see whether your business satisfies three criteria: first, that its money is secure, and in the case of new business it will probably ask for security to be in the shape of tangible items like fixed assets within the business or shares and other assets belonging to the owners in their private capacity in a ratio which may be as high as 1:1; second, that your firm is likely to have an inflow of enough liquid assets to enable it to recall its money, if necessary; third, that you will be able to make profitable use of it and pay the interest without difficulty.

There is a saying that banks will only lend you money if you do not need it and reading these requirements you may be coming to the conclusion that there is an element of truth in it. But what it really means is that it is no use going to a bank to bail you out of trouble. A business in trouble generally requires assistance on the management side at the very least and banks are just not in a position to provide such assistance, no matter how glowing the prospects might be if the firm could be brought back on track. So the bank manager is only going to be looking at present and quantifiable situations. He will not be very interested in often vague assets such as goodwill and even less interested in your hopes for the future.

If you have only just set up in business you may not have much more than hopes for the future to offer, and the bank manager will obviously be cautious in such cases. But can these hopes be quantified, and have you outlined a thorough cash flow budget? If you are opening, say, a new restaurant, facts such as that you and your wife are excellent cooks, have attended courses in catering and have established that there would be a demand for a good place to eat in a particular locality are relevant. But what the bank also wants to know is what your start-up costs are going to be, whether you have fully worked out what your overheads and direct costs are (ie items like rent, rates, gas and electricity, depreciation on equipment, staff wages and the cost of food), what relation these are going to have to your charges for meals, and what levels of seat occupancy you need to achieve to make a profit. This may take quite a lot of working out and it is advisable that you consult closely with your accountant in preparing your case for the bank. Indeed it may be a good idea to take your accountant along with you when you are approaching the bank for financial help.

It is, however, not impossible to do this by yourself. What you need is a 'business plan' and all the banks actually have kits which show you how to prepare them – the one produced by NatWest is particularly good. Even if you do not need finance it is a good idea to prepare a business plan because it will focus your mind on the main issues that are likely to determine the success of your venture. The salient points are:

- [ ] Your business experience.
- [ ] Your existing assets and liabilities.
- [ ] The product or service you are proposing to offer, the geographical market for it and how you propose to reach it.
- [ ] The likely demand for it – ie whether it is continuing and to what extent it is seasonal or susceptible to technological obsolescence.
- [ ] Competition. Where it is and how you propose to counter it by means of price, service, etc.
- [ ] Requirements for and likely costs of premises and/or equipment.
- [ ] How much of your own money you are proposing to put in.
- [ ] The amount of finance required and what it is going to be used for.
- [ ] What security you are able to offer.
- [ ] Cash flow and profit and loss forecast for the first 12 months.

On the basis of this information the bank manager will decide what form of help he is able to offer.

The commonest form of help, as far as the small business is concerned, is an overdraft rather than a bank loan. You will be given facilities to overdraw up to a certain amount, but the advantage of an overdraft, as opposed to a loan, is that interest (usually 2 to 3 per cent above base lending rate) is paid only on the actual amount by which you are overdrawn. Overdrafts are particularly useful, therefore, for the firm whose pattern of business fluctuates, such as the market gardener whose income is higher in spring than in winter, or a business which needs money to finance a large contract until the first progress payments are received. The disadvantage of an overdraft is that it can be called in. Though in practice this rarely happens, it is unwise to use money raised in this way to finance medium- and long-term requirements, particularly those which make no immediate contribution to profits, such as having your office done up! A more likely peril than the overdraft being called in, however, is the fluctuation of interest rates. If these go up sharply because of some economic crisis, you want to be in a position where you are keeping the facility you are using down to a minimum.

Overdrafts are not a suitable way to finance longer-term needs, such as plant, business equipment and premises. For them it is best to take out a bank loan, though for certain legal and technical reasons some banks now attach a minimum figure of £15,000 to such arrangements. The duration can be as long as 20 years, though 5 to 10 years is more usual. The longer the period of the loan and the larger the amount – size and duration usually being connected – the more detailed the business plan will have to be.

During the period of the loan, the borrower pays interest and repays the capital sum. As with overdrafts, interest rates are usually 2 to 3 per cent above base rate – sometimes more – but there is some minor scope for negotiation about that. This is worth some investigatory shopping around, because over a long period of time even a fraction of a percentage point can add up to a lot of money when larger sums have been borrowed.

Some schemes also offer the option between a rate of interest fixed at the time of borrowing and a variable one. The former type is advantageous if interest rates are low at this point, though the reverse is true if they are not. There are also schemes which give the option to switch between fixed and variable rates during the term of the loan.

For larger sums you might consider, with the help of your trusty financial adviser, an approach to the Investors in Industry (3i) Group. Its London office is at 91 Waterloo Road, London SE1 8XP, but it also has local offices in other cities. The advantage of 3i is that although it is a commercial body (it was in fact founded by the clearing banks and the Bank of England), it is rather less aggressive than some of its competitors in its approach to participation in the equity and management of the companies to which it lends money; but it is not, on the whole, interested in getting involved in businesses that are not yet established, especially small ones.

In the case of a limited company, the bank is likely to call on individual directors to guarantee any overdrafts or loans against their personal resources. There are certain pitfalls about some forms of guarantee and it is vital that you check with your solicitor when entering into such an arrangement. The most common cause of problems comes when you form a business with partners or shareholders outside your family. The bank will ask that your guarantee will be on a 'joint and several' basis. This harmless-sounding phrase means that if things go wrong and the bank calls in its guarantee, they will collect the money not from the individual guarantors but from the one or ones whom they have identified as being most able to pay. Those who have met their obligations are then left to make their own arrangements to collect from those who have not – the banks will not take action to pursue the defaulter. The enormous costs of litigation then mean that unless the sums involved are very large it is not worth while taking legal action. For instance, one group of 'joint and several' guarantors among whom such a problem arose were told by their bank manager that it would probably not be worth taking action over a default of under £3000. Legal costs would swallow up such a sum and even if they won their case they might not get costs.

If you find unacceptable the terms under which your bank is offering finance, it is worth shopping around to see if you can get a better deal elsewhere. The banks are now much more competitive with each other than they used to be and have become very well aware that the government is keeping a sharp eye on evidence of interest rate cartels between them.

You might also try one of the growing number of foreign banks now located in London. The American ones are reported to combine the highest degree of reputability with adventurousness in advancing risk capital.

Money from local authorities

Local authorities are empowered to spend a certain percentage of the rates in the general interest of the area, including business development. That means that grants may be available for such purposes as start-ups, job creation, rent or improvement subsidies.

The existence of grants for such purposes is not usually well publicised, but Local Enterprise Agencies (a complete list of these is given in the *Directory of Enterprise Agencies and Community Action Programmes*, available from Business in the Community – see address in Appendix 1) should have information on grants in their areas and who to contact about them at the local authority offices.

It is worth bearing in mind that these grants are not necessarily restricted to existing ratepayers. The object is to attract businesses and create employment, so if the local authority where you live refuses you a grant, a neighbouring one might take a different view – assuming, of course, that you agree to locate your business there.

In some cases local authorities will make loans even if they are unwilling or unable to offer a grant. The important thing is to find out what their criteria and objectives are in framing your application. In some London boroughs, for instance, special consideration is given to businesses which undertake to employ members of ethnic minority groups. Again, the Local Enterprise Agency should be able to shed some light on this. But whatever approach you decide to use, it will have to be based on a business plan similar to the one you use to borrow money from the bank which is described earlier in the chapter.

Private Loans

You may have friends or relatives who are prepared to lend you money, but private loans are a rich source of misunderstanding and so you should be clear about all the implications of such an arrangement. The best plan is to get a solicitor to draw up the terms of the loan, covering the rate of interest, the period over which the loan is repayable and the circumstances under which it can be withdrawn. It must also be made clear to what extent, if any, the lender has any say in the running of the

Getting It All *Together*

By the year 2000, 50% of all adults – worldwide – will be single. This fact alone substantiates the claim that personal introduction services are among the fastest growing industries in the world.

With over 110 franchise offices in the United States and Canada, Together is the world's largest personal introduction service, ranked Number 1 in the franchise service category by *Entrepreneur Magazine* an unprecedented three years in a row. Together is based on the vision that it can make a difference in the lives of thousands of people seeking companionship. Together offices enjoyed worldwide sales of $40 million dollars (US) in 1992, in excess of $50 million in 1993, and project an additional 25% increase in 1994 and beyond. Thousands of people have used Together's services with the vast majority achieving their goal of establishing a long-term relationship.

The company's enormous success led to the establishment of offices in the United Kingdom – in London, Kingston and Manchester – as trial centres for the European market. "All indications point towards a very strong potential market for European operations," said Brian Pappas, President of Together Introduction Limited, "and that's why we are offering a limited number, between ten and twelve franchise opportunities in England, Scotland and Wales."

During 1994, Together also expects to offer franchises in Spain, Germany, Belgium and the Netherlands. Towards the end of 1994, expectations are that planning will begin for similar operations in Asia, South Africa and Australia.

Personal introduction services are gaining greater acceptance everywhere. Couple this with the fact that 65% of sole proprietor businesses fail in the first year compared to the 94% success rate of franchises, and you have a compelling argument for joining the people who are working Together.

business and what the nature of this control is. Normally, however, the lender should not be entitled to participation in management matters; nor does the existence of his loan entitle him to a share of the profits, no matter how strong a moral claim he thinks he might have once your business starts making real money. In the case of a limited company, you must explain to the lender that a loan is not the same thing as a shareholding, though of course the offer of a loan might be conditional on acquiring shares or the option to acquire them. You should be clear about the implications of this: it entitles the shareholder to a percentage of profits in proportion to his holdings, and though loans can be repaid it is virtually impossible to dismantle issued share capital in this way.

Often private loans are not offered directly but in the form of guaranteeing an overdraft, on the basis that if the recipient of the overdraft is unable to repay it, the guarantor is liable for that amount. Losses incurred by the guarantor of a capital loan can be treated as a capital loss, to be set off against capital gains.

Over the last few years there have been various government initiatives to encourage investment in small enterprises and these have been developed into two main strands.

The Enterprise Investment Scheme. This scheme replaces the Business Expansion Scheme which was discontinued in 1993. Investors can still qualify for tax relief on funds invested in small, unquoted companies but the level of relief has been reduced from 40 to 20 per cent. However, the amount an individual can invest is now £100,000 per annum, a sharp increase on the £40,000 level under the old BES, and he or she gets capital gains tax relief on the sale of shares in an investment of this kind. The amount qualifying companies can raise by this method has also been raised to £1 million a year.

The Loan Guarantee Scheme. The government is clearly putting its weight behind this one and its support was emphasised in the 1993 Budget. The idea of the scheme, which was launched in 1981, is that the government guarantees the bank for a large proportion of a business loan when it feels the idea behind a proposition is basically sound but where the bank is unable to take the risk for other reasons.

There are two tiers to the scheme. Established businesses that have been trading for at least two years can borrow up to £250,000, with the government guaranteeing 85 per cent of that. A sum of that size requires DTI approval, but there is a small loan facility of up to £30,000 (the minimum is £5000) for less ambitious enterprises which can be processed much more quickly. That also carries an 85 per cent guarantee.

In both cases there is a small premium of 0.5 per cent payable for the guaranteed amount of the loan.

Money from the government

The government has millions of pounds available to foster the development of new and/or small businesses, the money being offered in the form of cash grants and special rate loans. In particular, it is trying to promote industrial development in the so-called special development areas, which in the main are those areas where traditional industries, such as shipbuilding, are on the decline and where unemployment is therefore apt to be high. The minimum project values go as low as £10,000 to £50,000 and though the authorities tend to look more favourably at established businesses which are relocating in development areas, the prospects are certainly worth investigating if you are in or are thinking of moving to such an area or to a New Town, where additional special aid may be available. Development areas offer the further advantage of usually having a large pool of local labour, and though the spectre of unemployment is no longer a guarantee for getting a cooperative labour force together, unions in such areas are often fairly realistic in their demands. Application forms for assistance in moving to a development area can be obtained from the Department of Trade and Industry, 1 Victoria Street, London SW1H 0ET.

If your proposed enterprise is in a small town, a run-down part of a large one, or a rural area in England, you should contact your Local Enterprise Agency (addresses obtainable from Business in the Community) and your local Training and Enterprise Council, or TEC.

A number of similar regional bodies also exist. These include the Welsh Development Agency, the Scottish Enterprise, Highlands and Islands Enterprise, and the Northern Ireland Development Unit. Your regional Small Firms Centre should be able to advise you on whether you have a case for approaching them.

But what about the marvellous invention that nobody will finance? Is the government prepared to sponsor British initiatives in new technology? The answer is a guarded 'yes'. There is such a body, but it is reputed to take an extremely cautious view of approaches made to it. Perhaps for this reason and because it demands a 50:50 share of the action if the idea works, it has been financially very successful. The body in question is the British Technology Group, 101 Newington Causeway, London SE1 6BU.

Business Start-Up Scheme

This scheme, formerly called the Enterprise Allowance scheme, has emerged as the most accessible and widely used of all grant sources. The target for the scheme is 100,000 entrants a year at least.

If you have been unemployed for six weeks, have a viable idea for starting your own business and are prepared to put £1000 of your own money into it (this can be a loan), you may be able to get a grant of between £20 and £90 per week, payable for between 26 and 66 weeks, depending on the assessment of the scheme's potential by the TEC, often acting on the advice of the Local Enterprise Agency. The TEC may also refuse applications. This emphasises the importance of having a well-prepared and convincing business plan.

Free literature
A number of useful free guides on government schemes to help small business have been issued by banks and major accountancy practices. Check with your bank to see what it has on offer in the way of loans or other schemes to assist new businesses.

Money through the EU

The bank, or possibly your Local Enterprise Agency, should be able to tell you whether you could be eligible for a loan from the European Investment Bank, which can lend up to 50 per cent of the capital cost of projects at subsidised rates in a defined range of industries. These loans are administered through UK banks and though they are mostly for larger sums and bigger projects than the average start-up, they also have medium-term loans for which the minimum amount is as low as £15,000, with a very competitive rate of interest.

Your best chance for an EU loan would be if you were located in an iron and steel closure area and were creating jobs for workers who have been made redundant from those industries. In fact with these European Coal and Steel Community loans there are special interest discount incentives for job creation.

Informal equity capital

Contrary to popular impressions, most venture capital companies are not interested in business start-ups, unless they are looking for an investment of upwards of £250,000 or so. That generally means enterprises which are already up and running. Management buy-outs and buy-ins are typical examples.

For start-up ventures of the kind we are mostly talking about in this book, a more likely source is what is called informal equity capital: 'business angels' to give them their more colloquial name. They are individual private investors, operating either singly or as syndicates, who are prepared to finance entrepreneurial businesses at an earlier stage and on a smaller scale than venture capitalists are likely to consider.

But where do you find your angel? The answer is through a Business Introduction Service. A directory of these is published by the British Venture Capital Association (3 Catherine Place, London SW1E 6DX;

071-233 5212). Firms listed there put together information about enterprises looking for capital – the usual minimum is £10,000. These are circulated to potential investors who usually pay an annual subscription to receive this information. When a deal is made, the enterprise receiving the investment pays a fee to the provider of the introduction.

In many ways, business angels operate like venture capital firms – indeed, the BCVA says that raising informal equity capital may well be the first stage on the way to approaching the venture capital market for bigger sums at a later stage. Business angels provide equity finance in return for a share in the business. They may want to play an active part in running it, which is why some prefer local firms. Business angels taking part in the Enterprise Investment Scheme introduced in the autumn 1993 Budget are allowed to be paid directors of the companies into which they have put money. This was not the case with the Business Enterprise Scheme (BES) which it has replaced.

Participation can be a good or a bad thing, depending on personal chemistry, whether the angel can make a genuine contribution, and whether the terms of participation have been clearly set out. The BCVA booklet notes that angels have no desire to take control of the businesses in which they invest, but obviously the potential for friction with an outside shareholder actively involved in running the show should not be discounted: getting the right angel is quite as difficult as it is for angels to find the right investment.

What angels look for is much the same as with venture capital providers: a thorough business plan, which covers not only the business itself, but also full details of the management team, when the investor can expect to get his or her money back and with what return. It follows, therefore, that a great deal depends on the introduction service's ability to find the right match. On the one hand, it should help firms looking for finance to present their case in a way which is likely to attract investors. On the other hand, it should be proactive in recruiting them. Venture Capital Report (tel 0491 579999), the market leader in this field, produces a monthly summary of opportunities and mails it to 600 subscribers, ranging from wealthy individuals to financial institutions.

The BCVA says that one of the big advantages of raising money via the informal equity capital market route is that business angels are quicker to make decisions and also less fixated on short-term gains. It may be that recognition of this situation has encouraged the government to give more scope to business angels under its Enterprise Investment Scheme.

Consider, however, the consequences of giving away an equity stake as opposed to raising a loan if you possibly can. The great success story, from the point of view of investing in a start-up, was that of the man who got 50 per cent of Body Shop for an investment of £4000 after Anita

Roddick had been turned down by the banks. But if your business grows into the kind of mega-success achieved by Body Shop, having parted with a large chunk of it for a modest investment might be a decision you will look back on with regret.

Hire purchase arrangements

Hire purchase arrangements can also be made with the help of a finance company. This is a useful way of financing medium- to longer-term commitments, such as the purchase of machinery, equipment and vehicles. The arrangements are basically similar to a private hire purchase contract, in that the buyer asks the finance company to buy the asset. He then hires it for a specific period, paying hiring charges and interest as he goes along, and can then exercise an option to buy goods at the end of an agreed period. Until that point they remain the property of the finance company, and there is thus no need, as a rule, for the hirer to provide security as is the case with a loan. On the other hand, the finance company will require him to maintain the asset in good order, to insure it and possibly to fulfil other special conditions such as providing satisfactory evidence that the money earned from it will at least cover the high interest charges involved.

The periods over which a hire purchase agreement may run vary with the nature of the asset, but in general terms the Finance Houses Association lays down that 'the goods should have a useful life greater than the period of the hire purchase agreement'. This, however, raises the question of what is a 'useful life'? It may be that the item in question, while still technically useful, will become hopelessly antiquated during the period of the agreement. In these days of rapid technological change, it is unwise to enter into unduly long-term commitments.

It is worth calculating the true rate of interest reflected in leasing or hire purchase charges over the given period of time. As in every other form of business, there are sharks around who turn out to charge astronomical rates of interest. It is worth getting more than one quote if there are several possible sources from which to obtain equipment on lease or hire purchase.

Other sources of finance

Investors who buy shares in small unquoted companies will be able to offset losses incurred in the disposal of such shares against taxable income, not just against capital gains. The problem, of course, is how do you find private individuals with risk capital? Surprisingly enough they do exist and, equally surprisingly, one way of getting at them is through stockbrokers. Stockbrokers have, in the past, been very coy about recommending investments of this kind, but the new legislation might, as it is intended to do, make them change their policy.

One is reluctant to suggest names of brokers because, as in the case of finance houses, there are horses for courses; but here again discreet inquiries by your accountant or bank manager might bear fruit.

Another source of information on private individuals with money to invest are solicitors and accountants in rural areas and small towns. They are often much more in touch with the situation on the availability of such funds than their brethren in larger, more imposing metropolitan offices.

LEntA, the London Enterprise Agency, publishes a monthly list of business propositions which occasionally includes details of private investors.

Using your own money

Inevitably you will have to put up at least some money of your own. Even if your form of business involves selling an intangible skill, as in the case of consultancy, you are going to need some basic equipment, not to mention the fact that you need to have enough money to live on until your business income builds up. You should bear in mind that any money of your own that you put into your firm should be earning a rate of interest comparable to what you could get outside (ie greater than its opportunity cost), and this must be reflected in your costing and estimating. This topic is dealt with in more detail in Chapter 1.7.

Apart from ready cash in the form of savings, jewellery and other liquid and saleable personal assets you will also have other, less immediate resources to turn to. The most obvious is your house and if you are in a part of the country where property prices are rising, its current value may be far in excess of your mortgage. You could take out a second mortgage on this basis, but interest rates on second mortgages are very high. Moreover, taking out a second mortgage will involve your spouse, since one person cannot obtain a second mortgage on the marital home without the other's permission. A better approach would be to take out a mortgage on another house and sell the one you are in.

Life insurance policies are also worth bearing in mind because companies will generally be prepared to lend money against up to 90 per cent of their surrender value. Interest rates on these loans are generally lower than on bank overdrafts.

It is possible in the case of a limited company for the shareholders to lend money to the company. This does not increase their liability in the same way as taking up issued share capital. However, outside lenders like banks do not take kindly to such arrangements because it indicates a certain reluctance by the shareholders to put their money where their mouths are!

HEMGLAS

DELIGHTFUL, DELICIOUS...DELIVERED!

The Hemglas Franchise

Delightful, Delicious...Delivered is the message to customers which is advertised on all vehicles operated under the Hemglas franchise.

From factory to freezer without any loss of temperature and therefore quality, is the boast of this company which delivers Frozen Food and Ice Cream Products direct to the consumer.

With a unique system of tours and distinctive chimes, operated under franchise from Hjem-Is Europa A.S. of Swedish origin, the U.K. Company Home Ice Products Ltd has embarked upon a programme of franchising its existing areas to individual franchisees.

Each franchisee who takes up an area is assured of existing trading income from Day 1 by virtue of the tours already being operated by the company.

In addition to the supply of a fully liveried vehicle, the company offers a 100% support system for all its franchisees by including management and accounting functions, marketing origination, product sourcing, pricing structure, provision for a replacement vehicle and additional sales support in case of emergency within its package.

The whole franchise has been designed to release the franchisee from worrying administration and other burdens so that all available time can be devoted to selling.

The four existing Regional Centres presently service franchisees in the West Midlands, East Midlands and East Anglia. The company will be actively expanding its operation into North Yorkshire and Kent during 1994.

With many imported products from Sweden and Denmark the company commands a large share of the take home Ice Cream market and is well placed to expand its activities nationwide through its franchise programme.

With Frozen Food and Ice Cream consumption set to increase dramatically in the U.K. the future for the business and its franchisees looks extremely rosy.

The best way to buy Ice Cream

Home Ice Products Ltd
Milnyard Square
Orton Southgate   Telephone: 0733 371711
Peterborough PE2 0GX   Fax: 0733 370175

Company Registered in
England and Wales
Registration No. 2695716

Raising money by effective cash management

Any method of raising money from the outside costs money. In a period of high interest rates, borrowing can be so costly as to swallow up the entire profits of a business that is overreliant on it. There are instances where borrowing huge amounts of money has made sense, for instance in the property market, where the value of assets in the early 1970s increased much faster than the value of the money borrowed to acquire them. But subsequent events showed that this is dependent on the assumption that the asset does go on appreciating in value at a very rapid rate, and certainly, from the point of view of the smaller business, one could state as golden rules the following: never borrow more than you have to, never buy until you need to. And when you need to, consider whether hire purchase or even leasing might not make more sense for you than committing cash to an outright purchase. Remember it is cash that pays the bills, not assets or paper profits.

A surprising amount of borrowing can be avoided by effective cash management. It is not dishonest to take the maximum period of payment allowed by your suppliers, and though you do not want to get the reputation of being a slow payer, once you have established a reputation of being a reliable account your suppliers may give you quite a bit of leeway before they start pressing you for payment even on an overdue sum. Nor is it dishonest to take note that some suppliers press for payment fairly quickly, whereas others are more lax. The former get paid first.

The reverse is true in the case of the customers you supply. Send out invoices as soon as the work is done. You are more likely to get paid at that point than some weeks later when the novelty has worn off and maybe quibbles have arisen. Send out statements punctually and make sure that your terms of payment are observed.

Take one simple example of how money can work for your business. If your VAT quarter is January to March you have to pay over the VAT you have billed to your customers minus the VAT you have been billed by your suppliers by the end of April. Thus, if you can send a lot of invoices out to customers on 1 January and get the money in quickly, all your VAT can sit in a deposit account for nearly four months. Equally, if you are planning to buy a large piece of equipment (say, a van) on which there are many hundreds of pounds in VAT for you to claim back, juggling with the precise date on which you make the purchase can minimise the damage to your cash flow.

Progress payments

In the case of work done on contract – say, a design or consultancy job involving sizeable sums of money over a longer period of time such as

three or four months – it is worth trying to persuade your customer to make advance and/or progress payments. After all, you are going to be involved in considerable expenditure before the final sum becomes due. Whether an approach of this kind should be made depends, of course, on how well you know the customer and how badly you think he needs you. If you need his work more than he needs your services, you should consider a bank overdraft, though the cost of this should be reflected in your charges.

Credit factoring

Credit management is a tricky business which has sunk more than one promising new enterprise which, hungry for business, too inexperienced or simply too busy to pay attention to time-consuming detail, has let its credit index – the length of time money is outstanding – get out of control. A possible solution is to have a credit factor to look after this aspect for you. The firm using such services continues to send out its own invoices but the factor, who, of course, gets copies of the invoices, takes over the whole business of collecting the receivables. He will also generally give advice on credit limits and, if required to do so, may be able to discount the invoices, ie allow you to draw cash from him against a percentage of the amounts he is due to collect. Naturally a fairly substantial fee is charged for this service, varying with turnover, and on the whole factors are not interested in firms whose annual turnover is less than £100,000, nor in those invoicing too many small amounts to small customers. Your bank should be able to advise you on the choice of a factor. Indeed a number of banks have subsidiaries which offer a factoring service. There is also now an Association of British Factors, made up of some of the largest firms in the business.

Coping with expansion

Edward Heath, when Prime Minister, came in for some derisive criticism when he described the dire state of the British economy at that time as 'suffering from the problems of success'. It is, nevertheless, a phrase which would ring a bell with many a businessman caught unprepared on a tide of expansion, even though at the level of the small firm the symptoms are somewhat different. They may emerge as problems with people, when the staff who were in at the beginning find it difficult to handle a larger-scale operation; or as mistakes made in interviewing and selecting people for new jobs in an expanding company; or simply when the owners are stretched in too many different directions to look at individual trouble spots in enough detail.

Most frequently these trouble spots turn out to be connected, directly or indirectly, with finance. You are producing something for which there is a demand; the world starts beating a path to your door; you appear to be selling your product profitably, and suddenly, in the midst of apparent plenty, you start running out of cash. What has probably happened is that you have forgotten that in general you do not get paid until you have delivered the goods, but your suppliers and the additional staff you have taken on have to be paid out of cash flow generated by a previous and smaller scale of operations.

The way to avoid this situation is to make complete budgeting and cash flow forecasts (see Chapter 1.7) because you will then be able to select the financial package that is appropriate: short-term loans and overdrafts to meet seasonal or fluctuating demands, such as the materials to supply a big contract; long-term finance for plant, machinery or vehicles, or to make a tempting acquisition; finance from within by tighter controls and better cash management to keep the ordinary course of expansion on an even keel. In other words the trick is to find the right mixture, not just to grab the first jar of financial medicine on the shelf. It may not contain anything like the cure you need.

Checklist: raising capital

1. How much do you need? Have you made an initial cash flow projection?
2. Is it to finance short- or long-term financial facilities?
3. Should you be looking to your bank for overdraft facilities? If so, to what limit?
4. Should you be looking for a loan from your bank or some other commercial or official body? If so, how much and over what period?
5. Have you considered leasing or hire purchase as an alternative to raising a lump sum? If this option is open to you, have you worked out the cost of leasing and credit finance as compared to interest charges on loans?
6. If your need for cash is related to difficulties with credit control, have you considered invoice factoring?
7. Have you considered turning personal assets into cash?
8. Assuming options 5, 6 and 7 have been considered and rejected, have you worked out how to repay the loan and interest charges?
9. What security can you offer a lender, and has it been independently valued?
10. Exactly how do you propose to use the money?
11. Have you prepared a written description of your firm, what skills the key people in it have to offer, what your objectives are, how

your product or service compares with the competition, what firm orders you have secured and what your realistic expectations, opportunities and goals are?

12. Do you have supporting evidence on orders you have obtained or are likely to obtain?

13. Have you (and your associates, if any) made as full a commitment to your enterprise in terms of time and money as can reasonably be expected of you?

14. Have you previously obtained financial help for this or any other business? Have you repaid it within the period due?

15. If you have any loans outstanding on the business, how much are they for, for what purpose and how are they secured?

16. Can you produce an up-to-date balance sheet showing the present financial state of your company?

17. Do you have a detailed cash flow projection, monthly over the first two years and quarterly thereafter, showing cash flow over the period of the loan?

18. Do you have annual projected profit and loss accounts and balance sheets over the period of the loan?

19. If you are approaching a merchant bank or private individual for venture capital how much of the equity in and control of your company are you prepared to let go?

20. If you are raising money to enable you to fulfil a large contract, have you talked to your customer about the possibility of his paying you in stages?

Professional and Other Outside Advisers

We have already touched on the importance of the role that professional advisers, particularly accountants and solicitors, are going to play in the formation of your business, whether it is to be a limited company or some other kind of entity. You are going to be using their advice quite frequently, not only at the beginning but also later, in matters such as acquiring premises, suing a customer for payment, preparing a set of accounts or finding out what items are allowable against your or your company's tax bill. Obviously, therefore, how you choose and use these advisers is a matter for careful thought.

Making the right choice

Many people think that there is some kind of special mystique attached to membership of a profession and that any lawyer or accountant is going to do a good job for them. The fact is, though, that while they do have useful specialist knowledge the competence with which they apply it can be very variable. A high proportion of people who have bought a house, for instance, can tell you of errors and delays in the conveyancing process, and some accountants entrusted with their clients' tax affairs have been known to send in large bills for their services while overlooking claims for legitimate expenses that were the object of employing them in the first place.

So do not just go to the solicitor or accountant who happens to be nearest; nor should you go to someone you only know in a social capacity. Ask friends who are already in business on a similar scale and, if possible, of a similar nature to your own, for recommendations. (If you already have a bank manager you know well, he may also be able to offer useful advice.) The kind of professional adviser you should be looking for at this stage is not in a big office in a central location. He will have bigger fish to fry and after the initial interview you may well be fobbed off with an articled clerk. Apart from that he will be expensive, for he has big office overheads to meet. On the other hand, a one-man operation can create a problem if the one man is ill or on holiday. The ideal office will be a suburban one, preferably close to where you intend to set up business because knowledge of local conditions and personalities can be invaluable, with two or three partners. Apart from that, personal impressions do count. You will probably not want to take on an adviser who immediately exudes gloomy caution, or one who appears to be a wide boy, or somebody with whom you have no rapport. Some people recommend that you should make a short list of two or three possibles and go and talk to them before making your choice. Stoy Hayward are particularly interested in the small business area and franchising; they have offices in London and the regions.

What questions do you ask?

Obviously, later on you will be approaching your adviser about specific problems, but at the outset you and he will be exploring potential help he can give you. Begin by outlining the kind of business or service you intend to set up, how much money you have available, what you think your financial needs are going to be over the first year of operation, how many people are going to be involved as partners or shareholders and what your plans are for the future. An accountant will want to know the range of your experience in handling accounting problems and how much help you are going to need in writing up the books, and he will advise you on the basic records you should set up. Remember to ask his advice on your year end/year start; this does not have to be 6 April to 5 April, and there may be sound tax reasons for choosing other dates. He may even be able to recommend the services of a part-time bookkeeper to handle the mechanics but, as we shall show in Chapter 1.5, this does not absolve you from keeping a close watch on what money is coming in and going out. It should be stressed at this point that, certainly in the case of a private limited company, the accountant you are talking to should be qualified, either through membership of the Institute of Chartered Accountants or the Chartered Association of Certified Accountants. Someone who advertises his services as a bookkeeper or merely as an 'accountant' is not qualified to give professional advice in the true meaning of that term, though a good unqualified man can do a very adequate job in preparing tax returns for something like a small freelance business.

A solicitor will also want to know the kind of business you are in and your plans for the future. But he will concentrate, obviously, on legal rather than financial aspects (so do not go on about money – he is a busy man, and this is only an exploratory visit). He is interested in what structure the operation is going to have and, in the case of a partnership or limited company, whether you and your colleagues have made any tentative agreements between yourselves regarding the running of the firm and the division of profits. He will want to get some idea of what kind of property you want to buy or lease and whether any planning permissions have to be sought.

How much is he going to charge?

This is rather like asking how long is a piece of string. It depends on how often you have to consult your adviser so it is no use asking him to quote a price at the outset, though if you are lucky enough to have a very clear idea of what you want done – say, in the case of an accountant, a monthly or weekly supervision of your books, plus the preparation and auditing of your accounts – he may give you a rough idea of what his charges will be. Alternatively, he may suggest an annual retainer for these services and any advice directly concerned with them, plus extra charges for anything that falls outside them such as a complicated wrangle with the inspector of taxes about allowable items. When calculating the likely cost of using an accountant remember that his fees are tax-deductible.

An annual retainer is a less suitable way of dealing with your solicitor because your problems are likely to be less predictable than those connected with accounting and bookkeeping. A lot of your queries may be raised, and settled, on the telephone: the 'Can I do this?' type. Explaining that kind of problem on the telephone is usually quicker and points can be more readily clarified than by writing a letter setting out the facts of the case (though you should ask for confirmation in writing in matters where you could be legally liable in acting on the advice you have been given!). However, asking advice on the telephone can be embarrassing for both parties. You will be wondering whether your solicitor is charging you for it and either way it could inhibit you from discussing the matter fully. You should, therefore, check at the outset what the procedure is for telephone inquiries and how these are accounted for on your bill.

A guide – not a crutch

For someone starting in business on their own, facing for the first time 'the loneliness of thought and the agony of decision', there is a temptation to lean on professional advisers too much. Apart from the fact that this can be very expensive, it is a bad way to run a business. Before you lift the telephone or write a letter, think. Is this clause in a contract something you could figure out for yourself if you sat down and concentrated on reading it carefully? Would it not be better to check through the ledger yourself to find out where to put some item of expenditure that is not immediately classifiable? Only get in touch with your advisers when you are genuinely stumped for an answer, not just because you cannot be bothered to think it out for yourself. Remember, too, that nobody can make up your mind for you on matters of policy. If you feel, for example, that you cannot work with your partner, the only thing your solicitor can or should do for you is to tell you how to dissolve the partnership, not whether it should be done at all.

Your bank manager

The other person with whom you should make contact when you start up in business is your bank manager. The importance of picking a unit of the right size which we have mentioned in connection with professional advice also holds true in this case. A smaller local branch is more likely to be helpful towards the problems of a small business than one in a central urban location with a lot of big accounts among its customers. You might also discuss, with your accountant, the possibility of going outside the 'big four'. It is necessary to be careful here because there have been some notorious failures of 'fringe banks', but there are a number of solid smaller banking houses which are more accommodating about charges on handling your account and loans. If you are changing banks, as opposed to merely switching branches, it will be difficult for you to get a sizeable overdraft until the manager has seen something of your track record.

You must inform your bank manager of your intention to set up in business, providing him with much the same information as you gave to your accountant. Indeed, it is quite a good idea to ask your accountant

to come along to this first meeting, so that he can explain any technicalities.

You may be operating a small-scale freelance business that does not call for bank finance. It is very important, in that case, to keep your personal and business accounts separate, with separate cheque and paying-in books for each one. Mixing up private and business transactions can only lead to confusion, for you as well as your accountant. Even if you are simply, say, a one-man freelance consultancy it is worth keeping your bank manager well informed about your business. Your cash flow as a freelance might well be highly erratic and unless he knows you and your business well he will be firing off letters about your unauthorised overdraft.

Insurance

If you are setting up a photographic studio and an electrical fault on the first day destroys some of your equipment you are in trouble before you have really begun. If you are a decorator and a pot of paint falling from a window sill causes injury to someone passing below you could face a suit for damages that will clean you out of the funds you have accumulated to start your business. Insurance coverage is, therefore, essential from the start for almost all kinds of business.

Insurance companies vary a good deal in the premiums they charge for different kinds of cover, and in the promptness with which they pay out on claims. The best plan is not to go direct to a company, even if you already transact your car or life insurance with them, but to an insurance broker. Brokers receive their income from commissions from the insurance companies they represent, but they are generally independent of individual companies and thus reasonably impartial. Here again, your accountant or solicitor can advise you of a suitable choice, which would be a firm that is big enough to have contacts in all the fields for which you need cover (and big enough to exert pressure on your behalf when it comes to making a claim), but not so big that the relatively modest amounts of commission they will earn from you initially are not worth their while taking too much trouble over, for instance when it comes to reminding you about renewals. Apart from these general points you will have to consider what kinds of cover you need and this will vary somewhat with the kind of business you are in. The main kinds are:

1. Insurance of your premises.
2. Insurance of the contents of your premises.
3. Insurance of your stock.
   (The above three kinds of cover should also extend to 'consequential loss'. For instance, you may lose in a fire a list of all your customers. This list has no value in itself but the 'consequent' loss of business could be disastrous. The same is true of stock losses. If a publisher loses all his books in a fire it is not only their value that affects him, but also the consequent loss of business while they are being reprinted, by which time the demand for them may have diminished.)
4. Employer's liability is compulsory if you employ staff on the premises, even on a part-time basis.
5. Public liability in case you cause injury to a member of the public or his premises in the course of business. You will also need third-party public liability if you employ staff or work with partners.
6. Legal insurance policies, which cover you against prosecution under Acts of Parliament which relate to your business (eg those covering unfair dismissal and fair trading).
7. Insurance against losing your driving licence – important if your business depends on your being able to drive.
8. Insurance of machinery, especially mechanical failure of computers, the consequences of which can be disastrous for most kinds of business.
9. Professional indemnity insurance. If you are offering a service, such as consultancy, many clients will demand that you are covered for loss that they might incur as a result of your advice.
10. Product liability insurance. The same principle as the above applies if you are manufacturing or supplying goods. Your customers will expect you to be covered against claims from faulty products.

Your broker will advise you on other items of cover you will need. You should check, for instance, that your existing policies, such as home and vehicle insurance, cover commercial use if that is what you envisage, but do not leave the whole business of insurance in his hands. Read your

DO YOU WANT TO EARN OVER £30,000pa AND WORK FROM HOME?

After 5 successful years of 'sparkling',we are looking for the right people to help take SPARKLERS* nationwide.

Our commitment to quality, reliability and training has enabled us to grow profitably through the recession in the face of intense competition. We are now offering a complete business package, fully supported with ongoing help and training to the right people who have the desire and ability to join us.

If you are hard working and feel that you could run your own business, in the knowledge that help is close at hand, write or telephone for more information.

WHY SPARKLERS*?
* *Established, Successful Business*
* *Good Brand Image*
* *Commitment to Training and Support*
* *Low Start-up Costs*

T.M.

**HOME CLEANING SERVICE
LUDLOW DRIVE, THAME, OXON OX9 3XS.
TELEPHONE 0844 217769.
HOT LINE & FAX 0844 261594**

In the PINK

"**I**nstantly recognisable," comments Claire Sebire on the corporate image of Sparklers, the domestic cleaning company she is now launching as a franchise.

Her pink uniformed team, all sporting the distinctive Sparklers logo, certainly do project a look of professionalism. "It's this image," comments Claire Sebire, "together with a reputation for quality and reliability, that has ensured our growth over the past five years."

She believes that Sparklers beats the competition thanks to "a degree of customer service rarely found among cleaning companies – that's why we don't need to advertise. Word of mouth from satisfied customers suffices."

"Priority is building a long-term customer base – we still have our first one! And franchising will permit sharing our success with others while gaining a nationwide presence."

Claire Sebire explains: "We're now looking for the *right* people to meet our strict selection criteria and code of practice for franchisees and workforce alike. This is vital to maintain the reputation we've built up over the years."

A former nurse, she understands the value of interpersonal relationships and wants franchisees capable of talking to people at all levels: "Our customer base ranges from ABC1 to estate semi-detached and elderly people. Although most work is in private homes, a homeowner may ask us to clean their office."

She argues that the franchise could be a "fantastic opportunity" for a housewife whose family is growing up – to gain independence from meeting the challenge of building her own business, gaining the satisfaction of direct rewards for her efforts, but without the daunting prospect of being totally on her own.

The company is committed to high quality support and training to help replicate Sparklers nationwide, she insists. "Our franchisees can benefit from our experience of cleaning and our knowledge of how to tap the market."

"We used experienced franchise consultant Gordon Patterson to confirm the business was suitable for franchising. Now that every aspect of the system is tried, tested and finetuned, we're ready to seek franchisees – but they must be the right ones. We won't rush into it."

She enthuses: "I've got exciting plans for the future growth of Sparklers, and the patience to do it properly, to develop a national network of franchisees, providing a local, conscientious service – and thus spread the brand name throughout the country and with it, the Sparklers reputation." ●

policies carefully when you get them and make sure that the small print does not exclude any essential item.

Insurance is expensive (though the premiums are allowable against tax inasmuch as they are incurred wholly in respect of your business), and you may find that in the course of time you have paid out thousands of pounds without ever making a claim. However, it is a vital precaution, because one fire or legal action against you can wipe out the work of years if you are not insured. For this reason you must check each year that items like contents insurance represent current replacement values and that your premiums are paid on the due date. Your broker should remind you about this, but if he overlooks it, it is you who carries the can.

The Federation of Small Businesses now includes automatic legal insurance in its membership subscription. This covers professional and legal fees of up to £10,000 for appeals to VAT tribunals, defence of Health and Safety at Work prosecutions, 90 per cent of the cost of an industrial tribunal award and defence of private and business motoring prosecutions. The FSB also runs a voluntary top-up scheme to supplement this basic legal cover.

Another interesting scheme is Allianz Legal Protection. Its Lawplan enables policyholders to pursue business-to-business debts. It also covers a wide variety of legal costs related to business activities, such as contract disputes. Obviously the need to get cover for such eventualities would depend on the kind of enterprise you are engaged in.

Other advisers and suppliers

In the course of transacting your business, you will probably need the services of other types of people: builders, to maintain and perhaps refurbish your premises; printers, to produce letterheads, advertising material, etc; surveyors and valuers to assess your property; and so on. You should apply the same criteria to these as to your professional advisers. Their services should be reasonably priced, and the service performed to the required standard. If the service is of a professional nature, the consultant should be a member of the relevant professional body. If this does not apply, it may be worth asking for recommendations from the local Chamber of Commerce, Small Firms Centre or Enterprise Agency.

In the case of designers, The Design Council (28 Haymarket, London SW1Y 4SU) provides a free design advisory service. One of their staff will come to see you, discuss your idea, product or service, maybe suggest how it could be modified to gain wider acceptance, and recommend a designer from the Council's designer selection service. You can call on the DAS even if your scheme has not got off the ground yet.

STANLEY R BRISTOW & CO

In Association with Hedley Dunk & Company

Chartered Accountants

A long-established practice with extensive experience in Business Start-ups, Business Management, Payroll, Book-keeping, VAT Returns, Personal and Corporate Taxation, Company Audits and Financial Advice.

377 Footscray Road, London SE9 2EN
Telephone 081-850 2195   Fax 081-859 6853

The designer's services, once you appoint someone, have to be paid for, but for larger firms with between 60 and 1000 employees there is actually a free scheme available – the Design Advisory Service Funded Consultancy Scheme.

Local Enterprise Agencies

Local Enterprise Agencies (LEAs) and Training and Enterprise Councils (TECs) have taken over from the Department of Employment's Small Firms Service as providers of advice and information to small businesses and the self-employed. There are LEAs throughout the country – a complete list is available from Business in the Community (see address in Appendix 1).

LEAs are sponsored by local firms or local branches of national companies, banks, accountancy practices and various public sector bodies. Apart from underwriting the running costs, sponsors often second members of their staff to them. Sometimes these are experienced managers on the eve of retirement, but quite often they are young high-flyers on the way up, being exposed, as part of a career development plan, to a wider variety of business problems than they would get in their own offices.

The quality of advice and their general helpfulness is high – for instance, they will help you to prepare a business plan and advise you on methods of obtaining finance. LEAs also run courses on basic topics like marketing and finance. They are less able to advise on the conduct of specific types of business activity, unless it is one that a seconded member of the LEA's staff happens to know about. Many do, however, operate 'marriage bureaux', putting small businesses in touch with potential customers or investors. Some also maintain registers of suitable properties for small businesses.

Calling in to your Local Enterprise Agency in the early stages of setting up business increasingly ranks with visiting your bank manager as one of the vital first steps of working for yourself.

The Department of Trade and Industry

The Department of Trade and Industry runs a number of programmes, many at regional level, to help small businesses. They fall into three main groups:

1. Consultancy help, ranging from initial advice on the telephone to troubleshooting visits by approved independent consultants.
2. Information and technology transfer, which covers issues like specialised advice on how to protect intellectual property.
3. Grants for research and development.

The initial contact in all these cases is the DTI itself (Ashdown House, 123 Victoria Street, London SW1E 6RB; 071-215 5000) but it is as well to be able to describe, before you ring them, exactly what the nature of your problem or request is.

Checklist: professional advisers

Solicitors

1. How well do you know the firm concerned?
2. What do you know of their ability to handle the kind of transactions you have in mind?
3. Is their office convenient to the place of work you intend to establish?
4. Do they know local conditions and personalities?
5. Are they the right size to handle your business affairs over the foreseeable future?
6. Have you prepared an exhaustive list of the points on which you want legal advice at the setting-up stage?

Accountants

1. Have they been recommended by someone whose judgement you trust and who has actually used their services?
2. Are the partners members of one of the official accountants' bodies? If not, are you satisfied that they can handle business on the scale envisaged?
3. Is their office reasonably close by?
4. Does it create a good and organised impression?
5. Can they guarantee that a member of the firm will give you personal and reasonably prompt attention when required?
6. Have you thought out what sort of help you are going to need?
7. Have you prepared an outline of your present financial position and future needs?
8. Have you considered, in consultation with your solicitor, whether

you want to set up as a sole trader, a partnership or a limited company?

Bank manager

1. Is your present bank likely to be the right one for you to deal with in this context?
2. Have you informed your bank manager of your intention to set up a business?
3. Have you established a separate bank account for your business?
4. Have you discussed with your bank manager the possibility of switching your account to a local, smaller branch?

Insurance

1. Do you have a reliable reference on the broker you intend to use?
2. Is he efficient, according to the reports you receive, about reminding you when policies come up for renewal?
3. Has he any track record of paying promptly on claims?
4. Have you prepared a list of the aspects of your proposed business which require insurance cover?
5. Are you fully insured for replacement value and consequential loss?
6. Have you read the small print on your policies or checked them out with your solicitors?

Simple Accounting Systems and Their Uses

Any bank manager will tell you that at least 80 per cent of all business failures are caused by inadequate record keeping. Unfortunately, this fault is by no means uncommon in small businesses because the entrepreneurial person who tends to set up on his own is often temperamentally different from the patient administrative type who enjoys paperwork and charting information in the form of business records. He is apt to feel that what really keeps the show on the road is obtaining and doing the work, or being in the shop to look after customers. However, unless you record money coming in and going out, owed and owing, you will never have more than the haziest idea of how much to charge for your products or services, where your most profitable areas of activity are (and indeed whether you are making a profit at all), how much you can afford to pay yourself and whether there is enough coming in to cover immediate commitments in the way of wages, trade debts, tax or professional fees, rent, rates, etc.

Legally, in fact, only a limited company is obliged to keep proper books of account: the definition is that they have to do so 'with respect to all receipts and expenses, sales and purchases, assets and liabilities and they must be sufficient to give a true and fair picture of the state of the company's affairs and to explain its transactions'. This is actually no bad objective for anyone carrying on a business on a full-time basis; the only trouble is that keeping and entering up a full set of books is very time-consuming and, though not inherently difficult, does require a certain amount of training and some natural aptitude for organising facts and figures if you are to avoid getting into a muddle.

As a rule of thumb, if your scale of operations is big enough to come within the orbit of VAT (that is, if your turnover is, or is likely to be, over £45,000 a year) we suggest you get qualified help with bookkeeping. But first of all, let us look at the very basic records you ought to keep if you are in business for yourself at all, even as a part-time freelance.

Two starting points

At the small-scale sole trader end, one reason why you need to keep records is to justify your expenditure claims to the tax inspector. For this purpose you may find that your most useful investment is a spike on which incoming receipts, invoices, statements and delivery notes can be placed. This ensures that essential documentary evidence of expenditure is retained and kept together, not used to put cups on or carried around in your wallet for making odd notes on the back. As your business grows you may find that the spike should be supplemented by a spring-loaded box file in which all such items should be placed in date order.

However, not all expenditure can be accounted for in this way. Fares, for instance, are not generally receipted, nor is postage, or you may be buying items for personal use at the same time as others that are directly connected with your business. Thus it is a good idea to carry a notebook around with you and enter up any expenses that you have incurred that are not documented. You will find that the taxman will accept a certain level of claims of this kind provided they bear a credible relationship to the business you are in. For example, if you are earning income from travelling round the country giving lectures he will accept a fairly high level of claims for fares, but not if the nature of your business is carrying out a local building repair service.

For larger outlays you may find credit cards a useful record-keeping aid. Apart from the fact that when card companies render their account for payment they provide a breakdown of where, when and how items were purchased, they also, in effect, give you six weeks' credit. During periods of high inflation this is a real consideration.

Keeping a cash book

The next stage is to keep a cash book. It does not have to be anything elaborate. The object of the exercise is to provide a record from which an accountant or bookkeeper can write up a proper set of books and to save him the time and trouble (which you have to pay for) of slogging through dozens or possibly hundreds of pieces of paper in order to do this. Since your professional adviser will have to work from your records it is a good idea to ask him what is the most convenient way of setting them out. He may suggest that you buy one of the ready-made books of account such as the *Complete Traders Account Book* or the *Self-employed Account Book*, though such books are not suitable for every kind of self-

INCOME

Date	Invoice No	Date paid	Details	Amount (£)	VAT (£)
2.5.94	8061		Six tables	224	39.20
6.5.94	cash		Desk	400	70.00
10.5.94	8062		Dining table	300	52.50
12.5.94	cash		Repair of wooden chest	160	28.00

EXPENDITURE

Date	Invoice No	Cheque/ Credit card	Details	Amount (£)	VAT (£)
3.5.94	-	911112	Wooden Top timber yard	850	148.75
4.5.94	Petty cash voucher 23	cash	Stamps	6	-
5.5.94	Petty cash voucher 24	cash	Expenses: trip to Harwich to inspect timber	40	7
13.5.94	-	911113	Electricity bill	80	14.00

Table 5.1 *Sample entries from the cash book of a cabinet-maker*

employment. If you find it difficult to follow his instructions, or you are using a ready-made book and are having trouble with it, here is something very simple you can do (see Table 5.1).

Buy a large (A4) ruled notebook and open it up at the first double page. Allocate the left-hand page to sales and the right-hand page to expenditure. If sales and expenditure fall into further categories which you want to keep track of, say, if you want to keep travel costs separate from the cost of materials, or if you are registered for VAT, divide up the page accordingly. You should also rule up columns for the date, the invoice number and the details of the invoice. Enter up these details at the end of each day's trading and you will find that it works both as a discipline in checking that all your sales and purchases are logged and that you now have a further record in addition to the documents on your spike or in your box file.

More elaborate systems

This sort of record is fine as far as it goes and in a small business engaged mainly in cash transactions your accountant may not need very much more than this to produce a set of accounts. In a larger concern, or one that operates extensively on taking and giving credit, it has some obvious limitations. For example, keeping track of when payments are made or received can become rather messy and difficult, and you will need to have a separate record, called a ledger, of the customers and suppliers with whom you do business so that you can see at a glance how much you owe or are owed in the case of individual accounts. Such details will be taken from further books – purchases and sales daybooks and a more elaborate kind of cash book than the simplified one we have described above. Though we have recommended that you leave the details of this kind of bookkeeping to a qualified person, let us look briefly at what is involved.

1. *Cash book.* Shows all payments received and made, with separate columns for cash transactions and those made through the bank (ie payments by cheque). Amounts received from customers are credited to their account in the ledger (see below). Payments made to suppliers are debited to their account in the ledger.
2. *Petty cash book.* Shows expenditure on minor items – postage, fares, entertainment and so forth, with a column for VAT.
3. *Sales daybook.* Records invoices sent out to customers in date order, with some analysis of the goods or service supplied and a column for VAT.
4. *Purchases daybook.* Records similar information about purchases.
5. *Ledger.* Sets out details, taken from sales and purchases daybooks, of individual customers' and suppliers' accounts and serves as a

record of amounts owed and owing. Details from the analysis columns of the sales and purchases daybooks are also transcribed, usually monthly, under corresponding headings in the ledger. This enables you to see at a glance where your sales are coming from and where your money is going.

6. *Capital goods ledger*. If you own expensive capital equipment – cars, lorries, machine tools, high-class film or photographic equipment, etc – you should have separate accounts for them in the ledger because the method of accounting for them is somewhat different. Capital items depreciate over a period of time (as you will know if you have ever sold a car) and this fact must be reflected both in your balance sheet and profit and loss account, and in the way you price your goods and services.

Writing down capital goods affects your tax liability. With some items you can write down the full value in the year of purchase, but it may not pay you to take advantage of this concession. How you deal with depreciation is very much an area where you are dependent on your accountant's expert advice.

Trading and profit and loss account

From the books described above, your accountant can draw together the information needed to compile the trading and profit and loss account (see Table 5.2). The function of the account is to tell you whether you have been making a gross profit and a net profit on your trading. It must be compiled annually and preferably more often than that, quarterly for instance, to enable you to measure your progress and make your VAT return.

To put together the account he begins by identifying the period you want to cover. He then totals up the value of all sales, whether paid for or not. Then he takes your opening stock and adds it to the purchases (but not expenditure such as rent or repayment of interest on loans). From this he takes the value of your stock (based on cost or market value, whichever is lower) at the end of the period you want to cover. Deducting the value of opening stock plus purchases from the value of sales will give him your gross trading profit (or loss) over the period.

Using this information he can work out the net profit and loss over the same period. The gross profit figure from your trading account appears at the top and against it he sets all the items from the various expenditure accounts in the ledger. He also includes in this figure the depreciation on capital equipment, but not its actual cost (even if you purchased it during the period in question) because that crops up later, in the balance sheet.

Deducting these from the gross profit gives you your profit over the period. If the total expenditure exceeds the gross profit you have obviously incurred a loss.

The balance sheet

We have mentioned in the previous section that capital equipment does not figure in the profit and loss account, but goes into the balance sheet. The balance sheet is a picture, taken at a particular point in the year (usually at the end of a company's financial year), of what the firm *owes* and what it *owns* (see Table 5.3). (This is not the same as a profit and loss account, which covers a period of time.)

In a balance sheet the assets of the firm used to be set out on the right and the liabilities on the left but it is modern practice to display them as below. However, all the assets and all the liabilities are generally not lumped together, but distinguished qualitatively by the words 'fixed' and 'current'.

'Fixed assets' are items which are permanently necessary for the business to function, such as machinery, cars, fixtures and fittings, your premises or the lease on them. 'Current assets', on the other hand, are

Trading and Profit and Loss Account for year ended 31.12.93		
	£	£
Sales		65,000
Purchases	30,000	
Opening Stock	5,000	
	35,000	
Less Closing Stock	6,000	29,000
Gross Profit		36,000
Rent and Rates	3,000	
Salaries	9,000	
Heat, Light	600	
Phone	350	
Travel	800	
Repairs	500	
Depreciation	1,800	
Professional Advice	450	
		16,500
Net Profit		19,500

Table 5.2 *Example of a trading and profit and loss account*

things from which cash will be realised in the course of your trading activities. These include the amount owed to you by your debtors (from the customers' accounts in the ledger), and the value of your stock (from the trading account). It also, of course, includes cash at the bank (from the cash book).

With liabilities, the position is reversed. 'Fixed liabilities' are those which you do not have to repay immediately, like a long-term loan from a kindly relative. What you do have to repay promptly, however, is the interest on that loan and this goes under 'current liabilities' if it is due, but has not been paid at the time the balance sheet has been prepared. The same is true of any amounts you owe to your suppliers' accounts in the ledger. Another item that goes on the 'liabilities' side is the share capital in the business and the profit from the trading account because both these amounts are ultimately owed by the company to the shareholders. Where, on the other hand, the company has been making a loss, the amount is deducted either from profits retained from earlier periods or from the shareholders' capital.

Balance Sheet as at 31.12.93		
	£	£
Fixed Assets		
Vehicles	3,200	
less depreciation	800	2,400
Fixtures and fittings	2,000	
less depreciation	500	1,500
		3,900
Current Assets		
Stock	6,000	
Debtors	1,800	
Cash	150	
	7,950	
Less Current Liabilities		
Trade Creditors	1,590	
Net Current Assets		6,360
Total Assets		10,260
Represented by		
	Authorised	Issued
Capital (2,000 shares at £1 each)	1,000	1,000
Loan repayable 1993		2,000
Profit		7,260
		10,260

Table 5.3 *An example of a balance sheet*

What should you be looking for in your records?

You will want to know whether you are making or losing money, but there are many other useful bits of information to be gleaned as well. If you are making a profit, what relationship does it bear to the capital employed in the business? You can calculate this by subtracting total liabilities from total assets. If you are making less than a 15 per cent return on capital, you are not, on the face of things, making much progress, though, of course, you could be paying yourself a very handsome salary before the profit figure was arrived at.

The percentage return on capital can be calculated by the following sum:

$$\frac{\text{profit}}{\text{capital employed}} \times 100$$

Another thing you can work out from your balance sheet is whether you are maintaining sufficient working capital to meet your requirements for new stock or materials or to pay for wages and rent. Here you look at current assets and current liabilities. The calculation:

$$\frac{\text{current assets}}{\text{current liabilities}}$$

gives you your *current* ratio. If you have, say, £1000 of each you are said to have a current ratio of 1:1. Clearly, in that case you would be in trouble if a major debtor were to go bankrupt. So it may be that you should cut back on some item of expenditure you were planning on. Furthermore, the current ratio includes certain items, like stocks, which may not be immediately realisable. If your current ratio is low, and you are still in two minds whether or not to buy that new machine, you might apply what is known as the *acid test ratio*, which shows your ability to meet liabilities quickly if the need arises. Here you simply deduct stock from your figure for current assets to give you a figure for liquid assets, ie debtors and cash. If the ratio of liquid assets to current liabilities is too low you may have more money tied up in stock than you should have.

Even the acid test ratio assumes that your debtors are going to pay you in a reasonable period of time: most likely within the terms of trade you are allowing. But is this assumption really correct? Look at the annual sum:

$$\frac{\text{debtors}}{\text{sales}} \times 365$$

If your sales are £10,000 and your debtors owe £1000, they are near enough to meeting net monthly terms for you not to worry about it. But if your debtors, on the same sales turnover, are running to £3000, there is something wrong with your credit control and you are probably heading for serious trouble.

Another important ratio is profit to sales. What this should be depends on the sort of business you are in. Your accountant should be able to advise you here on the basis of his knowledge of similar traders. If your percentage is on the low side you may be buying badly, failing to pass on cost increases, or possibly incurring losses from pilferage.

There are other ratios to look out for, but we hope that you will now be clear that the balance sheet and trading and profit and loss accounts are not just a financial rigmarole you have to go through, but very valuable indicators of the way your business is going, or the financial state of some other business you are thinking of buying. They are also useful for:

1. Assisting the bank manager to determine the terms of an overdraft.

2. Selling your business to a proposed purchaser.
3. Agreeing tax liabilities with the inspector of taxes.

Checklist: simple accounting systems

1. Do you carry a notebook to record smaller items of business expenditure, such as taxi fares, as soon as they are incurred?
2. Have you considered using credit cards for larger outlays?
3. Do you have a system for filing incoming invoices as soon as they are received?
4. Have you asked your accountant what books and records he advises you to keep?
5. Do you know and understand the procedures involved? If not, have you asked your accountant to recommend someone who can help you on a regular basis – at least once a week or once a month, depending on your scale of operations?
6. Do you have any idea of the ratios current in your type of business, so that you can measure your performance against the norm?

CHAPTER 1.6

Invoicing and Credit Control

Time is money, as the old saying goes. It ought to be written large in the minds of anyone giving credit, that is, any business that supplies goods and services which are not on a strictly cash-on-the-nail basis.

In these days of tight money there is a tendency for many customers, including large and reputable firms, to delay payment as long as possible because, as noted in Chapter 1.3, taking credit long – and preferably giving it short – is one way to maintain a flow of cash in the business. The supplier who does not demonstrate that he is in a hurry for payment, therefore, is the one who comes last in the queue.

Sending out invoices and statements

The first step towards ensuring that you are not in this position is to issue an invoice for work done or goods supplied as soon as possible after you deliver. On the invoice you should give the customer's order number. If it was a telephone order and you forgot to get an order number, you should at least give the date of the order. You should also state when you expect to receive payment. The usual period is between seven and 30 days after delivery. Many private individuals, in fact, pay on receipt of an invoice. Business firms, on the other hand, expect to receive a statement of their account at the end of the month, setting out invoices due or sent during this period: their dates, invoice number, the nature of the goods and the amount. You can have statement forms printed, but if you are not a limited company you can use your letterheads for this purpose, simply typing the word STATEMENT at the top. Every customer who has received an invoice and not paid at the end of the month when it is due should get a statement, which should repeat your payment terms.

The particulars of the invoice(s) are drawn from your customer's ledger, though it is essential to keep copies of the actual invoices as well, filed in date order. You are going to need them for VAT purposes, or to check queries. When you receive payment, check that it tallies with the amount due on the customer's ledger entry, mark off the details against each individual item as shown in the previous chapter and enter the amount in the cash book. If the customer requires a receipt, ask him to return the statement (or the invoice if he has paid on that) with his remittance – otherwise you will be involved in time-consuming typing – tick off the items paid, and attach a receipt form or bang on a rubber stamp, 'Paid'. Be uniform about your systems. If you have two different ones for the same part of your operation you are going to waste a lot of time looking in the wrong place when you come to check a document.

Do not neglect the process of checking payments because any amounts unpaid must go into next month's statement. Some invoices which have appeared on your statement will not be paid because they are not yet due for payment. For example, if your terms are 30 days and you have invoiced an item on the 20th of the month, a business customer is unlikely to pay until the month following. Quite often he only activates payments at the end of the month, unless he is unusually punctilious, efficient or being offered extra discount for quick settlement.

What happens if payment becomes overdue? This is extremely annoying, because at best it is going to involve you in extra correspondence. You must be tactful and patient if you want more business from your clients, and remember that some large organisations are slow in paying, not by choice but because they are dictated to by their computer accounting systems. But if your patience is exhausted, there are usually three stages. The first is a polite reminder of the amount due, how long it has been due and of your terms of supply. This should be coupled with asking the customer whether he has any queries on any of the invoices which might explain the delay. If there is no reply by the end of that month, write again, referring to your first reminder and setting a deadline for payment. A telephone call to the customer is often opportune at this stage. If that deadline is not met, you will have to write again, referring to your previous reminders and threatening legal action unless a new and final deadline is met. (If you have a large number of credit accounts, it may pay you to have sets of blank letters for each stage prepared in advance.)

In most cases the threat of legal action will do the trick, but how you proceed after that depends on the amount of money involved. Fortunately the Court and Legal Services Act of 1990 has simplified procedures. Debts of any amount can be recovered in the County Court, without involving solicitors – though, of course, their services may ultimately be necessary if the claim is disputed by the debtor.

Then there are three important points to establish before starting legal action:

ROOKE HOLT
Chartered Accountants

83 Ebury Street, London SW1W 9QY
Telephone: 071-730 2257   Fax: 071-730 0229

76 Trull Road, Taunton, Somerset
Telephone: 0823 323959

SPECIALISING IN SMALL COMPANY AUDITS, START UP'S AND TAXATION

---

1. Can the defendant actually pay? Wringing blood from a stone is a notoriously fruitless exercise.
2. Can you prove the claim by producing documentation about what was actually agreed, such as a confirming letter? Bounced cheques, reminders to pay, etc are also relevant.
3. Are you sure you have got hold of the right person? You may have been dealing with an individual acting on behalf of a company. In that case the claim is against the company.

The next stage is to issue a default summons in the County Court. It does not have to be in the area where the defendant lives, which could be in your favour if the case is undefended. If it is defended, the matter will automatically be heard in the defendant's County Court, though here again there is an option to full-scale proceedings. If the amount involved is less than £1000 the matter automatically goes to arbitration. That means both parties are obliged to accept the arbitrator's judgment.

The default summons involves a certain amount of paperwork. The court officials will brief you if you choose to do this yourself rather than getting your solicitor to do so. Remember he may charge you anything from £50 to £200 per hour, depending on how high-powered a firm you choose.

In the first place the summons is sent by post. The defendant then has 14 days in which to pay and if he fails to do so or to announce his intention to defend the action, then you as the plaintiff are entitled to judgment, which will include the amount claimed, plus court costs: a maximum of £70 for claims of under £5000, plus extras which can mount up if the case drags on. The problem is not so much the court costs but the time and trouble that it all takes. However, the good news is that few defendants will let matters go as far as this and the ultimate sanction of having bailiffs called in on them, if they can pay and unless they intend to defend the case.

You can, of course, ask for references before giving credit though this is a matter which has to be approached with some delicacy; but if you receive a sizeable order out of the blue from some business firm with whom you have not previously dealt, it is advisable to ask for a couple of references in acknowledging the order. Ask the referees to what amount they give credit to this particular customer, how long they have been doing business with him and whether he pays promptly.

If your business consists of making or repairing goods to order – tailoring, for instance – it is not unusual to ask the customer to pay up to 50 per cent on account where an estimate of over £50 or so has been given. This helps cash flow as well as protecting you against possible default. Equally, if goods of resaleable value are left with you for repair you should display a notice reserving the right to dispose of them if the customer does not come to collect them within a reasonable time of completion of the work.

A common delaying tactic, or it may be a perfectly legitimate query, is for the customer to ask for copy invoices on receipt of your statement. Do not part with your file copy. You will have to send a photocopy if you do not keep duplicates for this purpose.

Credit cards

For larger personal transactions and for items such as the settlement of restaurant bills, credit cards are a popular method of making payment. A business which wants to offer credit card payment facilities to its customers has to make application to the company concerned, which then sets a money limit to the transaction per customer for which the business in question can accept payment on that company's cards. Above that limit, which is based roughly on the applicant's average transaction per customer, the sale has to be referred back to the credit card company. This can be done over the telephone.

Each sale, as it is made, is entered up on a voucher supplied by the credit card company. The voucher is paid into the bank by the seller and the amount is debited to the card holder's account. The advantage of credit cards from the seller's point of view is that he receives guaranteed payment. Against this, he has to pay to the bank a small percentage on every transaction, the amount of this percentage being negotiated at the time he joins the scheme.

Most credit card companies operate on lines very similar to the scheme we have just outlined. Diner's Club vouchers, for instance, though not paid into a bank are sent to the Club organisation on certain specified dates, whereupon payment is made to the seller.

Checking incoming invoices and statements

Unless you transact your business by paying in cash or by cheque on the spot (which is likely in only a few business spheres), you will also be at the receiving end of invoices and statements from your suppliers. The moment they come in, put them on the spike. Then, daily if possible, enter the details in the suppliers' ledger, as described in Chapter 1.5. File incoming invoices in date order, for you will need them for VAT purposes.

When you receive your statement make sure it tallies with the amounts and details which you have entered in the suppliers' ledger, mark off all the items paid and write up the amount in the cash book.

If you are paying by cheque there is no need to ask for a receipt (which only adds to the paperwork) since an honoured cheque is itself a receipt. Make sure, though, that you enter up the stubs, unless you write up the cash book at the same time as you draw the cheques.

Checklist: invoicing and credit control

Invoicing

1. Are you invoicing promptly, on or with delivery?
2. Do your invoices clearly state your terms?
3. Do you ensure that the customer's name, address and order number (if any) or date are correctly stated on your invoice?
4. Are your statements sent out promptly at the end of the month? Do they state your payment terms?
5. Are they clear and easy to follow? Would they make sense to you if you were the recipient?
6. Are you checking payments received against ledger entries?

Credit control

1. Does every account have a credit limit?
2. Is it based on first-hand knowledge of the customer as a credit risk or personally, his track record as a payer with you or others in your line of business, on representatives' reports or reliable trade references, or on bankers' references, in that order of usefulness?
3. Do you exercise special vigilance on new accounts?
4. Do your statements show the age of outstanding balances and do you or your credit controller look at outgoing statements to check on customers whose payments situation seems to be deteriorating?
5. Do you have a system for dealing with customers who exceed their credit limit?
6. Do you have a sequence of reminder procedures for dealing with overdue accounts by telephone calls and/or letters?

7. Do you check orders received against a list of customers who have exceeded their credit limit or who are proving to be reluctant or non-payers?
8. Does the person in charge of credit control liaise with those responsible for supplying the account in question to make sure that there are no special reasons for non-payment before sharper warnings are delivered?
9. Do you regularly check on the debtor:sales ratio to make sure you are not heading for a liquidity problem by being too generous about extending credit?
10. Do you have a list of people you can contact in your principal customers' accounts departments if there are payment problems?

CHAPTER 1.7

Budgeting and Cash Flow Forecasting

One principle that it is vital to grasp is the importance of liquid cash in running a business. This should not be confused with profitability. Because of the way the profit figure is arrived at on the trading account (see Chapter 1.5), it is perfectly possible for a business to be trading profitably and yet be quite unable to pay the tax bill or the rent because its resources are tied up in stock or, even worse, in equipment.

Failure to understand the distinction between profit and cash flow is not uncommon and it can be disastrous. For example, you may be offered very persuasive financial inducements to carry or manufacture additional stock. If it is a good product and one for which there is a consistent demand you may say to yourself that you are going to need more anyway in six months' time, so why not stock up for a whole year at a bargain price? This can be a valid argument, but before you accept it consider that when the bills come in they have to be paid with money, not with stock. Profitability means very little unless cash is there when it is needed.

This is true even for businesses that do not carry stocks, like a photographic studio producing goods only to order, or a design consultancy selling more or less intangible skills. You are still going to have outgoings on travel or materials; and even if your premises are a back room in your own house there are still bills to be met, apart from the matter of needing money to live on.

Planning your cash requirements

Planning your cash requirements is crucial from the outset of your career as a self-employed person. It will determine much of your policy towards what kinds of work you take on. It is far better, if you are short of liquid capital, to take on a number of small jobs which will keep money coming in than one big, tempting, potentially profitable one where you might run out of cash three-quarters of the way through. For, unless you make provision to receive progress payments from your customer, backed up possibly by a bank overdraft, your suppliers are going to be pressing you for payment before you are in a position to send your bills to the customer.

Even at best, in most businesses which are not taking cash across the counter there is going to be a lag between the time you are being asked for payment and when your customer pays you.

In order to estimate what your needs for cash are going to be you should set up and revise, at three- or six-monthly intervals, a cash flow budget; and in order to refine it, you should also check it back against what actually happened. Indeed, before you begin you should have (and the bank manager will want to see) a fully worked out cash flow projection for the first 12 to 18 months.

The words 'cash flow budget' sound intimidatingly technical, but mean simply that you should make a realistic forecast of money coming in and going out over the period. Again, how accurate you can be depends somewhat on the circumstances and the type of business you are in. If you have bought a going concern there may be regular contracts that you hope to maintain, or in the case of a retail business or a restaurant some kind of predictable pattern of trade which can be established from the cash book or general ledger. If you have started a new business of your own, on the other hand, you may not have much to go on in the way of facts on cash coming in. You might only have enough certain information on the next two or three months, though if you have asked yourself the questions we outlined in Chapter 1.1 you will have ensured, as far as possible, that there is a continuing demand for your product so that orders will go on arriving while you are completing the work you have already lined up. But even in cases where you do not know where the penny after next is coming from, at the very least the cash flow budget will tell you what commitments you have to meet and, therefore, what volume of sales should be your target to this end. You can include this sales target in your budget, but do not forget that in order to achieve it costs of materials and additional overheads will also be involved. Moreover, both in cases where income is firmly expected and where it is only a forecast of expectations, the cost of materials and wages will have to be met before you actually get paid.

Let us take a hypothetical case here to illustrate a cash flow budget in operation over the first four months of the year, for a small offset printing business with two partners and one employee. Over these months they have a contract to print the spring catalogue from a local firm of nursery men, a monthly list from a firm selling militaria by mail order and a booklet on the town for the Chamber of Commerce. They also have some orders for what is known as 'jobbing' – small jobs such as wedding invitations, brochures, printed labels and the like – with the prospect that a regular flow of such work can be picked up. Against this, they have to meet wages, rent, PAYE, VAT, telephone, the running of a van, the purchase of materials, rates, electricity, National Insurance contributions, etc.

As you will see from the forecast (see Table 7.1), the partners budgeted for a deficit in the first two months, but they were not worried because they knew that in March and April they could expect a couple of big payments from Rosebud Nurseries and from the Chamber of Commerce. However, in order to keep solvent they had to borrow £2000 from the bank, interest payments on which had to be paid at intervals. They also had to plan the purchase of their most costly item, paper, as close as possible to the month in which they would actually be using it for their two big jobs. There is no point in holding expensive stock which cannot be used at an early date. Even though, with inflation, it might actually have been cheaper for them to have ordered all their paper for the first four months back in January, their bank overdraft would not have been sufficient to meet the bill.

In March they had to allow for three quarterly items, electricity, telephone and their VAT return, and as the year progresses they will have to make plans to meet such major items as rates and taxes. Note also that expenditure which is central to the activities of the business, in this case paper, has to be forecast more carefully than incidentals such as postage where a monthly average has been extended. If postage was a more crucial factor, as might be the case with a mail-order firm, this part of the cash flow budget would have to be worked out in more detail.

Regarding the revenue part of the forecast, the partners had enough orders for jobbing work to budget fairly accurately for the first two months. For March and April they guessed a figure, hoping spring weddings and a general upturn of business after the winter would lead to a modest growth in incoming funds after that point.

The overall March and April figures look quite rosy, but after that it was clear that they would have to turn up some more jobs like Rosebud Nurseries and the Chamber of Commerce booklet because the over-heads – wages, rent, the maintenance contract on their machines, bank interest – plus the cost of paper and materials needed to fill forecast work were running slightly above the expected income. So even though they are running well ahead of the game at the end of April, they would be unwise to start reducing that bank overdraft just yet.

There are many other lessons to be learned from your cash flow budget. They vary from business to business, but the essential points are that it is an indispensable indicator in making your buying decisions both of stock and materials, that it helps you to decide your priorities between getting work (and what sort of work) and devoting all your

	January		February		March		April	
Income (£)								
From	December Statement		January Statement		February Statement		March Statement	
Militaria Ltd	500		500		Rosebud Nurseries Ltd	5,300	Chamber of Commerce	2,000
Other work	400		250		Militaria Ltd	500	Militaria Ltd	500
		900		750	Other work	500	Other work	500
						6,300		3,000
Expenditure (£)								
Wages, salaries, PAYE, National Insurance	750		Wages, etc 750		Wages, etc	750	Wages, etc	750
Rent	100		Rent 100		Rent	100	Rent	100
Maintenance contract	20		Maintenance 20		Maintenance	20	Maintenance	20
Petrol	40		Petrol 40		Petrol	40	Petrol	40
Postage	20		Postage 20		Postage	20	Postage	20
Travel and Entertainment	40		Travel, etc 40		Travel, etc	40	Travel, etc	40
Paper	1,500		Materials 100		Materials	150	Materials	100
Other materials	200		Bank Interest 60		Electricity	70	Paper	1,500
		2,670		1,130	Telephone	40		2,570
					VAT	300		
					Paper	1,000		
						2,530		
Cash surplus (deficit)	(1,770)		(380)		3,770		430	

Table 7.1 *An example of a cash flow budget*

energies to executing it, and points to the importance of getting the maximum credit and allowing the minimum!

Checklist: budgeting and cash flow

1. Is the forecast of money coming in based on firm orders or at least reasonable expectations or does it include an element of fond hope?
2. Are the customers concerned likely to pay you at the times forecast?
3. Can you persuade any large customers to offer you progress payments to help you over difficult months?
4. Have you included everything in the outgoings section of the budget, including allowing for things like VAT and the heating of premises in winter months?
5. Do you have the resources to see you through deficit months, or have you secured finance to this end?
6. Is there any way you can cut down on the expenditure element by delaying or staggering buying decisions of stock or leasing rather than buying equipment?

CHAPTER 1.8

Costing, Pricing and Estimating

How much should you charge your customers? Or, to put it more searchingly, on what factors should your charges be based? It is surprising than many self-employed people would be hard put to it to give a clear answer to that question. There are such things as 'going rates' and 'recommended' (or generally accepted) prices, but often these are in the nature of broad guidelines and unless you know what all your costs are, not just the cost of materials, or how long the job took you, you are sooner or later going to be in the position of either undercharging or making an actual loss.

There are some self-employed occupations where the scope for how much you can charge is either narrow or non-existent. This applies particularly to many areas of the retail trade, where goods tend to have recommended prices printed on them by the suppliers; but even there you may want to consider *reducing* some prices in order to undercut a competitor and the question arises whether you can afford to do so. This depends on your overall costs – rent, rates, power supplies and many other factors. Equally, some freelance jobs are subject to generally accepted 'going rates' and the more commonplace such jobs are (ie the smaller the degree of service or expertise that is involved) the more strictly you have to keep within that rate. But the corollary of this statement is also true: the more unique your product or service, the more you can afford to charge for it.

This can apply even in the ordinary retail trade where, on the face of things, the prospect of getting away with charging more than the competition is not promising. Recently a small supermarket opened near my house. It is open late at night, on Sundays and on public holidays and, quite rightly, it charges for that extra time. Most things cost a penny or two above what they do in the larger shops down the High Street, but it is offering something more than they are, and meets competition not by charging less, but by providing more – a much-needed neighbourhood service for out-of-hours shopping.

The same principle can be applied to even rather routine freelance jobs. Provide a straightforward typing service and you will have to stick pretty much to the going rate; but offer something special, like accurately typing mathematical material or unusually high turn-round speeds, and you can move into a different price bracket.

Determining your costs

You could say to yourself: 'I'm going to charge as much as I can get away with' or, 'I'm going to charge the standard rate for the job.' These are quite sensible guidelines to be going on with, but at some point you are probably going to be in the situation of wondering whether you should be charging a little more, or perhaps whether you can afford to reduce your price in order to land some work that you badly want. It is then that you have to get to grips with what your costs really are.

The most obvious one is your own time, and curiously enough it is an element that self-employed people are often confused about, because they tend to regard it as being somehow different from the time taken by employees. If a job involves your working flat out for a 100-hour week, you are underpricing the product of that work if your remuneration is less than that of an employed person doing the same kind of work at full overtime rates. There may be a reason why you *should* be undercharging: you may want a 'loss-leader' introduction to a particular customer, or to undercut a competitor, or you may simply need the money that week. But if you undercharge, you should be clear in your mind why you are doing so.

Another factor that is sometimes overlooked is that in most cases there are overhead costs incurred in running your business, irrespective of whether you have work coming in or not. We will deal with these overheads in more detail in a moment, but the point to be made here is to correct any misconception that the margin between what you charge and your basic costs in time and/or materials represents your profit. True, it is a profit of a kind – gross profit. But the real profit element in a job, the net profit, only emerges when the overhead costs have been met. So the right way to work out your price to the customer, or to determine whether a job is worth taking on, is to establish whether it will pay for materials, overheads, wages (if you employ others) and still leave you with a margin of net profit that adequately reflects the time and skill you are putting into it.

Once you have been in business for a few months you should have accumulated enough facts and figures to establish what your overhead costs are. To what extent you can control the situation beyond that

London Society of Chartered Accountants

BOTHERED? CONFUSED? Feeling in need of practical advice and assistance in starting a business, with VAT or talking to the bank manager or the tax inspector?

The London Society of Chartered Accountants Enquiry Service can help to put you in touch with a chartered accountant in your area who can provide help and advice. *Please contact:*

London Society of Chartered Accountants
52 Tabernacle Street, London EC2A 4NB
Telephone: 071-490 4390

depends, again, on what sort of business you are in. If you are running an ordinary retail shop, operating on margins that are more or less fixed by the supplier, there is not much you can do about pricing your goods, but at least you will know whether you can afford to spend more on extra fittings or take on more staff, or whether you should be staying open longer to attract extra trade. But if you are manufacturing something, you can work out a rule-of-thumb method in the form of a percentage to add on to your materials costs in quoting prices or, in the case of a service, an average hourly rate. It is important, though, to keep on monitoring these rule-of-thumb procedures against what actually happened, so you should keep a record detailing the specification of each job, in which actual costs can be compared against your original estimate. Over a period of time, in this way you should be able to build up a reliable set of costs which can be referred to when an assignment which sounds similar comes up.

At the beginning, though, you will have very little to go on, so let us look in more detail at the factors you will have to take into account.

Costs connected with your premises

Rent, heat, light, telephone, rates, insurance, finance (if you own or have bought a lease of the premises), cleaning and maintenance contracts.

A cost that particularly has to be watched now is the effect of the uniform business rate. Anyone moving into a property for business purposes has to bear the full increase in rateable values that came in 1990. If you are already occupying business premises, the increase is staggered over five years at 20 per cent a year, plus inflation.

In some parts of the country rates have actually been lowered, but in the more prosperous areas, where new business formation is most likely, they have increased sharply.

Costs of finance
Interest charged on overdrafts or loans. You should include in this calculation interest on any money you yourself have put into the business, because it should be earning a rate of return equivalent to what you could get on the open market.

Costs of equipment
If you are renting equipment or buying it on hire purchase this item of expenditure presents no problems. The issue is more complicated if you have bought equipment outright, because you have to figure out some way of recovering the purchase price and this is done by bringing in the concept of 'depreciation'. What this means is that you gradually write off, over a period of time based on the item's useful life, most of the amount you paid initially; not all, because it will have some resale value at the end of the depreciation period.

Supposing you bought a second-hand van for £6000 and you think it will last you for four years, at the end of which time you could expect to get £1000 for it. This leaves you with £5000 to depreciate over four years – £1250 per annum. There are also a number of other ways to calculate depreciation and your accountant will advise you on the method most advantageous to your kind of business. The important point to bear in mind, though, is that depreciation is a real factor, not just an accountancy device. Assets like motor cars and equipment do wear out and have to be replaced. Financial reserves should be built up to enable you to do this.

Administrative costs
Running your business will involve general expenditure which cannot be directly related to particular assignments: stationery, publicity, travel, postage, entertainment of clients, fees to professional advisers, and so forth.

Salaries and welfare
Salaries are best calculated at an hourly rate, based on an average working week. In the case of employees these rates are usually determined by the market for that particular kind of employment. The

problem is deciding how much you should pay to yourself. Again, this obviously varies with the kind of business you are in, but as a rough guideline you should, after meeting all your expenses, be earning at least as much as an employed person with the same degree of skill and responsibility. It is most important to cost your time properly; let us, therefore, look at a worked example of what might be involved in the case of a person in full-time self-employment.

Supposing you were aiming to earn £18,000 a year. To start with you would want to take into account four weeks' annual paid holiday (three weeks, plus statutory holidays) and you would assume an eight-hour day and a five-day working week. However, not all your time would be directly productive: some of it would be spent travelling, on administration and on getting work. So let us say your productive time is 32 hours a week. That would give you an hourly rate based on 32 × 48 hours a year: 1536 hours. Divided into £18,000, that means a rate of about £11.70 per hour. On top of that you have to allow for welfare items: your National Insurance stamp, possibly contributions to a retirement pension scheme and certainly insurance against sickness or death. Let us assume this comes to another £1000 a year. Divided by 1536 working hours, this adds another 65 pence to your hourly rate.

Similarly, when costing the time of any full-time staff working for you, it is not just a question of calculating basic rates of pay. You have to allow for holidays, the employer's contribution to National Insurance stamps and to the graduated pension scheme. These items can add 6 to 8 per cent to the cost of wages.

Variable costs

All the costs we have just described are fixed costs. You incur them whether you have work coming in or not. Variable costs are items like materials which can be attributed to specific jobs. There are circumstances in which what we have described as fixed costs can vary slightly. If you are running a lot of overtime, this will mean an increase in your fuel bills and extra payments to your staff or to yourself. But the benefit of achieving properly costed increases in productivity, for example in the case of a shop staying open late to attract more trade, is that, provided you are able to keep fixed overheads stable, this element will form a smaller proportion relative to your turnover, and that means a more profitable business.

Establishing your prices

You now have a set of basic data on costs which can be applied to your prices when you are asked to quote for a job or in making up your invoice. If you are supplying a service, the best way to do this is to take all your fixed costs, establish an hourly rate based on your usual working

week and then estimate how long the job will take you. The effect of this is that if jobs do not materialise in the way the 'usual working week' concept implies, you yourself are going to be carrying the can for the fixed overheads which are being incurred during all the hours in that week when you are not working. And if you only get 20 hours' work during a week in which you had budgeted for 40, loading your charges to the customer to make up for the shortfall could mean that you will come up with an unacceptable quotation or a price that will discourage your customer in the future.

The other lesson to be learned is that fixed overheads should be kept as low as possible. For instance, if you are planning a freelance design service to earn extra money in the evenings you should be chary of acquiring expensive equipment. In the limited hours of work which a part-time freelance operation implies, you may never be able to charge enough money to do more than pay the overheads. As far as possible, keep your costs in the variable category by hiring or renting equipment only when and for as long as you need it.

This is also true of businesses that produce manufactured articles (and activities which operate on lines similar to manufacturing such as a restaurant, where the product is created in the form of a meal), though in these cases some machinery and equipment are usually essential. The price here will be based on a unit per item rather than on an hourly rate, but the principle is the same. Instead of fixing an hourly rate based on an expected working week, calculations should be made on a projected volume of costs spread over the number of units sold. Thus, if you aimed to sell in a week 20 chairs which cost you £5 each in materials your variable costs would be £100. If your fixed overheads, including your own remuneration, came to £300 a week, you would have to charge £20 per chair. And do not forget that even if your object is only to make a living wage out of your business, you should still be putting aside reserves to replace equipment as it wears out, and that the cost of doing so will, in periods of inflation, be a great deal higher than its original cost.

Preparing quotations

With many jobs, whether they are a service or a commission to manufacture something, you will be asked to supply a quotation before a firm order is placed. Once that quotation has been accepted it is legally binding on both parties, so it is important not only to get your sums right but to make it clear in the wording attached to them what exactly you are providing for the money. In the case of a decorating job, for example, you should specify who is providing the materials and, if you are, to what standards they are going to be. Consider also whether any out-of-pocket expenses will be involved (travel, subsistence) and whether these are to be met by your customer or whether they have been allowed for in your quotation.

Apart from variable factors such as these, every quotation should set out the conditions of sale under which it is being offered. Different businesses will involve different kinds of conditions, but here are some basic points to bear in mind:

1. Particularly in times of inflation, you should make it clear that the prices quoted are current ones and may have to go up if costs rise during the course of the job.
2. Terms of payment should be set out, for example 30 days net.
3. You will have to cover the not uncommon situation of the customer changing his mind about the way he wants the job done subsequent to his accepting your quotation. You should leave yourself free to charge extra in such circumstances.
4. If you have agreed to complete a job within a certain length of time, set out the factors beyond your control which would prevent you from meeting the agreed date.
5. You should make it clear what circumstances of error, loss or damage will be your responsibility and what would fall outside it.
6. You should stipulate that once the quotation is accepted, the order cannot be cancelled except by mutual consent and that the customer will be liable for all charges up to that point.
7. You should mention that the total is subject to VAT at the rate ruling at the date of invoice. This is particularly important when the customer is a private person who is unable to claim back his VAT inputs. (See Chapter 1.12 for details of VAT.)

Having gone to all the trouble to set out the quotation and conditions of sale, you should not neglect to check, before you start work, that the customer has actually accepted it in writing! It is all too easy to forget this or to imagine that an amicable verbal OK is sufficient. If a dispute arises, however, you will be very thankful to have carried out all the formal steps of documentation.

Every few months sit back for half an hour and consider your pricing policy. If you have set up as a consulting engineer and have no wish to get involved with renting offices and employing others, your workload capacity is limited to the number of hours you put in. To start with you will probably be glad of work at any price but as your business builds up to the point where you are working all hours the only way you will be able to increase your real income is to increase your prices. So if you have a reliable supply of work coming in which is giving you a reasonable income, do not be afraid to put in some highish quotes for new work. It is not always the case that the lowest tender wins the job, particularly in the field of consultancy.

Checklist: costing, pricing and estimating

1. How unique is your product or service? If it is not particularly uncommon, how can you make it more so?
2. How essential is it to the customer?
3. What is the competition charging for the same or similar product or service?
4. How badly do you need the job or order?
5. Is your customer likely to come back for more if the price is right, or is it a one-off?
6. Will doing business with this customer enable you to break into a wider market, and thus enable you to reduce your unit costs?
7. What is the element of risk involved (ie is the customer, to your knowledge, a quick and certain payer)?
8. Do you have any idea how long the job will take you?
9. Can you relate the time element to your fixed costs?
10. Have you made a full assessment of all your fixed costs?
11. Do you have any idea what your materials are going to cost you?
12. Have you costed your own time properly?
13. Will the job leave you a margin of net profit? Or should you forgo this in the interest of meeting fixed costs?
14. Have you prepared a quote, specifying exactly what you are going to provide or do, including terms of payment?
15. Has the customer accepted your quotation?
16. Are you keeping records of what the job cost you so that you can adjust your prices or quote more accurately next time?

CHAPTER 1.9

Marketing Your Work

Good ideas, it is sometimes dismissively said, are ten a penny, the implication being that the really difficult part is putting them into effect. Apart from the obvious virtues of persistence, hard work and technical know-how, this also requires a modicum of marketing skill. In other words, you will have to know whether there is a big enough demand for your product or service at the price you need to charge to make a living and how to identify and reach your potential customers.

Manufacturers

You may be the world's most skilful maker of hand-carved model sailing ships, but unless enough people want them you are going to have a hard time trying to make a living out of producing them commercially. So before you start in business, look around. Go to gift shops, luxury stores or wherever it is that the kind of item you are aiming to produce is being sold and find out about prices, quality standards and the extent of the demand. Any intelligent shop manager or assistant will be glad to give you such information, provided you do not buttonhole them at a busy time of the day. It may be that by modifying your idea in quite a minor way, you will come up with a much more saleable article than the one that was originally in your mind.

Another point to watch out for is whether there is a long-term future for your product. This is particularly true with regard to fashion goods. There may be a craze for some particular kind of accessory and for a while you will be able to sell everything you produce. But before long some large manufacturer will come along and make the same thing much more cheaply and distribute it more effectively than you can. When the craze dies down he will get off the bandwagon and on to something else. Are you going to be able to keep a step ahead of him by being in a position to meet the next craze before the big manufacturers become aware of it?

You also have to keep an eye on competitors of your own size. If you are making and selling pottery, consider how many other craft potters are active in your area and whether your work is so good and so competitively priced that it does not matter how many there are; or whether you can produce something commercially viable that they are not doing.

But no matter how good or unique your product may be, the ultimate key to success lies in effective sales and distribution. At the smallest level you might be selling direct to the public through your own shop, as is the case with many craft goods, but you have to bear in mind that you need to achieve a considerable turnover for a shop in a good location to be viable. This is difficult if the range of specialisation is very narrow, and many small-scale manufacturers, therefore, combine having their own shop with direct mail and mail order (which we shall come to in a moment) and with marketing to other retail outlets. Shop and workshop premises can be combined in the same floor area, so that you can switch readily from the sales counter to the workbench when the shop is empty. This requires permission from the local planning authority if a 'change of use' of what were originally shop premises is involved.

Starting-up costs will eat deeply into your capital, so unless you have enough experience of the marketing (as opposed to the manufacturing) end of your speciality to be absolutely convinced that you can sell it, it is a good idea to begin by making a few prototypes of the product and its packaging and by trying to get orders from retailers. Though your friends and family may think your idea is wonderful, the acid test is whether it will survive in the marketplace. In the course of investigating this, the natural conservatism of most branches of the retail trade may at times depress or irritate you, but it is worth listening to what people who are involved in it have to say. If the same criticisms keep on cropping up you should think seriously of modifying your prototype to take them into account.

Distribution can be another big headache and your premises should be big enough to enable you to hold roughly as many days' or weeks' supply of stock as it takes to replace it at its rate of demand. If a business is selling ten chairs a week and it takes two weeks to get that number of replacements, there should, ideally, be space for something like 20 chairs. A customer might be prepared to wait a week for delivery, but he is unlikely to wait a month.

Accessibility of non-selling areas is important too. Adequate entry for goods and materials at the rear or side of the premises is often essential and will always save time and energy.

Dealing with large companies

Winning an order from a large company can put a small business on its feet at a stroke, not only directly but in terms of gaining credibility with other customers. But pursuing orders of that kind is not without its perils. For one thing large firms are not necessarily rapid payers; nor, as some bankruptcies have shown, is a household name inevitably a sign of financial soundness. Careful checks with your bank are essential.

The implications of a big order also need to be thought out very fully in cash flow terms and if progress payments are not offered, other forms of finance will have to be found. A further point to consider is that it is highly likely that a major customer will seek to impose conditions not only of price, but of quality and delivery. Fair enough; but in combination these three can make what seems like a high value order look much less tempting on the bottom line of profitability.

The whole thing becomes even more complicated if you find you have to subcontract part of the job, as is often the case when a small business lands in the big time. Unless you can control the subcontractor's work very tightly by writing and being in a position to enforce a very clear set of specifications you can land yourself in the position one small book publisher got into once. It won an order from a major chain of multiples for many tens of thousands of copies of a number of titles. For cost reasons these had to be manufactured in the Far East and when they were delivered they did not match up to the very strict merchandising standards that had been stipulated. What had looked like a wonderful stroke of good fortune turned into a horrifying, litigation-laden loss.

Of course, large companies are anxious to avoid this sort of thing, so they seldom deal with small companies whose approach is less than 100 per cent professional. A lot of them, by all accounts, fall down at this first hurdle. However good your idea or product, it will never even come up for discussion unless your letter is clearly and neatly presented, reasonably well written and, above all, sent to the right person. Firms are full of stories of letters being sent to executives who had long left the company and whose names had been gleaned from some out-of-date directory. One phone call would have done the trick.

The lesson that small things make big impressions is also worth remembering when the big customer you have been courting finally sends his inspection team or his purchasing officer round. Nothing looks worse than a scruffy reception area or sounds worse than badly briefed staff. Indeed, you yourself should make sure that you can answer convincingly all the questions you are likely to be asked on such things as capacity, delivery, the quality of your workforce and whatever is connected with the business you are trying to win.

Shops and service industries

The first large shopping centre built in Britain was a flop because, among other disadvantages, it had no parking facilities and was situated in a working-class area a few minutes' walk away from a large, long-established and very popular street market. The developers, for all their vast financial resources, had ignored hotel magnate Conrad Hilton's three factors in siting a business serving the public: location, location and location. If you are thinking of setting up a shop, restaurant or some other service outlet, find out as much as possible about the area. What sort of people live there? Is the area declining economically or on the up and up? What is the range of competitors? How efficient do they look and how well are they doing? If you are thinking of opening a high-class restaurant and there are nothing but fish and chip establishments in the neighbourhood, does this mean that there is no demand for a good restaurant or a crying need for one?

Take the case of a bookshop. You would want to conduct some rule-of-thumb market research about the area before going any further. For example, you would want to know whether there were enough people in the area to support such a venture, whether they were the sort of people who regularly bought books, and how good the local library was. You would also want to know what impact the result of your market investigations might have on your trading policies. Thus, if there were a lot of families with young children around, you should be considering getting to know, and stocking, children's books; or, if there were a lot of students in the neighbourhood, it would be worth your while finding out what textbooks were being used in local educational institutions. Alternatively, if your bookshop is highly specialised – medicine, academic history, chess, or some other specific activity – an expensive High Street location is likely to be wholly inappropriate. You will want to be near the centre of that activity, or, more likely, will want to sell to your well-defined audience through direct mail.

The same broad principles apply to almost every kind of retail or service outlet and you will have to conduct this kind of research, which is really just plain common sense, whatever your venture. Do not be tempted to overlook it just because you are buying what is supposed to be a 'going concern'. One reason why it is up for sale may be that, despite the owner's or agent's protestations to the contrary, it was doing badly. If that was because the previous owner was a poor manager or stocked the wrong kind of goods for the neighbourhood you might be able to turn the business around, but if there was simply too much competition in the area from similar shops and there is no chance of trading viably in something else from the same address, you would be well advised to forget about those premises, however good a buy they may seem from a purely cost point of view. You will also be able to check on the vendor's assertions by looking, preferably with your accountant, at his profit and loss accounts, not just for the past year but the previous three to five years, to get a picture of the general trend of things. On the whole, buying a going concern has to be approached with great caution, particularly by the inexperienced, because of the difficulties of valuing stock and goodwill with any accuracy. See Chapters 2.2 and 2.5 for more detailed treatment of these points.

Freelance services

Most freelances agree that the way you get work is by knowing people who are in a position to give it to you. That sounds rather like a chicken-and-egg situation and, to begin with, so it is. You would be ill-advised to launch into freelance work, certainly on a full-time basis, until you have built up a range of contacts who can provide you with enough work to produce some sort of living for at least the first few months. Often these are people whom you have got to know in the course of a full-time job, or while doing temporary work. Many advertising agencies, for instance, have been started by a breakaway group taking a batch of clients with them when they start up.* And it may even be that your employer, having been compelled to make you redundant, will still be willing to put work out to you on a freelance basis.

Once you have got going and established a reputation for doing good, reliable work, things get much easier. For one thing, word-of-mouth recommendations have a strong effect in the freelance world. Moreover, you will be able to produce examples of work sold, or be able to refer prospects to other clients who have engaged you successfully. Evidence, for instance, that your fashion photographs have actually been used by national magazines is generally more impressive than a folder of prints, no matter how good they are. In freelance work, as in other spheres, nothing succeeds like success.

One problem with freelance work, though, is that clients often want something done in a hurry – over a weekend or even overnight. This can be highly inconvenient at times, but it is generally a bad idea to turn work down simply for this reason. If you have to be selective, turn away the smaller, less remunerative jobs or commissions from people who are slow to pay their bills. One thing you should never do is to let a client down. If you cannot, or do not want to, take on an assignment, say so immediately.

---

* To combat this trend many firms now include clauses in their employment contract expressly stating that it is not permissible to work for a client of the employer for two years after leaving that employer.

Press advertising

Advertising is a marketing tool and like any other tool you have to use it in the right place, at the right time and for the right job if it is going to be of any use to you. If you are a local building contractor, there is no point in advertising in national newspapers, because most of the circulation, which is what you are paying for in the rates charged, will be outside the geographical area you are working in. On the other hand, if you are making a product to sell by mail order, the bigger the circulation the better. There are, however, still provisos; there is, for example, no point in advertising a product aimed at 'top people' in a mass-circulation tabloid.

The first rule is to pick the right medium for the product or service you have to sell. Do not be dazzled by circulation figures. What matters is the *quality* of the circulation in relation to your marketing needs, and a trade or local paper may often provide the best value for money. A few years ago the author was responsible for marketing a very expensive American book on Japanese flower arranging. It turned out that there was a small journal with a circulation of a few hundred copies to devotees of this arcane hobby and a full-page advertisement (which then cost a mere £15), combined with an order coupon, produced a quite extraordinary response. Of course, full-page advertisements normally cost a good deal more than that and in the nationals they can run to thousands of pounds. A small, regular insertion in a local or specialist paper is what you should be thinking of, and the keyword is 'regular'. People's needs change from week to week, and unless you happen to hit them in the week they need your product you will not hit them at all.

Regular advertising need not be expensive. An advertisement in the 'classified' section (but be sure to specify the right classification!) costs only a few pounds, and there may be bulk rates for regular insertions. You can also have a display advertisement. These are charged by column inches (or centimetres) rather than by line as is the case with classified. It costs more, but the advantage is that you may be able to control the position in which your advertisement is to appear. The top and outside edges are more eye-catching than, say, the inside corners. 'Facing matter' advertisements, particularly when they are facing a feature article relating to your kind of product, can also be very effective. It is a good idea to get a graphic designer – you will find plenty of addresses in Yellow Pages or your Thomson local directory – to do a layout for you. It will only cost you a few pounds and the result will be infinitely more attractive and eye-catching than if you leave it to the printer's typesetter.

Some days are reckoned by admen to produce a better response than others, although there are divided opinions on what these days are. The best advice is to experiment with different days. It is worth

HEMGLAS

DELIGHTFUL, DELICIOUS...DELIVERED!

The Hemglas Franchise

Delightful, Delicious...Delivered is the message to customers which is advertised on all vehicles operated under the Hemglas franchise.

From factory to freezer without any loss of temperature and therefore quality, is the boast of this company which delivers Frozen Food and Ice Cream Products direct to the consumer.

With a unique system of tours and distinctive chimes, operated under franchise from Hjem-Is Europa A.S. of Swedish origin, the U.K. Company Home Ice Products Ltd has embarked upon a programme of franchising its existing areas to individual franchisees.

Each franchisee who takes up an area is assured of existing trading income from Day 1 by virtue of the tours already being operated by the company.

In addition to the supply of a fully liveried vehicle, the company offers a 100% support system for all its franchisees by including management and accounting functions, marketing origination, product sourcing, pricing structure, provision for a replacement vehicle and additional sales support in case of emergency within its package.

The whole franchise has been designed to release the franchisee from worrying administration and other burdens so that all available time can be devoted to selling.

The four existing Regional Centres presently service franchisees in the West Midlands, East Midlands and East Anglia. The company will be actively expanding its operation into North Yorkshire and Kent during 1994.

With many imported products from Sweden and Denmark the company commands a large share of the take home Ice Cream market and is well placed to expand its activities nationwide through its franchise programme.

With Frozen Food and Ice Cream consumption set to increase dramatically in the U.K. the future for the business and its franchisees looks extremely rosy.

The best way to buy Ice Cream

Home Ice Products Ltd
Milnyard Square
Orton Southgate   Telephone: 0733 371711
Peterborough PE2 0GX   Fax: 0733 370175

Company Registered in
England and Wales
Registration No. 2695716

experimenting with the wording, too. Try several variations on the same theme and use the one that brings you the best response. But avoid trying to cram in too many words. People do not, on the whole, respond to overcrowded ads.

One important feature is that your advertisement should be very specific about how the goods and services advertised can be obtained. Your address should be prominent and if you are only available at certain times of the day or in the evenings this should be stated. If you are selling a product, an order coupon (stating price *and* postage) reinforces this point. It will also enable you to measure the extent of the response. You should, in fact, keep a close eye on where most of your sales or assignments come from: the type of customer and how he is getting to hear about you. This will enable you to concentrate future marketing efforts in the most rewarding sectors.

Public relations

It may be possible, particularly if you have a specialist line of business, to obtain free coverage in trade journals and local newspapers by sending them press releases to mark events such as the opening of an extension or the provision of some unique service. You simply type the information on a slip marked PRESS RELEASE; 'embargo' it – ie prohibit its use – until a date that suits you, and send it to newspapers and magazines you choose as the likeliest to use it. Newspapers and other news media – don't forget about local radio and even local TV – are, however, only interested in *news* and the mere fact that you have opened a business may not interest them much. Try to find a news angle; for instance, that you have obtained a large export order, or are reviving a local craft or are giving employment to school-leavers. If you have any friends who are journalists ask their advice on the sort of information that is likely to get the attention of editors. Better still, ask them if they will draft your press release for you.

There are many other PR activities – sponsorship, stunts, celebrity appearances at your premises, public speaking, and so on. All are designed to publicise who you are and what you do, and suggest to the public that you provide a worthwhile and reliable service. PR for the small business is covered thoroughly in Michael Bland's *Be Your Own PR Man* (published by Kogan Page).

Direct mail and direct response promotion

Direct mail selling is a considerable subject in its own right. It differs from mail order in that the latter consists of mailing goods direct to the customer from orders engendered by general press advertising, whereas in the case of direct mail selling the advertising is a brochure or sales letter specifically directed at the customer. Direct response promotion consists of an ad plus coupon placed in a newspaper or journal, to be posted to the manufacturer as an order. If you use these methods, remember to allow for postage in your pricing and since the response to direct mail averages around 2 per cent, the postage cost per sale is quite a considerable factor. It can, however, be a very effective way of selling specialised, high-priced items (£15 is around the viable minimum these days) or of identifying people who are likely to buy from you regularly if you are selling variations on the same product. Unless you are very skilful at writing brochures or sales letters you should get this done for you by an expert. Such people are employed by mailing list brokers (you will find those in the Yellow Pages), who will often provide a complete package: they will sell to you, or compile for you, specialised lists, address and stuff envelopes and produce sales literature.

Their services are not cheap and before you plunge into a direct mail campaign there are relatively inexpensive ways of testing the market for yourself. Pick 100 specialist addresses of the type you want to reach on a bigger scale – again, you may find them in the Yellow Pages. A small want ad in one of the advertising industry's trade papers will soon raise the services of freelance copywriters and designers if you need such help. From the percentage reply to the sample mailing you will be able to gauge whether a bigger campaign is worth mounting and you will also get some idea of how to price the product to take into account the likely mailing costs per sale. It is generally essential, by the way, with direct mail advertising, to include a reply paid card or envelope with your sales literature. Details of how to apply for reply paid and Freepost facilities are available from the Post Office.

Mail Order Protection Schemes

Before you can start selling by direct response advertising in a newspaper or periodical, you will have to get permission to do so from its mail order protection scheme (MOPS). These schemes have been set up under the auspices of the Office of Fair Trading to protect consumers from fraudulent advertisers. Essentially, the various media act as insurers and undertake to refund readers' money if the advertiser absconds or fails to deliver for some reason or other. Before accepting the insurance risk, papers and periodicals will therefore try to satisfy themselves that the advertiser is above board. In the case of national media their requirements will be quite searching; they may want to see accounts, take up credit and other references and even look over your premises. Applications for MOPS clearing at this end of the advertising market have to be accompanied by a fee which can go well into four figures and which has to be renewed every year. Requirements in local and trade media are less exacting, but you still need clearance before they will take your advertisement.

Checklist: marketing your work

Manufacturers

1. Have you tested your idea by discussing your proposed product with potential customers? Or, better still, by showing it to them?
2. Is the market for it big enough? How accessible is it?
3. Can the customers you have in mind afford a price that will produce a profit for you?
4. Have you studied the competition from the point of view of price, design quality, reliability, delivery dates, etc?
5. Should you modify your product in some way so as to get the edge on the competition? Have you worked out what this will do to your costs?
6. Is there a long-term future for your product? If not, do you have any ideas for a follow-up?
7. Can you handle distribution? Do you have access to a van if the market is local? Do you have adequate parking facilities if it requires dispatching?
8. In the latter case, have you taken post and packing costs into account in working out how much the product will cost the customer?
9. Do you have adequate space to hold stock, taking into account production time?
10. Do you have someone who can deal with customer queries and complaints? Or have you allowed for the fact that you will have to take time out yourself to deal with them?

Shops and service industries

1. How much do you know about the area?
2. Is the location good from the point of view of attracting the kind of trade you are looking for?
3. What competitors do you have?
4. How are they doing?
5. Based on your study of the area, and the people who live in it, how does this affect the type of goods or the nature of the service you are going to offer?
6. If you are buying a going concern, have you checked it out thoroughly with your professional advisers?

Freelance services

1. Do you have any contacts who can give you work?
2. Have you made a realistic appraisal of how much you can expect to earn over the first six months?
3. Have you allowed for the fact that you will need a good deal of spare time to go around looking for more business?
4. What evidence can you produce of your competence to do freelance work in your proposed field?
5. Have you shown that evidence to the sort of person who might be a customer to get his reaction on whether it is likely to impress?
6. Who are your competitors, what do they charge and what can you offer that is superior to their services?

Advertising and promotion

1. Have you chosen the right medium to promote your product or service?
2. Do you have any idea of the circulation and how this is broken down, geographically or by type of reader?
3. Have you worked out any way of monitoring results, for instance by including a coupon?
4. Have you included the cost of advertising and promotion in your cash flow budget and in costing your product?
5. Have you worked out how many orders you need to get from your advertising/promotion campaign to show a profit?
6. In the case of a display advertisement, have you specified a position in which it is to appear?
7. Again, in the case of a display ad or a brochure, have you had it properly designed?
8. Does your advertising/promotion material state where your product or service can be obtained and, if relevant, the price?
9. Is the wording compelling? Does it clearly describe the product or service and does it motivate the customer? Would you buy it, if you were a customer?
10. In the case of a classified advertisement, have you specified under which classification it is to appear?
11. Are all the statements and claims you are making about your product or service true to the best of your knowledge and belief, bearing in mind that untruths can leave you open to prosecution under the Trade Descriptions Acts?

CHAPTER 1.10

The Fun of Exporting

'Exporting is fun,' said Harold Macmillan when he was Prime Minister, though it may perhaps be doubted whether he knew much about filling in bills of lading in sextuplicate or waiting for an onward flight in a corrugated iron shed in Burkina Faso. At any rate it has taken a long time for the export message to sink in with British firms and even now many small companies put export fairly low on their list of priorities. But while it is true that it is usually essential to get one's place established in the domestic market, there are many attractions about exporting.

- □ It increases sales and therefore lowers unit costs.
- □ It decreases dependence on the UK market – some companies, for instance, owe their survival to having moved into the Middle East in the early seventies, when business was booming there but in recession almost everywhere else.
- □ It can produce increased profits in countries where you can charge higher prices or where sterling has a poor exchange rate.
- □ It broadens one's awareness of other markets and sometimes gives warning of competing products being developed or on sale elsewhere.
- □ It gives you a chance to see the world 'on the company'.

Even if you find none of these reasons compelling enough to make you want to leave your home patch, there are circumstances under which you can become an exporter without really wishing to. If you have a good product, it is very possible that someone abroad will get to hear of it and want to buy it. Indeed, that is how many small companies first become involved, having made the wise decision that business should never be turned away.

If, however, you decide to play a more active role as an exporter than just meeting the demand as it occurs, what special factors should a small business look at? Actually, in many respects they are not very different from those that apply domestically: that the product has to be competitive in price and quality or that it has a unique feature which places it in a class of its own, but for which there is also a viable demand at a price you are reasonably sure the market will pay. Where export does raise special problems is that you also have to make sure that the product meets local specification in terms of technical requirements and consumer laws; that it can thrive under what may be quite different environmental and climatic conditions; that manuals and user instructions are intelligible, either in English or in translation; and that it does not breach any cultural taboos. The last named is often more important and wide ranging than people realise. One Australian meat company nearly lost a huge Middle East order because their house symbol was stamped on their cheques. It was a pig, an unclean animal in Moslem countries.

Indeed, all markets have their peculiarities and the advice generally given to exporters is first to visit one country or region and get to know it rather than trying to sell to the world. Even Sir Terence Conran, one of Britain's outstanding marketing men, lost heavily at first with his New York venture because he had not appreciated the Americans' appetite for continuing 'sales', however bogus. Apart from that, exporters to the US market often fail to realise that America is such a huge country that the characteristics of the Midwest are different from those of California and that both are different from the South or New York City. Freight is a factor there too – freight costs can eat deeply into margins and you have to consider that the price of your goods to the customer has to include the cost of physically getting them to him.

Similar lessons can be drawn from Africa with its widely different climatic conditions and its heavy ingredient of political risk, from Asia and Australia where sheer distance from the UK means that it can take months to get the goods there and further months to get payment, and even from the EU.

Where to get help

Fortunately, there are quite a few sources of help and advice for those who want to become exporters.

- ☐ Local Chambers of Commerce are often well informed about major markets.
- ☐ Many of Britain's major trading partners maintain trade associations in London (eg the German Chamber of Trade and Industry, the Arab-British Chamber of Commerce) and though some of them are more concerned with exporting to this country than

importing into their own, they do also know what the requirements are in the latter case.

☐ The customer service division of the overseas departments of the big four banks.

☐ The Department of Trade and Industry (DTI). They produce inexpensive booklets of basic information on all the major countries which do business with British firms and you can also get special reports on particular countries, which cost somewhat more. They can also tell you about buying missions from overseas buying organisations established in this country by major foreign department stores, for instance.

   Equally usefully, they organise trade missions through local Chambers of Commerce or trade associations. These enable you to visit major markets as part of a group with a substantial government subsidy. Since contacts can be arranged in advance, this is a considerable saving in time as well as money. Usually, if you go on your own to another country, it takes days simply to find your bearings and set up meetings.

☐ The Overseas Trade Services Department of the DTI produces a *Guide to Export Services* which is well spoken of. The DTI also organises local seminars for small exporters – call 071-215 5000 for details.

Setting up sales arrangements

Few firms will want to move so far, so fast, though. Usually it is a question of setting up some kind of sales operation by appointing a local agent; you may already have been approached by one keen to handle your business. Flattering though such interest is and though it certainly helps to start out with someone who feels optimistic about your prospects, agents do have to be checked out. Bad ones may not only hinder your progress, but may cost you a lot of money by alienating dealers or by taking commission on business which you would have got anyway and which they have made little effort to expand.

   For a small fee the DTI provides status reports on agents, but the best plan is undoubtedly to go out to the territory and meet the prospective agent personally. Apart from any impressions you form of him and his office – you should certainly see the latter – you should find out who else he is working for and preferably get a statement of that in writing. You will be known in that territory by the company you keep. Quite apart from the fact that the agent's other clients should be appropriate to your business – there is no point in having someone handling medical supplies when all their other agencies are office equipment – they should also be reputable. Preferably, the principals in some cases should be known to you so that you can make further inquiries back in the UK. Once you have satisfied yourself of his *bona fides*, there should be a written agreement, defining:

- ☐ The territory
- ☐ The period of time the agreement is to run for
- ☐ Payment terms
- ☐ Whether the agency is exclusive or not; and, if customers are still free to buy direct from you, whether the agent gets commission on such business
- ☐ Whether or not he is to be a stockist and, if he is, on what terms he has the right to return unsold goods
- ☐ What you undertake to provide, free or otherwise, in the way of promotional back-up.

Once you have appointed an agent it is equally important to keep taking an interest in his activities. If he never hears from you, he will assume that you have forgotten his existence. A word of praise, or even complaint, never comes amiss. Remember the American saying, 'The wheel that squeaks loudest gets the most oil.'

Documentation

What chiefly deters small businesses – and some larger ones – from actively pursuing export sales is the documentation it involves. This is particularly true in countries with a strong bureaucracy or where the purchasing is done by the State. Invoices have to be correct in every detail and to conform exactly to quotes or other documents to which they relate; otherwise the goods may not be collected or, worse, not paid for. There are also problems in some countries with certificates of origin of the goods, usually because of political considerations. Quite a number of countries, for instance, do not buy – or at any rate profess not to buy – goods from countries of which they disapprove politically, and demand certified invoices attested by a Chamber of Commerce in multiple copies. In some cases, it must be said, the documentation is literally not worth the trouble it costs – it has to be a matter of judgement related to the value of the goods being supplied or the importance of the customer otherwise.

As an exporter you will also have to familiarise yourself with the arcane vocabulary of export documentation – phrases like CIF, CIP, FOB, FRC and so forth. An excellent account of this and other matters is given in *Selling to Europe* by Roger Bennett published by Kogan Page.

Fortunately, freight forwarders – a list of them can be obtained from the British International Freight Association – will handle the documentation for you, for a fee, which is quite modest considering the hassles involved: about 5 per cent of the total freight costs. Some freight forwarders are less than competent, though. Ask your colleagues in other firms for their recommendations and the name of the person they deal with. Good service quite often depends on one particular individual, who is well worth rewarding with some good Scotch at Christmas time.

The VAT situation on exports to other EU countries is at present a maze of confusion, and you should check the current state of play with the UK Customs & Excise. At present you have to charge VAT at UK rates to non-VAT registered customers in the EU, unless you are trading on a big scale in the country concerned, at which point local arrangements come into place. If the customer is VAT registered, you have to charge him import tax at the equivalent of local VAT rates. Strictly speaking it is not VAT, but you have to show the customer's VAT number on your invoices and record these sales in your UK VAT return.

Getting paid

One thing freight forwarders cannot do for you is to collect payments, and the mechanics of this are a great deal more complicated than in the UK. The reason for this is largely that invoices, which trigger the payment process, also have to serve as a Customs clearance document and must therefore have all kinds of data on them which are not required in the UK: weight, value, origin of the goods and so forth. The requirements vary from country to country and are set out in a book called *Croner's Reference Book for Exporters*. Your bank should be able to help you with them. They should also be able to advise you on the best method of getting paid once the invoice has been presented. Generally, it involves some method of transferring money from the customer's bank to yours so you need feel no hesitation in calling on your bank for assistance.

If you just receive the occasional order from abroad and don't want to get involved in extended payment procedures, the best plan is to send a *pro forma* invoice. This still has to have details which are shown on the commercial invoice, but it means the customer has to pay in advance if he wants the goods. However, you should wait to clear his cheque before dispatching them unless payment is made by some form of mail transfer; again through the bank.

The devaluation of sterling on 'black Wednesday' in 1992 brought handsome profits for those who had quoted prices in one of the currencies that appreciated against the pound. However, sterling rose by a good 10 per cent against some of these currencies during 1993, so those who went on quoting in them lost some of the money they had gained earlier. Most exporters agree that the safest bet is to quote in your own currency. You won't make any windfall profits that way, but at least you know you will be able to pay your UK suppliers in the currency at which you have bought from them, namely pounds sterling.

CHAPTER 1.11

Employing People

A fairly common observation about employing people has been to say that this is when your troubles begin. Apart from the difficulty of finding Mr or Ms Right – a task which even experienced personnel people admit, in their more candid moments, is something of a lottery – employers also have to comply with various articles of employment legislation, though since the early 1980s much of this has been relaxed. However, the main aim of protecting longer-serving employees (and these may include staff in a business you have bought who were taken on by the previous owner) from arbitrary hiring and firing remains in place. Whole books could be and have been written about the legal technicalities involved, but all we can do in this section is to draw your attention to some of the major pitfalls you should look out for when you start employing people.

The terms of employment

The terms of employment statement which has to be issued in writing to every employee who is going to work for you for eight hours or more per week within eight weeks of joining is in fact not a pitfall, but a rather sensible document which clarifies right from the outset what the terms of employment are. From the employer's point of view, the necessity of drafting a terms of employment statement should concentrate the mind wonderfully on issues about which it is all too easy to be sloppy at the expense of subsequent aggravation, such as hours of work, holidays and, above all, exactly what it is the employee is supposed to be doing. The following points have to be covered in the contract, and you must say if you have not covered one or other of them:

- ☐ The normal hours of work and the terms and conditions relating to them

- ☐ Holidays and holiday pay
- ☐ Provision for sick pay
- ☐ Pension and pension schemes
- ☐ Notice required by both parties
- ☐ The job title
- ☐ Any disciplinary rules relating to the job
- ☐ Grievance procedures.

A further requirement is that employers must issue on or before each payday and for each employee an itemised statement showing:

- ☐ Gross wages/salary
- ☐ Net wages/salary
- ☐ Deductions and the reasons for them (unless these are a standard amount, in which case the reasons need only be repeated every 12 months)
- ☐ Details of part-payments, eg special overtime rates
- ☐ The rate of pay and how it is calculated
- ☐ Whether it is paid weekly or monthly
- ☐ The period of employment, if it is temporary.

Unfair dismissal

Probably the area of legislation which it is easiest and most common to fall foul of is that relating to unfair dismissal. Every employee, including part-timers if they work for you in other than a freelance capacity for more than 16 hours a week, who has been on your staff continuously for 104 weeks or more must be given a written statement of your reason if you want to dismiss him.

You must also give him one week's notice (or payment in lieu) if he has been with you continuously for four weeks or more and, after two years, one week's notice for every year of continuous employment. Fair enough, you might say, particularly as, on the face of things, what the law regards as fair grounds for dismissal are perfectly reasonable: incompetence, misconduct or genuine redundancy. The problem is that the employee is at liberty to disagree with you on the fairness issue and to take his case to an industrial tribunal, which stipulates that the employer's grounds for dismissal must be *reasonable*.

The 1980 Employment Act made four changes of particular relevance to small businesses employing staff:

1. The qualifying period for alleged unfair dismissal claims was extended from 6 months to 12. For firms with fewer than 20 employees it has been extended to two years in respect of new employees; an important simplification since redundancy has a similar two-year qualifying period.

2. Industrial tribunals are directed to take account of the size and resources of the employer. For example, where an employee proves unsatisfactory in one job, a large employer might be able to offer him another position, but a small employer would find this more difficult in most cases.
3. Post-maternity reinstatement is waived for firms of five employees or less, if reinstatement is not practicable.
4. Frivolous claims are to be deterred by a liability to costs.

If the employee has been guilty of gross misconduct, such as persistent lateness, you will probably win your case, provided you warned him in writing to mend his ways well before you dismissed him. The point here is that not only must you have good reasons for dismissing him, but also you must have acted reasonably in the dismissal situation. This means that you have got to follow a proper sequence of written warnings – not less than three is the number generally recommended – stating his inadequacies, telling him what he has to do to put them right and spelling out the consequences if he fails to do so.

When it comes to matters of competence, though, things are rather less clear-cut, particularly if the task involved is not one where performance can be readily quantified or where there are many imponderables. It would be relatively easy to argue a case against a machine operator who was consistently turning out less work than his colleagues on similar machines, but far more difficult in the case of a salesman who could plead that a poor call-rate was the result of difficulties in finding car parking or inefficient back-up from the office.

The fact is that in all matters affecting competence you really have to do your homework very carefully before dismissing someone. The inexperienced employer may unwittingly contribute to a judgment by the tribunal going against him by such steps as including the person concerned in a general salary rise not long before informing him he is not up to the job.

There may be cases where you, as the employer, are satisfied that dismissal is fair, but where the law does not agree with you. One where you have to be very careful is dismissal on medical grounds. No reasonable employer would dismiss anyone in such circumstances if he could help it, but if you get stuck with someone who is persistently off sick and is able to provide satisfactory medical evidence, you would have to show proof that the absences were of such a nature as to cause disruption to your business before you could discharge him. Even more tricky is the case of employees who are engaged in public duties, such as being on the local council. You have to give them reasonable time off to attend to those duties, though not necessarily with pay.

We have used the word 'he' of employees so far (in the interests of brevity, not for sexist reasons) but, of course, all these provisions extend

136

to women as well. The Sex Discrimination Act and the Equal Pay Act mean that women have in all respects to be treated on an equal footing with men, though since 1982 firms with fewer than five employees have been exempt from the former provisions. There are also occupations where discrimination is legal on common-sense grounds – for instance, lavatory attendants!

There are some additional hazards to employing women of child-bearing age. Provided she works until 11 weeks before her confinement a woman who has been continuously in your employ for two years or more is entitled to take up to 40 weeks off if she becomes pregnant and to return to her original job, without loss of seniority, at the end of that time. Furthermore, she is entitled to remuneration at nine-tenths of her normal salary less NI maternity allowance, for the first six weeks of her absence, although the employer can recover the money from the Department of Employment. And if you bring in a replacement for her, or any other employee who is off for any longer period of time, be very careful. Her replacement could sue you for unlawful dismissal unless you notify him or her in writing that the appointment is a temporary one and give notice when it is coming to an end. From October 1994, a pregnant employee is entitled by law to 14 weeks' maternity leave, irrespective of how long she has been working for you, or the size of your business – though you will not have to pay her salary while she is away. However, she will also be entitled to reinstatement in her original job, if she gives her employer 21 days' notice of her intention.

The penalties for losing an unfair dismissal case can be ruinous for a small firm. In the most extreme instances you could be in for a compensation award of £11,000, plus any redundancy pay to which the employee is entitled, plus a basic award related to age and length of service. On top of all this, in the most aggravated cases, there is a further substantial additional award of up to £5330 – even higher where sex or race factors are involved. Thus if you are in any doubt at all about a dismissal you should consult a solicitor who is versed in this aspect of the law.

Redundancy

Redundancy is a ripe area for misunderstanding. Redundancy occurs when a job disappears, for example, because a firm ceases trading or has to cut down on staff. It does not have the same restrictions as dismissal, but nevertheless does involve some financial penalties for employers if the employee has been continuously employed by the firm concerned for two years or more. In that case he will be entitled to redundancy pay on a formula based on length of service and rate of pay. About half of this can be recovered from the Department of Employment, which you should notify if you intend to make anyone redundant. As usual, there is a good deal of form-filling involved. The law also requires you to give advance warning to the relevant unions if any of their members are to be made redundant.

What happens if you buy a business, lock, stock and barrel, together with the staff? You may find that you do not like some of the people the previous owner took on, or that you want to change or drop some of the things he was doing, with the result that staff will be made redundant. Irrespective of the fact that you did not hire the people concerned, you are still stuck with your responsibility towards them as their current employer, so that being the proverbial new broom can be a very costly exercise. Before buying a business, therefore, it is very important to look at the staff and at the extent of any redundancy payments or dismissals situations you could get involved in.

Statutory sick pay

Under the Social Security Contributions and Benefits Act (1992), employers are responsible for paying Statutory Sick Pay (SSP) to virtually all employees earning more than £56 a week after 13 weeks' employment, for up to 28 weeks' sickness in the year. The obligation begins after the employee has been off work sick for more than four consecutive days. These need not be working days, though. They could include the weekend, or days when he or she would not normally be working. SSP is treated as earnings, so you should deduct PAYE and pay the employer's National Insurance contribution on it.

After these four days, and once the employee starts qualifying for SSP, it is only payable for the days when he or she would have been working. This means that when you employ part-timers – a growing part of the workforce – you would be well advised to specify their working days in the terms of employment, rather than having a loose 'as and when needed' arrangement.

Good paperwork in SSP situations is all the more important because you claim back the payments you have made by deducting the amounts from the employer's National Insurance contribution.

The employee can offer self-certification for up to seven days. After that the employer should ask for a doctor's certificate. Careful records have to be kept of SSP payments and retained for three years. When you start employing people you should get guidance from the DSS on how they require this to be done.

Guidance leaflets on employment
A great many leaflets giving guidance on employment matters are available free from the Department of Employment. For an up-to-date

list, write to the General Office, Information 4, Department of Employment, Caxton House, Tothill Street, London SW1H 9NF.

In the same context, another Act of Parliament you should keep an eye open for when buying a business is the Health and Safety at Work Act, which lays down standards to which working premises have to conform. Before putting down your money you should check with the inspectors of the Health and Safety Executive that any premises you are buying or leasing as part of the deal meet those standards.

In this connection it is important to be aware of the concept of 'constructive dismissal'. If an employer changes the terms of employment by action such as substantively lengthening hours, reducing pay or benefits or even adversely changing the status of an employee, that can be tantamount to unfair dismissal.

Recruitment

The cost of discharging staff, whether because of redundancy or by dismissal, makes it imperative that you should make the right decisions in picking people to work for you in the first place. We have said that the sphere of personnel selection is something of a lottery. It could equally be described as a gamble and there are ways in which you could cut down on the odds against you.

The most obvious question to ask yourself is whether you really do need to take someone on permanently at all. The principle we have put forward for the purchase of equipment – never buy anything outright unless you are sure you have a continuing use for it and that it will pay for itself over a reasonable interval of time – also applies to personnel. The legal constraints that cover part-time or full-time employees do not extend to freelances, personnel from agencies or outside work done on contract, and this could well be the best way of tackling a particular problem such as an upward bump in demand until you are sure that it is going to last.* It is worth remembering, too, that when you take on staff you take on a good many payroll and administrative overheads in addition to their salary. These can add quite significantly to your costs.

Sooner or later, though, if you want your business to grow (and growth of some kind seems to be an inevitable concomitant of success) you are going to need people. But even then you should ask yourself

---

* However, in some cases freelances have successfully argued retrospectively that since they were subject to the same conditions as the ordinary employees of a firm, they were covered by employment law. It is not enough to say that 'A' is a freelance and 'B' is not; there must be recognisable differences in the way they work. The freelance must not be under your direct supervision and control, or he will be likely to be classified (for the purposes of redundancy pay, etc) as an employee.

what exactly you need them for and how much you can afford to pay. Clarifying these two issues is not only important in itself, but will also give you the basis of a job description which you can use in your press advertising or approach to a recruitment agency, at the interview and, finally, in the contract of employment. Around it you should also build a series of questions to ask the interviewee that should give you some indication of his competence to do the job. Such questions should call for a detailed response rather than a 'yes' or 'no' type of answer. For example, if you are interviewing a sales representative, asking him how long he has been in the business will tell you something, but not nearly as much as the answer to a question that tries to elicit which buyers he knows and how well he knows them.

Competence is part of the story. Equally important is the interviewee's track record: how many previous employers he has had and whether his progress has been up, down or steady. Too many job changes at frequent intervals can be a bad sign and it is fair to ask searching questions about this if it is part of the employment pattern. It is also wise to be cautious about people who are willing to take a large drop in salary. In these days when good jobs are hard to come by there can be a perfectly good reason for this, but you ought tactfully to find out what it is.

Possibly the references will give you a clue and you should always ask for and check references. They are not always reliable – most employers are reasonable people and they will not speak ill of an ex-employee if they can help it (though they should be aware that it is illegal to misrepresent the abilities or overstate the capability of an employee or ex-employee to another employer) – but they will generally alert you to real disaster areas. Telephone reference checks are widely reckoned to be more reliable than written ones because referees are nearly always more forthcoming in conversation than in a letter, since the law of libel and industrial relations law loom large in any written deposition.

Conditions of work

Numerous regulations affect working conditions and you should be conversant with those relevant to your area, particularly if it is a potentially dangerous trade. Length of hours, minimum wages, employment of young persons, etc will tend to apply to all businesses and, though you may escape prosecution for a while, to fall foul of the law is likely to be embarrassing and expensive.

Checklist: employing people

1. Do you really need to take on staff? Will there be enough to keep them busy a year from now?

2. Have you worked out a job description which sets out the purpose of the job, the duties involved and who the person appointed will report to?
3. Have you decided how much you can afford to pay?
4. Does your advertisement or approach to a recruiting agency spell out the job description, the salary and the approximate age of the person you are looking for?
5. Does it in any way contravene the Sex Discrimination Act or the Race Relations Act?
6. Have you prepared a series of questions that will throw some light on the interviewee's competence, personality and previous record of employment?
7. Have you taken up and checked references?
8. Are you satisfied, before making the appointment, that you have seen enough applicants to give you an idea of the quality of staff available for this particular job?
9. Do you have a procedure for reviewing the employee's progress before the expiry of the 104-week period after which he can claim unfair dismissal if you decide he is not suitable?
10. Do you make a practice of putting important matters in writing to the employees concerned?

Taxation

How you are affected by taxation depends on the nature of the commercial activity in which you are engaged. Virtually everyone pays tax on income from some source, whether this be from full-time employment, from dividends or interest or from self-employment, or from a combination of several of these elements. The various kinds of income are assessed under several headings or schedules and the ones we will be particularly concerned with are:

1. Schedule D. Case I and Case II: Income from trades, professions or vocations. (In the interests of simplicity we will refer to this as Schedule D, though there are four other 'Cases' of Schedule D income.)
2. Schedule E: Wages and salaries from employment.

There are also other ways in which you may be involved in tax matters. You may be paying capital gains tax on the disposal of capital assets. If you are employing people full-time, you will be responsible for administering their PAYE payments; also, in certain circumstances, your own PAYE. If you are a shareholder in a limited company, it will be paying corporation tax on its profits. Lastly, you may – and if your turnover exceeds £45,000 a year, you must – for the supply of certain goods and services collect VAT from your customers and pay it over to Customs and Excise, less any VAT on goods and services supplied to you in the course of business.

One cannot, in a book of this nature, deal exhaustively with a subject as complex as taxation. But, with this proviso, let us look in broad outline at some of its principal implications. There are certain income tax advantages in working for yourself, or even in earning a supplementary income from part-time self-employment. To some extent these advantages were eroded by the National Insurance contributions for the

DO YOU WANT TO EARN OVER £30,000pa AND WORK FROM HOME?

After 5 successful years of 'sparkling',we are looking for the right people to help take SPARKLERS* nationwide.

Our commitment to quality, reliability and training has enabled us to grow profitably through the recession in the face of intense competition. We are now offering a complete business package, fully supported with ongoing help and training to the right people who have the desire and ability to join us.

If you are hard working and feel that you could run your own business, in the knowledge that help is close at hand, write or telephone for more information.

WHY SPARKLERS*?
* *Established, Successful Business*
* *Good Brand Image*
* *Commitment to Training and Support*
* *Low Start-up Costs*

T.M.

HOME CLEANING SERVICE
LUDLOW DRIVE, THAME, OXON OX9 3XS.
TELEPHONE 0844 217769.
HOT LINE & FAX 0844 261594

In the PINK

"Instantly recognisable," comments Claire Sebire on the corporate image of Sparklers, the domestic cleaning company she is now launching as a franchise.

Her pink uniformed team, all sporting the distinctive Sparklers logo, certainly do project a look of professionalism. "It's this image," comments Claire Sebire, "together with a reputation for quality and reliability, that has ensured our growth over the past five years."

She believes that Sparklers beats the competition thanks to "a degree of customer service rarely found among cleaning companies – that's why we don't need to advertise. Word of mouth from satisfied customers suffices."

"Priority is building a long-term customer base – we still have our first one! And franchising will permit sharing our success with others while gaining a nationwide presence."

Claire Sebire explains: "We're now looking for the *right* people to meet our strict selection criteria and code of practice for franchisees and workforce alike. This is vital to maintain the reputation we've built up over the years."

A former nurse, she understands the value of interpersonal relationships and wants franchisees capable of talking to people at all levels: "Our customer base ranges from ABC1 to estate semidetached and elderly people. Although most work is in private homes, a homeowner may ask us to clean their office."

She argues that the franchise could be a "fantastic opportunity" for a housewife whose family is growing up – to gain independence from meeting the challenge of building her own business, gaining the satisfaction of direct rewards for her efforts, but without the daunting prospect of being totally on her own.

The company is committed to high quality support and training to help replicate Sparklers nationwide, she insists. "Our franchisees can benefit from our experience of cleaning and our knowledge of how to tap the market.

"We used experienced franchise consultant Gordon Patterson to confirm the business was suitable for franchising. Now that every aspect of the system is tried, tested and finetuned, we're ready to seek franchisees – but they must be the right ones. We won't rush into it."

She enthuses: "I've got exciting plans for the future growth of Sparklers, and the patience to do it properly, to develop a national network of franchisees, providing a local, conscientious service – and thus spread the brand name throughout the country and with it, the Sparklers reputation." ●

self-employed (Class 4) which came into force in April 1975 and imposed what was, in effect, an additional and much resented tax on the self-employed. The amount of the contribution is subject to a certain amount of annual tinkering. It is payable by men under 65 and women under 60 and it currently stands as a levy of 7.3 per cent on profits/gains between £6490 and £22,360 (1994). However, 50 per cent of the Class 4 contributions can be deducted from income for tax purposes.

There have also been some changes in real terms in the flat-rate weekly (Class 2) National Insurance contribution additionally payable by people who have an income from self-employment as well as a salary from another source. The earnings rate from self-employment above which this additional contribution has to be paid is currently £3200 a year and the weekly contribution is now £5.65, payable irrespective of whether or not it is a full-time activity, or something you do in addition to another job as an employee where you are also taxed on PAYE.

The weekly contribution for the full-time self-employed is also £5.65 and the best way to pay it is by direct debit from your bank. If your earnings are likely to be below £3200, you may not have to pay this. In that case you should report the circumstances to your local DSS office and ask for a leaflet which will give you further details on how to proceed – NI 27A: *People with small earnings from self-employment.*

If, in addition to some self-employed activity, you also have a regular job in which you are making Class 1 contributions, paying the Class 2 contribution in addition to that could take you over the maximum earnings limit on which your NI contributions are based. That is currently £430 a week. If you believe your total earnings for the tax year will exceed £22,360 (ie 52 × £430) you can apply for deferment of Class 2 contributions until the level of your earnings is established. That has to be done before the end of the tax year on Form CF 359, obtainable from the DSS, Class 4 Group, Newcastle upon Tyne NE98 1YX.

Like the income of employed persons, the income from self-employment in its various forms is subject to an ascending rate of tax, starting at a flat 20 per cent on the first £3000 per annum, 25 per cent up to £23,700 and rising to a maximum of 40 per cent. These figures are subject to certain personal tax reliefs, such as allowances for dependent relatives, for part of the premiums on life assurance policies, etc, which you can deduct from your total income in arriving at the rate at which you pay tax.

Where income from self-employment or even part-time employment differs from ordinary wage- or salary-earning status is that you are allowed, in assessing your earnings, to deduct from your profits any revenue expenditure 'wholly and exclusively incurred' in carrying on your trade or profession. Under the heading of revenue expenditure comes business expenses, and since your profits and your earnings will be either synonymous or closely related, the first point to observe is that you must claim all the business expenses to which the taxman entitles you.

Principal allowable business expenses

1. *The cost of goods bought for resale and materials bought in manufacturing.* This does not include capital expenditure such as cars or machinery, though certain minor items like small tools or typewriters may be allowed under this heading.
2. *The running costs of the business or practice.* Under this concession come heating, lighting, rent, rates, telephone, postage, advertising, cleaning, repairs (but not improvements of a capital nature), insurance and the use of special clothing. If you are using your home as office you can claim up to two-thirds of the running costs of the premises as a business expense – provided you can convince the taxman that you are indeed using as high a proportion of your house as this exclusively for business purposes. Some people have been advised not to make this type of claim at all, because of the probability that, on selling, they might have to pay capital gains tax on the 'business' part of the sale, thus outweighing any income tax advantage. There are also potential VAT implications. If you claim that more than 40 per cent of your gas bill is attributable to business use, you will have to pay VAT on that portion.
3. *Carriage, packing and delivery costs.*
4. *Wages and salaries.* Any sums paid to full-time or part-time employees. You cannot, however, count any salary you and your partners are taking from the business, but you can pay your wife a salary (provided she is actually doing a reasonably convincing amount of work for you). This is an advantage if her income from other sources is less than £3445 a year, because that first slice of earnings is free of tax – one of the reliefs we mentioned earlier.
5. *Travel.* Hotel and travelling expenses on business trips and in connection with soliciting business. You are not, however, allowed the cost of travel between home and office, if you have a regular place of work. In addition to these expenses you can claim for the running costs of your car (including petrol) in proportion to the extent to which you use it for business purposes.
6. *Interest.* Interest on loans and overdraft incurred wholly in connection with your business. This does not include interest on any money you or your partners have lent to the business.
7. *Hire and hire purchase.* Hiring and leasing charges and hire element in hire-purchase agreement (not the actual cost, because this is a capital expense).

8. *Insurance.* Every kind of business insurance, including that taken out on behalf of employers, but excluding your own National Insurance contributions and premiums paid on your personal life insurance (though these premiums are subject to an ascending scale of personal tax relief, from 17.5 per cent if you are under 35, to as high as 40 per cent for those between 61 and 75).

9. *The VAT element in allowable business expenses (unless you are a taxable trader for VAT purposes).* This would include, for instance, VAT on petrol for your car. The VAT on the purchase of a motor car is allowable in all cases, since this cannot be reclaimed in your VAT return.

10. *Certain legal and other professional fees.* You are allowed to claim for things like audit fees or court actions in connection with business, but not for penalties for breaking the law (eg parking fines!).

11. *Subscriptions to professional or trade bodies.*

12. *Bad debts.* These are bad debts actually incurred, though provision is generally allowed against tax in the case of specific customers whom you can show are unlikely to meet their obligations; for instance, if their account is overdue and they are failing to respond to reminders. A general provision for a percentage of unspecified bad debts is not allowable against tax, however sensible it may be to make such provision in your accounts.

    Trade debts owing to you count as income even if they have not been paid at the end of the accounting period. Likewise, debts owed by you count as costs, even if you are not going to pay them until the next accounting period.

13. *Gifts.* Business gifts costing up to £10 per recipient per year (but excluding food, drink and tobacco). All gifts to employees are allowable, but generous employers should remember that the employee may have to declare them on *his* tax return if their value is substantial.

Capital allowances

You are allowed to write off against taxable profits 25 per cent of the cost of capital equipment on a reducing balance basis after the first year. For instance, in the second year, if you buy a piece of equipment for £1000, you will be granted £250 writing-down allowance. For the following year, it will be 25 per cent of £750 (ie £187.50) and so forth.

The writing-down allowance also extends to private cars used for business, up to a maximum of £3000.

Equipment bought on hire purchase is eligible for the writing-down allowance in respect of the capital element.

The hire charges themselves can be claimed as business expenses, spread over the period of the agreement.

In calculating your writing-down allowances you will have to take into account whether or not you are a taxable trader for VAT purposes, which depends on whether your annual turnover exceeds £45,000. If you are, you will already have claimed the VAT on your purchase in your quarterly or monthly VAT return. Thus capital allowances will be calculated on the net amount excluding VAT (except in the case of motor cars).

Stock valuation

If you are in a business which involves holding stock (which may be either finished goods for resale, work in progress or materials for manufacture), it must be valued at each accounting date. The difference in value between opening stock and closing stock represents the cost of sales. Obviously, therefore, if you value your closing stock on a different basis from the opening stock, this will affect the profit you show. If you value the same kind of items more highly it will depress the cost of sales and increase the apparent profit. If you value them on a lower basis the cost of sales will be increased and the profit decreased.

Example A		**Example B**	
Sales	£150	Sales	£150
Opening Stock		*Opening Stock*	
100 Rose bushes		100 Rose bushes	
@ £1.00: £100		@ £1.00: £100	
Closing Stock		*Closing stock*	
50 Rose bushes		50 Rose bushes	
@ £1.50: £75		@ 60p: £30	
Cost of Sales	£25	Cost of Sales	£70
Profit	£125	Profit	£80

Table 11.1 *An example of stock valuation*

Plainly, then, it does not make sense for you to up-value your closing stock in order to show a paper profit. Equally, you are not allowed to depress it artificially in order to achieve the reverse effect. However, if you can make a genuine case that some stock will have to be sold at a lower margin than the one you normally work to in order to be able to sell it within a reasonable time, a valuation in the light of this fact will generally be accepted by the taxman.

Computing taxable profit

Normally your accountant will prepare a set of accounts for you for each year you are in business. Your accounting date need not coincide with the tax year (ending 5 April). The profits shown in these accounts will be the basis of your assessment.

As we stated earlier, certain costs which are genuine enough from the point of view of your profit and loss account are nevertheless not allowable for tax purposes: for example, entertaining customers other than foreign buyers or their agents. You are also not allowed to charge depreciation against your profit (though remember that you will receive a writing-down allowance which, in the end, has a similar effect). These and other non-allowable expenses must be added back to the profits.

Equally, certain profits which you have made are to be deducted for the purposes of Schedule D assessment because they are taxed on a different basis and are subject to a return under another heading. Examples are gains from the disposal of capital assets, income from sub-letting part of your premises or interest paid by the bank on money being held in a deposit account.

In recent years some new kinds of business spending have come in for tax relief, notably incidental costs of raising loan finance and start-up costs incurred before you begin trading.

Losses

If your business or professional occupation has made a loss on its accounting year (and remember that from the tax point of view non-allowable expenses are added back to profits and you will have to do the same in your return), you can have the loss set off against your other income for the tax year in which the loss was incurred and for the subsequent year. However, you cannot set off business losses against liability for capital gains tax.

If your income for the year in which you made the loss and that of the subsequent year still does not exceed that loss, you can set off the balance against future profits; or you can carry the loss back and set it against earlier profits.

In the case of traders and partnerships, losses incurred in the first four years of a business can be carried back against income from other sources, including salary, in the three years before commencing business as a self-employed person or partner. However, it should be noted that this does not apply to losses incurred by a limited company of which you are a shareholder – such losses can only be set off against profits chargeable in the form of corporation tax. Even if you invest your money in your own company and it fails, you can only set off your loss against capital gains from other sources – not against income tax.

The basis of assessment

For businesses which are up and running on 5 April 1994 Schedule D tax is assessed on the profits for the preceding tax year. Thus your tax assessment for the year ending 5 April 1994, which you have to pay in 1994, will relate to the accounting year which ended in the tax year finishing 5 April 1993. Your *accounting* year, as we have just said, need not coincide with the taxman's year: 6 April to 5 April. You can, if you like, run it to the anniversary of your commencing business, or on a calendar year. However, in the first year of operations, you will be assessed either on the proportion of profits for the accounting year represented by the time from your starting date to 5 April, or the actual profits during these months. You cannot, in respect of the first year, ask to be assessed on a preceding year basis.

Thus, if you commenced business on 1 October 1993 and your profit for the year ending 30 September 1994 is £1000, you will be taxed on the basis of six months' profit (1 October 1993 to 5 April 1994). This assessment will have to be met in 1994. It is not on a preceding year basis.

In the second tax year, in this instance the one ending 5 April 1995, your Schedule D tax will be based on the actual profit for the first 12 months of business: here, £1000.

In the third tax year, you will be assessed on your declaration for the preceding year which, as we have seen, is still the profit in your first 12 months of operations; in this case again £1000. Thereafter you will be paying tax on the normal basis of the preceding year's profits.

The object of these somewhat tortuous manoeuvres is to put you into phase for paying tax on the latter basis; but all that was changed in the autumn 1993 Budget. From 5 April 1994, new businesses will be assessed on a current year basis right from the beginning. Existing enterprises will change over to current year assessment in 1997/98, but the mechanics of this are still being worked out. Check with your accountant how to prepare for the changeover.

Spare-time work

Even though you have a full-time job which is being taxed under Schedule E and thus being taken care of under your employer's PAYE scheme, you may also have earnings from part-time employment in the evenings and weekends which you have to declare. Your employer need not know about this second income because you can establish with your tax inspector that the tax code which fixes the amount of PAYE you pay (see below) only relates to the income you receive from your employer.

Your spare-time income is also eligible for the allowances on expenses 'wholly and exclusively incurred' for business purposes. This means that it is most important that you should keep a proper record of incomings and outgoings. If your spare-time activities are on a small scale, you will not need to keep the kind of detailed books of account described in Chapter 1.5; but you should certainly maintain a simple cash book, from which at the end of the year you or your accountant can prepare a statement to append to your income tax return.

Tax on spare-time work is payable in two half-yearly assessments: on 1 January within the year of assessment and on 1 July following the end of it.

Probably the largest item you will be able to set off against spare-time income is any sums you can pay your wife for her assistance up to the level of her tax-free allowance of £3445, provided she is not earning as much as this from another source.

Partnerships

Partnership income is assessed between the partners in the same ratio as that in which they have agreed to split profits. However, the ratio will be the one that actually exists at the time the assessment is made, which, since the tax is on a preceding year basis, may not necessarily be the same as that which obtained the year the profits were established.

Salaries, and interest on money put into the business by partners, are considered as profits for tax purposes and have to be added back as such in order to arrive at taxable profits.

For the purposes of assessment, the partnership is treated as a single entity, so the tax will be collected from the partnership as a whole, not from the individuals who constitute it.

Corporation tax

Corporation tax is payable by limited companies. Its provisions are somewhat complicated and it must be assumed, for the purposes of this brief chapter on taxation, that readers who are intending to set up businesses in this form will seek professional advice on tax aspects. However, the salient points are as follows:

1. For small companies corporation tax is charged at a rate of 25 per cent on profits up to £250,000 for 1993/94.
2. Dividends are paid to shareholders without deduction of tax, but 25/75ths of the dividends must be handed over to the Inland Revenue by the company within three months of the date of payment of the dividend. This is known as 'advance corporation tax' and is set off against corporation tax payable on profits.
3. Unlike Schedule D income tax, corporation tax is normally payable nine months from the end of each accounting period.

4. Allowable expenses against profits for corporation tax purposes are roughly the same as those for other forms of revenue expenditure, with the important addition that salaries paid to employees (who include the owners of the company, if they are working in it) are deductible. However, in certain circumstances, the interest on loans made to the company by directors will not be treated as an allowable expense, but as a distribution of income on which advance corporation tax is payable.

If you are a director of a limited company, your income from this source will not be liable to the National Insurance levy of 7.3 per cent on income between £6490 and £23,360 a year. Your National Insurance contributions will be at the employed rate and you will be paying PAYE on your salary.

Inheritance tax

This tax is in some ways similar to the older concept of death duties in that a charge is made on transfers of assets at death, up to a maximum of 40 per cent on amounts over £150,000. On outright gifts made more than seven years before death a limited amount of tax relief is available.

There is also another concession which is important to owners of small businesses. Inheritance tax on the value of these is charged at half normal rates, no doubt to prevent their having to be broken up to pay the tax. What are regarded as private and business assets at death are, however, bound to be a subject of potential dispute with the Inland Revenue, so it is vital to seek professional advice on the implications of this tax in making a will.

Capital gains tax

This tax has acquired the inevitable battery of judgments of what is and is not a capital gain. But, in essence, the situation is that if you sell or give away assets, which are usually cash, shares, property or other valuables, and your real or notional gain in any tax year from such transactions is more than £5800, you are liable for capital gains tax at the same rate as your 'top slice' of income tax. The gain is calculated on the difference between the value of the asset at 31 March 1982 and its current net value, less the costs incurred in acquiring it, or improving its value.

Two loopholes have been created in this particular tax fortress which may benefit small businesses. First, if you sell a business and buy another one within three years you can defer payment of the tax until you finally dispose of the one you have bought and cease trading. Second, people who have been owners of a business for more than 10 years can, at the age of 55 obtain relief from CGT if they do sell their assets, up to a maximum of £250,000. Gains between £250,000 and £750,000 are taxed at 50 per cent of the full rate of CGT.

The second benefit could be of particular value to people who have been using part of their private house as business premises and claiming tax relief on the charges incurred (heating, lighting, rates, etc) on a proportionate basis. Before 1978 they would have had to pay CGT on that proportion when they came to sell the house and this deterred quite a number of people from making such a claim, understandably when you consider the level of capital gain reached on house prices in many parts of the country. Now the capital gain relief on the sale of a private residence, part of which had been let, is £40,000.

Appeals

Every taxpayer, be he an individual or a corporation, has the right to appeal against his tax assessment, if he has grounds for believing he is being asked to pay too much. Such appeals have to be made in writing to the Inspector of Taxes within 30 days of receiving an assessment. They are usually settled by more or less amicable correspondence, but ultimately can be taken to a hearing by the General or, in more complex cases, Special Commissioners.

PAYE

If you employ staff you will be responsible for deducting PAYE from their wages. The same applies to your own salary from a partnership or a limited company. The sums have to be paid monthly to the Inland Revenue by the employer.

You will receive from the tax office a tax deduction card for each employee, with spaces for each week or month (depending on how they are paid) for the year ending 5 April. On these cards, weekly or monthly as the case may be, you will have to enter under a number of headings, details of tax, pay for each period and for the year to date. You will know how much tax to deduct by reading off the employee's tax code number, which has been allotted to him by the tax office, against a set of tables with which you will also be issued. Without going into technicalities, the way the tables work is to provide a mechanism, self-correcting for possible fluctuations of earnings, of assessing the amount of tax due on any particular wage or salary at any given point of the year.

At the end of the tax year you will have to make out two forms:

1. Form P14 for each employee for whom a deductions working sheet has been used in the year just ended. Two copies are sent to the tax office. The third copy is called Form P60, and is issued to

each employee. This gives details of pay and tax deducted during the year, as well as any SMP or SSP.

2. Form P35 for the Inland Revenue. This is a summary of tax and graduated National Insurance contributions for all employees during the year. It is a covering certificate sent with the Forms P14.

Before 6 May you have to send the tax office Forms P11D or P9D, which give details of your employees' expenses and benefits for the tax year just ended.

When an employee leaves, you should complete another form, P45, for him. Part of this form, showing his code number, pay and tax deducted for the year to date, is sent to the tax office. The other parts are to be handed by the employee to his new employer so that he can pick up the PAYE system where you left off.

VAT

If the taxable outputs of your business, which for practical purposes means what you charge your customers for any goods or services that are not specifically 'exempt', exceed, or are likely to exceed, £45,000 in a year you will have to register with the Customs and Excise (not the tax office, in this case) as a taxable trader for VAT purposes. This means that you will have to remit to Customs and Excise, either monthly or quarterly, 17.5 per cent of the price you charge on your 'outputs', this being the current standard rate of VAT. However, you will be able to deduct from these remittances any VAT which you yourself have been charged by your suppliers – your 'inputs'. This item covers not only materials used in producing the goods or services you supply to your customers, but everything which you have to buy to run your business, including such things as telephone charges. There are now severe penalties for making late returns.

Not all goods and services carry VAT. Some are 'zero rated' – basic foodstuffs, newspapers and exported goods being notable examples. Full details are contained in VAT Notices 700 and 701, issued by Customs and Excise, New King's Beam House, 22 Upper Ground, London SE1 9PS, and you should obtain from them these Notices together with any others about VAT which are relevant to your trade or profession. You will find your local office listed in the phone book. The significance of zero rating is that even though you do not charge VAT on goods of this nature that you supply, you can still claim back VAT on all your inputs, excluding the purchase of cars and business entertainment of domestic customers.

Zero rating is not, however, the same as 'exemption'. Zero rating carries a theoretical rate of VAT, which is 0 per cent. Exemption means that no rate of VAT applies at all and examples of exempt suppliers are bookmakers, persons selling or renting land and buildings, and various types of medical services. The exempt status is not particularly desirable, because if you are exempt you still have to pay VAT on all your inputs but have no outputs to set the tax off against.*

In this sense exempt traders are like private individuals and the question, therefore, arises as to whether you should, as you are entitled to do, ask to be registered as a taxable trader even though your outputs are less than the mandatory £45,000 a year level. Customs and Excise may, of course, refuse to register you on the grounds that your outputs are too low, though no hard-and-fast minimum figure for this has been fixed. Your accountant should be able to advise you on this point, but the main consideration would be the level of your taxable inputs. Thus if you are a part-time cabinet-maker you would be buying a lot of materials which carry VAT. But, if you were doing something like picture research, the VAT inputs might be quite low and the administrative work involved in being a taxable trader might not be justified by the amount of VAT you could claim back against your outputs.

The point to be realised is that if you register as a taxable trader, voluntarily or otherwise, you are going to be involved in a fair bit of extra administration. At the end of each VAT accounting period (quarterly or monthly, the latter being more usual with traders in zero-rated goods), you will have to make a return of all your outputs, showing their total value and the amount of VAT charged. Against this you set the total of your inputs and the amount of VAT you have paid. The difference between the VAT on your outputs and that on your inputs is the sum payable to Customs and Excise. This obviously causes problems for retailers making a great many small sales and particularly for those supplying a mixture of zero-rated and standard-rated goods (eg a shop supplying sweets, which are taxable, and other items of foods, which are mostly zero rated). It also underlines the vital importance of keeping proper records and retaining copy invoices of all sales and purchases, because although your VAT return need only show totals, Customs and Excise inspectors are empowered to check the documents on which your return is based and require you to keep these records for six years. There is obviously, therefore, a link between the records you have to maintain for ordinary accounting purposes and those that are needed to back up your VAT return.

There is also a close connection between VAT and the problem of cash

---

* The distinction between zero-rated goods and exempt goods is important in determining whether you should be registered for VAT. Exempt goods do not count towards total 'turnover' for this purpose, but zero-rated goods do. Thus, if your turnover is over £45,000 including exempt goods but under that figure without them, you are not liable to pay VAT.

flow. When you receive an invoice bearing VAT, the input element can be set off against the VAT output on your next return, irrespective of whether you yourself have paid the supplier. Therefore, if you are buying an expensive piece of capital equipment it will make sense for you to arrange to be invoiced just before your next return to Customs and Excise is due.

The boot is on the other foot, though, when you yourself are extending credit to a customer. The sale is reckoned to have taken place when the invoice has been rendered, not when you have received payment. Therefore you will be paying VAT on your output before you have actually received the cash covering it from your customer. This also means that except in some special cases no relief is given in respect of bad debts.

It is also worth noting that if you are liable for VAT, inputs can be claimed on goods purchased for the business before it opens which are in place at the time of opening. VAT can also be claimed back on services such as professional advisers' fees supplied within six months of starting to trade.

Once you have registered for VAT, you will receive, at the end of each quarter, a form on which to make your return to Customs and Excise. It is very important to do this within the time stated, because there are financial penalties for making late returns, which can go as high as 30 per cent for repeated defaults.

There are also penalties for 'serious misdeclarations'. If you find, however, that you have accidentally underdeclared any of your taxable outputs, you can apply to the Customs and Excise to make a 'voluntary disclosure for accidental underpayment'. This would not make you liable to a penalty.

Before making a quarterly return, it is a good idea to check your own figures. Dividing the VAT total by the net total should show that the VAT is 17.5 per cent of the net, or at least very close to it. Customs and Excise will accept a tolerance like 0.25 per cent. But anything more than that suggests a mistake in your arithmetic somewhere. Better to pick it up yourself than to invite a visit from the VAT man.

The black economy

One cannot these days write about taxation without some reference to the 'black economy'. There is a good deal of evidence to suggest that the response to the way rising wages and salaries are pulling an increasing number of people into higher tax brackets has been tax evasion on a large scale by a variety of means, such as straightforward non-declaration of earnings, making or receiving payments in cash, arranging remuneration in kind or, simply, barter deals. Some of these methods are easier for the tax inspectors to spot than others, but this is not the place to give advice on a highly contentious topic, except to say that all forms of tax evasion are illegal. In fact, there are enough loopholes and 'perks' available to self-employed people with a good tax consultant at their elbow to render law-breaking an unacceptable and unnecessary risk.

The challenge to self-employed status

In recent years there has been an increasing tendency for the Inland Revenue to challenge taxpayers' claims to be assessed under Schedule D and to try to bring them within the PAYE scheme. The challenge hinges round the nature of the relationship between the provider of work and the performer of it. If the provider of work is in a position to tell the performer the exact place, time and manner in which the job is to be done, then the relationship between them is, to use an old-fashioned phrase, a master-and-servant one and clearly does not qualify for Schedule D taxation. On the other hand, if the performer of the work is merely given a job to do and is absolutely free as to how he or she does it, except in so far as it has to be completed within certain specifications of time, quality and price, then the performer can be regarded as self-employed. There are, however, some potential grey areas here; for instance, a freelance working mostly for one client may be straying into a master-and-servant situation. The Inland Revenue is also now treating any income derived under a contract of service as liable to PAYE – even if it is only for one or two days a month. This means that formal contractual arrangements should be avoided when worthwhile payments are involved. A guidance note has been issued (IR56) under the title *Tax – Employed or Self-Employed*, but the inspector of taxes is still entitled to take his own view of your situation.

The Inland Revenue has a degree of autonomy which is not generally realised by the general public. It is not, for instance, answerable to Parliament except in the widest political sense, so it is no use writing to your MP, no matter how unjustified you may feel a tax decision is. Your only recourse is to take the matter to an Independent Appeals Tribunal, but unless a large sum of money is involved it is probably not worth the trouble – though self-employed people who are members of a professional association may find it willing to take up on their behalf something that looks like a test case.

Introducing Personal Computers and Other Gadgets

Personal computers

Personal computers are now in the same price range as the fancier, but by no means the most expensive and outlandish bits of gadgetry which a self-employed person or a small office might consider getting; a far cry from the fairly recent past, when installing a computer was a major undertaking for any company with a turnover of less than a couple of million or so.

Computers have become easier to operate ('user friendly', as the jargon has it) as well as much cheaper; the National Computing Centre estimates that computing costs only 1 per cent of what it did a decade ago. None the less, the possibilities of making expensive mistakes, both in purchasing and in application, still abound. The only difference is that whereas large businesses can afford to make mistakes, there is much less margin for error in the case of small ones.

In itself, buying a PC these days is no 'big deal'. The less expensive ones cost no more than a middle range electronic typewriter, and if you have to make a choice between the two, a PC costing £400 to £500 is much better value than an electronic typewriter. There are, however, still problems of choice between the various PCs themselves. Selling PCs has become a big and competitive business and there are shoals of salesmen and advertisers who will try to convince you that their product is the answer to your problems. The question is, what really are your problems? What are your needs likely to be in the foreseeable future?

Unless you have established those things, you may end up with the wrong machine or with one that is much more sophisticated – and therefore more expensive – than you really want. Conversely, you may also be spending too little and buying a machine which your business needs will soon outgrow. For instance, a bottom-of-the-price-range PC is wonderful value for someone like a freelance copywriter or journalist who wants a basic word processor to create documents and produce invoices. It is not suitable for a consultant producing professional-looking reports which include graphics; and though there are some business-oriented programs available for it, they are generally considered to be cumbersome in use. The first step in choosing a PC, therefore, is to list the things you want it to do – now and in the foreseeable future.

Getting to know computers

If you are over 40 or so, your knowledge of computers may be limited. In that case it may pay you to read a simple book on the subject. If that thought fills you with terror, it should be stressed that there is absolutely no need whatever to get involved with the technicalities of how computers work, or how to write a program – all you need to know are the basics of what they can do; in other words, the applications.

Your local library or a friend who knows about computers should be able to point you in the direction of some books for beginners. But by way of a preliminary run-in, here are a few terms and concepts which those who know absolutely nothing about computers may find useful.

First of all, any computer system has two components – hardware and software. Roughly they mean what they describe. The hardware is the machine itself and the software is the programs which instruct it to carry out a range of tasks. These begin with information being put in (eg a customer's account number) and this stage is called *input*. The next thing to happen is *processing*, when the input is acted on by the current program (eg the program instructs the computer to turn the customer's account number into her/his full name and address and maybe to check that her/his account is up to date). If a transaction has taken place the details would go into *storage* in the computer's *memory*; in this case, it might be the information that the customer's account should be debited with the value of the transaction. Finally, the whole transaction itself should be displayed on a screen and/or printed out as hard copy: this is known as *output*.

In order to carry out these processes the computer employs various pieces of hardware and software. The input is typed on to the *keyboard*. It is processed in the computer's 'memory' – what might be called its brain. As with the human version, speed of reaction counts as well as size. PCs now on the market are configured as either 286, 386 or 486; the higher the number, the greater the processing speed – and the higher the cost.

Some of the grey cells here are the computer's own memory, technically known as RAM. RAM is used by the manufacturer to store

the computer's instructions to operate itself. A second level of memory is installed by the user when he or she works on the hard disk, a built-in feature which is standard on almost all PCs now. Its memory is measured in megabytes, and most PCs now have at least 40 megabytes of memory. That is the minimum needed to run what are now fairly standard applications packages, like Windows. They take up a fair bit of memory space, even before you start putting your own data on them.

The third level of memory is the floppy disk, which is used in two ways. Firstly, when you buy an applications program, it comes on a floppy disk, the contents of which you transfer to the hard disk by means of what you hope will be intelligible instructions, either in a manual that comes with it or by a series of step-by-step 'prompts' which appear on the screen while you install the program.

The program will stay there as long as you want it, or until a better or more up-to-date version of it comes along. Loading the program from the floppy to the hard disk can be quite tricky for the uninitiated and unless you are computer-literate (in which case you will probably have skipped this section anyway), it is a good idea to ask the dealer to do it for you as a condition of purchase. Otherwise try a computer-literate friend.

A typical program would be one which included order processing. The operator types in a customer number; the program converts this into an actual name and address which would appear on the TV-like screen (properly called a VDU – Visual Display Unit). The operator then types in a number for the item ordered and if it is out of stock or nearing a re-order point and appropriate instructions have been written into the program by the supplier of the software, it will inform the operator accordingly. Furthermore, and again if the program allows for it to be done, the fact that the item in question should be re-ordered will be stored in the memory to be called up by the operator when he or she is running the re-order part of the program. This transaction will most likely be printed out as hard copy on the *printer*.

The other use of the floppy disk is to transfer information you want

HOW SAFE IS YOUR BUSINESS?

Your wastepaper basket could be a rich source of information for your competitors and other prying eyes.

All sorts of confidential information is entrusted to paper but notes, copies of letters or mistyped letters, financial information and computer print-outs are invariably crumpled up and thrown away without a second thought about security implications.

And any company handling personal data including mailing lists needs to maintain utmost confidentiality in order to comply with the 1987 Data Protection Act.

Our shredding machines guarantee that confidential documents remain confidential.

They range from desk side companions such as the Geha Crocodile to industrial machines able to destroy everything from complete lever arch files to floppy discs.

If you want to ensure nobody else is making your business their business then call Paul Brabazon today on 0488 72011.

Yorkberry Business Machines Ltd.
Lowesden Works, Lambourn Woodlands,
Newbury, Berks RG16 7RU
Tel: 0488 72011
Fax: 0488 72895

to keep to the floppy from the hard disk. This is a safety measure, but one well worth adhering to for essential records in case someone has an accident with the hard disk. Ghastly things can happen if you issue a wrong command, even though the program will probably offer a warning first.

Cans and can'ts of computing

The moral of all this, sometimes overlooked by eager buyers, not to mention eager salespeople, is that the computer can only do the things which the programs running at the time will allow it to do. An analogy might be hiring a secretary. If you want a shorthand-typist and that person has not been trained (or programmed, if you like) to carry out either of these functions, he or she will not be a success.

In the case of a secretary, or any other person you take on to the staff, you will have analysed at least to some extent what you want him or her to do and you will look for someone who by virtue of a mix of experience, track record and qualifications can carry out those tasks. In essence this is what you should do if you are contemplating buying a PC. In fact it is much more necessary to have a clear 'job description' for a machine like a computer, because unlike a human being it is not flexible: you cannot say to it (unless of course the program allows you to do so), 'Hey, wait a minute. While you're doing x, could you also check on y and z?'

As we have said, a computer can be programmed to do all sorts of tasks, but this requires writing special programs, which can be very costly indeed. It has to be done by experts – and the stories of experts getting it wrong, at vast expense to their client, are legion – and it will usually cost you several times what you paid for the computer in the first place. There are, however, standard tasks which are common to most types of business and for these, program packages are available which can cost as little as a hundred or so pounds, and indeed are often bundled in when you buy the hardware. Such programs carry out, at the operator's instructions, tasks like invoicing, preparing statements and reminders, stock control and sales analyses of various kinds. All the experts advise that you should pick the software first, then get the hardware to run it on. Never be seduced by sales talk which recommends the opposite course. There are any number of computer disaster tales about firms being persuaded to buy expensive hardware on a promise that the software package needed would 'shortly' become available.

In addition to the computer itself, you will also need a printer and here the choice is between a dot matrix and a laser printer. Laser printers are much more expensive, but as with the power of the PC itself, your choice depends on what you are going to use it for. If you need high quality printed outputs, then a laser printer would be the one to choose. If all you are doing is producing letters and invoices, the dot matrix variety is perfectly adequate. The near letter quality is hard to tell from typing, while for purely utilitarian purposes like turning out consignment notes, the draft mode operates at a high speed even in cheaper models like the Amstrad.

Consultants

If a computer is going to be essential to the kind of business you are engaged in, the plan of campaign recommended by nearly everyone who has had any experience in the matter is to get in a consultant. This need not necessarily mean an expenditure of thousands. At this stage all you need is to get someone to have a look over your operation to tell you whether computerisation is the right answer for you, to check out suppliers and, later on, to help with implementation. There are lots of computer consultants advertising in the Yellow Pages, but a word-of-mouth recommendation is always better than pulling a name out of the telephone book. It is also best to find a local firm rather than one that has to travel a long way to come to see you.

If someone can give you a recommendation, make sure you get the name of the actual consultant he or she saw, because the quality of advice depends not so much on the firm as on the person. Failing personal recommendations, you should ask the consultants you are approaching to name a couple of their customers and check them out. You should also ask whether the consultants in question are tied in with any particular manufacturer. The roles of consultants and salesmen do not always mix to the advantage of the customer, to put it mildly.

As we have recommended in the case of other kinds of advisers in Chapter 1.4, you should specify exactly what you want them to do and ask them to quote a price on it. This will not only give you an idea of how much you will be paying for, but will also simplify the consultant's task and should hence make his service cheaper for you. For this purpose you will have to break down the nature of your operation and set out what you want done by the computer. For instance, a typical trading operation might fall into such headings as these:

- □ *Input:* orders and returns from customers.
- □ *Processing:* invoicing and updating stock records.
- □ *Storage:* lists of customers and their credit limits.
- □ *Output:* creating the physical invoices, credit notes, statements, reminders, etc.

As well as the routine items and their present and expected volumes, you should have an idea of exceptions and overrides, how often they occur and what particular problems you have. You should also think about future additional functions you want the computer to perform. Finally, and by no means least important, you should have a clear idea of how much you can afford to pay for the system, both initially and by way of annual service charges.

Quis custodiet custos ipse? (Who guards the guardian?), as the Romans pertinently asked. Or, in this case, how will you know whether the consultant knows his stuff? One way to do so is to get to know more about computers yourself: the National Computing Centre offers some good introductory courses for small businessmen. There are also many magazines aimed at first-time buyers of PCs. A fairly regular feature in these are questions you ought to ask the supplier – the principal ones are in the checklist below.

You ought also to be aware of your obligations under the Data Protection Act if you are proposing to use a PC in order to keep mailing lists or record personal data about your customers. The Act does not apply if you are using your machine only for internal administrative purposes, though theoretically word processors, which have the capacity to store lists of names, have to be registered. Fuller details are given in Chapter 1.14 (Legal Basics), but there is also a free explanatory booklet available from the Data Protection Registrar.

Checklist: key computing questions

1. The cost of the system.
2. What extras are required, why and how much they will cost.
3. Delivery time for hardware and software.
4. Whether hardware and software are being supplied by the same firm or not (the reason for this question is that where the two are being supplied separately, it is all too easy for the one to blame the other for failures, leaving you as piggy-in-the-middle).
5. Whether additional software is needed and how long it will take to create.
6. Guarantees.
7. Availability and cost of induction courses.
8. Storage/memory capacity (the less the computer has, the less it will be able to do, which is why very cheap computers are unlikely to be suitable for business purposes, whatever their other virtues may be).
9. Capacity for expansion (adding on more VDUs as your business expands may slow up the memory hopelessly, unless additional storage/memory capacity can be added). Costs as well as feasibility of upgrading should be checked.

10. Range and relevance to your needs of free software being bundled in with your purchase.
11. Arrangements for security of data (this does not mean theft so much as the existence of inbuilt precautions against damage to programs or loss of vital data – too bad if you accidentally deleted all your accounts receivable, for instance).
12. Length of warranty period.
13. Maintenance and servicing costs (who pays for what).
14. Maintenance and servicing efficiency (how long it will take for someone from the supplier to turn up if something goes wrong).
15. Written commitments (what written commitments, as compared to verbal promises and assurances, the supplier is prepared to make about performance and after-sales back-up).
16. How many of the make recommended are installed and working and for how long.
17. Whether it is being used by other companies similar to yours and what the problems, if any, are likely to be.
18. Whether the suppliers will let you 'play with' the PC for a reasonable period of time (and without obligation) so that you at least get to grips with the most basic difficulties.
19. How much training is needed, who will supply it and at what cost.
20. Whether the price includes all the accessories and peripherals you need.
21. Whether you could talk to some users comparable to yourself and ask them how good the manual is, how easy the software is to use, and whether the manufacturer or dealer provides any help when you run into problems.
22. The cost and speed of the printer, and the quality of its output where this is a relevant factor.
23. Whether the system has been commented on in the computer press.
24. Whether the PC and the printer will be connected up and tested before being delivered to you.

Satisfactory answers to these questions will not, of course, in themselves guarantee that your computer will be a success. But they should protect you from some of the more grievous and expensive errors that have been, and continue to be, made by businesses large and small.

Computers and printers are only two of the growing range of technological aids available to self-employed people. It's easy to become a gadget freak and the more technically literate you are, the greater the temptation to spend a lot of money on gadgetry and a lot of time fiddling around with it. Probably all you really need, though, are an answering machine and a fax. These are now so much a part of the standard home office that you run the risk of denting your credibility if you don't have them. Fortunately, their widespread use has also made them much cheaper.

Answering machines now cost as little as £60. You can record an outgoing message to play to people who phone while you are away. The machine will record an incoming message from them which you then play back when you return. At the more expensive range you get further 'bells and whistles', such as the facility to interrogate your machine from a distance and to get it to play back, over the phone, any messages that have come in for you. Another optional extra is a recording facility, which enables you to record your telephone conversations. By law, such machines have to sound an electronic warning to alert the other party that your conversation is being recorded.

Stand-alone answering machines can be connected to your ordinary telephone line. Alternatively, you can buy an integral phone and answering machine. BT and Mercury both issue useful booklets about their products for small business users.

One piece of telephone equipment that has come into fashion over the last couple of years is the mobile phone. Though heavily hyped, mobile phones are expensive to run: apart from the cost of the phone itself, there is a line connection charge, a monthly line rental fee and a fairly high call charge per minute. Because this is a competitive market it abounds in special offers of one kind or another, such as rent-free periods. But before taking the plunge, make sure that the supplier is not taking away with one hand what is being given with the other. My own view is that mobile phones are little more than a status symbol, unless your occupation is genuinely one where you are away from base a lot and need to keep in touch with clients or with your office while on the trot.

Fax machines are another matter. Like word processors, you wonder how you did without them. Fax time is charged at the same rate as telephone calls, so sending a long document can work out expensive, especially if it contains illustrations which take longer to transmit. But as a quick response tool – say, to give a quote or confirm acceptance of an offer – fax is ideal. Bear in mind, though, that a fax is not a legal document. When you need to give legal weight to a communication, it may be advisable to send hard copy through the post as well. Many people who send faxes regularly also use a 'cover sheet' which states how many pages the total message consists of.

Like answering machines, they are available either on a stand-alone basis, connected to a telephone line or as part of an integral telephone/ answering machine/fax system. My own preference is for the fax to be a separate piece of equipment. If you have too many integrated bits and pieces in your communications system you run the risk of being cut off from the outside world if one item goes wrong and needs to be taken away for repair.

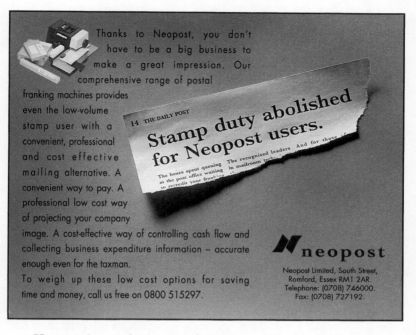

How much more in the way of electronic aids you will need depends on the sort of business you are in, but before buying a new piece of office equipment ask yourself:

- ☐ Will it increase my income?
- ☐ Will it decrease my costs?
- ☐ Will it free me to do other things that will have the above effect?
- ☐ How long has it been around – and therefore how reliable is it likely to be?
- ☐ Will it mean that other equipment that I am using will be obsolete because it isn't compatible with the new stuff?

CHAPTER 1.14

Legal Basics

Going to law is a process where the cure, in money terms, is often worse than the disease – which is why so many settlements are made out of court. Even seeking legal advice is an expensive business: £30 to £50 an hour is now the going rate, depending on where you are, and few legal bills come to less than this minimum, even for a short consultation. In complex disputes or where larger sums of money are involved legal action may ultimately be the only course open. But at the more basic levels of trading law there are some straightforward principles laid down, though they are sometimes blurred by old wives' tales – for instance, that a shopkeeper is obliged by law to sell anything he displays for sale. Knowing what the law actually says about this and other everyday trading transactions will help you to sort out minor disputes and, very often, save costly legal fees.

The Sale of Goods Act 1979

This Act places some clear but not unfair obligations on you as the seller once a contract has taken place, an event which occurs when goods have been exchanged for money. Nothing needs to be written or even said to make the contract legally binding and you cannot normally override it by putting up a notice saying things like 'No Refunds' or limiting your responsibilities in some other way. This is prohibited under the Unfair Contracts Act of 1977.

The Sale of Goods Act has three main provisions concerning what you sell.

1. The goods must be 'of merchantable quality'. This means that they must be capable of doing what the buyer could reasonably expect them to do – for instance, an electric kettle should boil the water in it within a reasonable length of time.

2. The goods must be 'fit for any particular purpose' which you make known to the buyer. For instance, if you are asked whether a rucksack can carry 100 lb without the strap breaking and it fails to match up to your promise of performance, you will have broken your contract.

3. The goods must be 'as described'. If you sell a bicycle as having five speeds and it only has three, then again you are in breach of contract – as well as of the Trade Descriptions Act, if you do so knowingly.

But what happens if you yourself have been misled by the manufacturer from whom you bought the item in question? You cannot refer the buyer back to him: the Sale of Goods Act specifically places responsibility for compensating the buyer on the retailer, no matter from whom the retailer bought the goods in the first place.

Thus, if the goods fail on any of the three grounds shown above, you will have to take them back and issue a full refund, unless you can negotiate a partial refund, with the buyer keeping the goods about which he has complained. However, they need not accept such an offer, nor even a credit note. Furthermore, you may be obliged to pay any costs the buyer incurred in returning the goods, and even to compensate him if he had a justifiable reason to hire a replacement for the defective item; for instance, if he had to hire a ladder to do an urgent DIY job because the one you supplied was faulty.

The only let-out you have under the Act – which also covers second-hand goods – is if you warned the buyer about a specific fault, or if this was so obvious that he should have noticed it. In the case of the bike, he probably would have found it difficult to spot that a couple of the gears were not working, but he could reasonably be expected to notice a missing pedal.

The Supply of Goods and Services Act 1982

This is essentially an extension of the Sale of Goods Act into the sphere of services. The point you have to watch out for is this: if you are offering a service, say, for repairs or some form of consultancy, the implied terms, which the Court will read into the arrangement whether they are written down or not, are: (1) that the supplier will carry out the service with reasonable care and skill; and (2) that it will be carried out in reasonable time and at reasonable cost.

A recent example of the Supply of Goods and Services Act in operation was when an architectural student carried out a small flat conversion job for a client. He neglected to obtain planning permission for some of the work and, even though he was not fully qualified at the time, it was held that, in offering his services, he should have known that this was a basic part of the service he had been offering.

169

Disclaiming responsibility for your actions under either of these Acts is not the answer; that would make you liable under another piece of legislation – the Unfair Contract Terms Act 1977.

Obligation to sell

By law, all goods have to be priced but, contrary to some widely held beliefs, there is no obligation on you to sell goods on display for sale if you don't want to. For instance, an assistant in an antique shop might wrongly price a picture at £2.50 rather than £250. The intending buyer cannot force you to sell at that price, even though it is publicly displayed. However, once the goods have been sold at £2.50, even in error, a contract has taken place and cannot be revoked without the agreement of both parties.

This also applies when the buyer has paid a deposit and this has been accepted. Supposing he had paid £1 and offered to return with the balance, a bargain would have been made which you would be obliged to complete. It is, however, binding on both parties. If the buyer, having paid a deposit, decided to change his mind you would be within your rights in refusing to refund the money.

Estimates and quotations

Self-employed people supplying services such as repairs are often asked for a quote or an estimate. How binding is the figure you give?

This is a grey area in which even the Office of Fair Trading finds it difficult to give a legal ruling. They recommend, however, that a 'quote' should be a firm commitment to produce whatever the subject of the inquiry is at the price stated, whereas an 'estimate', while it should be a close guess, allows more leeway to depart from that figure. Therefore, if you are not sure how much a job is going to cost, you should describe your price as an estimate and say it is subject to revision. This may not, of course, satisfy the customer, in which case he would press you for a quote. If you really find it difficult to state a fixed sum because of unknown factors, you can either give some parameters (eg between £x and £y) or say that you will do £x-worth of work – which on present evidence is what you think it would take – but that you will notify the customer if that sum is likely to be exceeded to do the job properly. In general, though, an itemised firm quotation is the document that is least likely to produce disputes.

Completion and delivery dates

If you give a time for completing a job you will have to do it within that time – certainly if it is stated in writing.

In the case of delivery of goods ordered by customers the same is true. If you give a date you have to stick to it or the contract is broken and the customer can refuse the goods and even, in some cases, ask for compensation. Even if no date is given, you have to supply the article within a reasonable period of time, bearing in mind that what is reasonable in one case, such as making a dress, may not be reasonable in another – obtaining some ready-made article from a wholesaler, for example. The relevant law here is the Supply of Goods and Services Act 1982.

Trading associations

In addition to legal obligations you may also belong to a trading association which imposes its own code of conduct. Such codes sometimes go beyond strict legal requirements, on the principle that 'the customer is always right'. This is not a bad principle to observe, within reason, whatever the legalities of the case. A reputation for fair dealing can be worth many times its cost in terms of advertising.

Leases

Apart from trading law, the other area where it is important to be aware of the basics is in looking at the terms of your lease if you plan to trade from rented premises. This would include your own home. There are likely to be restrictive covenants in the lease which will prevent you from carrying on a trade in premises let to you for domestic use. This may not be an insuperable obstacle, but you would certainly have to get the landlord's permission if you wanted to use your home for any purpose other than just living there.

Even when you rent commercial premises there are likely to be restrictions on the trade you carry on in them. An empty flower shop, for instance, could probably be used as a dress shop without complications, but its use as a furniture repair business might be disallowed because of the noise involved in running woodworking machinery. You and your solicitor should examine the lease closely for possible snags of this sort.

Equally important is the existence of any restrictions which would prohibit you from transferring the lease to a third party. This would mean that the purchaser would have to negotiate the lease element in the event of the sale of the business with the landlord, not with you, and this could drastically affect the value of what you have to sell. For instance, if you took a gamble on renting premises in an improving area which fulfilled your expectations by coming up in the world, you would not be able to reap the benefit of your foresight and courage if you could not transfer the unexpired portion of the lease.

Commercial leases, unlike most domestic ones, run for relatively short periods: usually between three and seven years, with rent reviews at the end of each term or sometimes even sooner. This adds an unknown factor to the long-term future of any business in rented premises and is one you need to take into account in buying a business – again, particularly in an improving area. In Covent Garden, for instance, a number of small shops which moved in when it was a very run-down part of central London with correspondingly low rents were hit by huge increases when these rents were reviewed in the light of the improved status of the area subsequent to the redevelopment of the market building and its surroundings.

The other point to watch for in leases is whether you are responsible for dilapidations occurring during the period of your lease. If you are, you could be in for a hefty bill at its end and for this reason it is advisable to have a survey done and its findings agreed with the landlord, before you take on the lease.

The Trade Descriptions Act 1968

Another piece of legislation you need to watch out for, especially in advertisements and brochures, is the Trade Descriptions Act. This makes it a criminal offence knowingly to make false or misleading claims, verbally or in writing, about any goods or services you are offering.

The notion of a trade description covers a wide range of characteristics, such as size, quantity, strength, method and place of manufacture, ingredients, testimonials from satisfied customers and claims that the goods or service are cheaper than the same bought elsewhere.

It is possible by cunning wording to stick to the letter of the law, but not its spirit. For instance, the words 'made with' some desirable substance or other may indicate that it was made with only a minute quantity of it. But on the whole it is better to stick to the truth, since a successful claim against you could result in a compensation award of up to £1000 – not to speak of loss of reputation.

The Data Protection Act 1984

This Act came in towards the end of 1985, with the object of protecting individuals from unauthorised use of personal data about them; for instance, by computer bureaux selling mailing lists to direct sales organisations. Registration under the Act had to be completed by May 1986. Though failure to register is a criminal offence, the indications are that very few small businesses have actually done so, other than those which are directly affected such as computer bureaux. In theory, though, the obligation to register is quite widespread because anyone with a word processor that can store personal data may be liable to register at a cost of £22.

Application forms and guidance notes are available from post offices. Essentially, data users have to disclose to the Registrar what lists they hold, how and where they obtained the details on them and for what purposes they intend to use them. They must also undertake not to disclose them to any unspecified third party, or to use them for any purposes other than the declared ones. However, data used for internal administrative purposes, such as payrolls, are exempt if they are used only for that function.

The Price Marking Order 1991

This is an EC Directive. It obliges you to state the price of goods offered for sale in writing.

CHAPTER 1.15

Pensions and the Self-employed

It is scarcely possible these days to open the financial pages of any newspaper without seeing at least one advertisement for self-employed pensions. It is also a fair bet that these are studied more closely by financial advisers than by the self-employed at whom they are aimed, unless of course the latter are nearing the age at which pensions begin to become of immediate interest – by which time it may be too late to do anything about it. The trouble is that the self-employed, by temperament, are more interested in risk than security and tend to place provisions for retirement rather low on their scale of priorities.

However, there are compelling reasons why you should take self-employed pensions seriously and find out what they involve, to outline which is the object of this chapter. In urging you to read it, we promise to avoid the mind-boggling pension jargon which generally sends readers of newspaper articles on the subject straight to the less demanding pastures of the sports pages.

State schemes

Everyone in the UK now has a pension provision of some kind, by law. You belong and contribute either to the basic state scheme (even if you are self-employed – through your NI contributions) or to a scheme set up by your employer, which has to provide benefits at least equal to those offered by the state earnings-related scheme. This scheme provides a small basic pension topped up by an earnings-related amount and it has a number of serious disadvantages. One is that the earnings-related element is calculated on a formula based on your earnings over 20 years from the start of the scheme and, without going into the details of this, the effect is that you cannot get the full benefit of it if you retire before 1998. A second disadvantage is that there is no lump sum provision on retirement or death, as is the case with most private schemes. A third drawback is the top limit on earnings, on which the earnings-related benefit is limited to £350 a week. Thus, the more highly paid you are on retirement, the worse your benefit is in comparison.

However, from the point of view of the self-employed, the biggest drawback of the lot is that you are not eligible for earnings-related benefit at all, on the grounds that the fluctuating nature of self-employed earnings makes it difficult to set up such a scheme. All you are entitled to is the basic pension, which is generally admitted to be quite inadequate on its own.

Tax benefits

This is in itself a reason why you should make additional arrangements as soon as you possibly can, but for the self-employed there is another compelling incentive. Investing in a pension scheme is probably the most tax-beneficial saving and investment vehicle available to you at this time. Here are some of its key features:

1. Tax relief is given on your contributions at your top rate of tax on earned income. This means that if you are paying tax at the top rate of 40 per cent you can get £1000 worth of contributions to your pension for an outlay of only £600.

2. Pension funds are in themselves tax exempt – unlike any company in whose shares you might invest. Thus your capital builds up considerably more quickly than it would in stocks and shares.

3. When you finally come to take your benefits – and you can take part of them as a lump sum and part as a regular pension payment (of which more later) the lump sum will not be liable to capital gains tax and the pension will be treated as earned income from a tax point of view, as distinct from investment income, which is regarded as 'unearned' and taxed much more severely.

4. Lump sum benefits arising in the event of your death are paid out to your dependants free of inheritance tax. This may enable you to build up pension funds to the extent where liability to inheritance tax is reduced quite drastically on other assets from which income has been siphoned to provide a pension.

The advantage of all this over various DIY efforts to build up a portfolio of stocks and shares – even if you are more knowledgeable about the stock market than most – should be obvious; you are contributing in that case out of taxed income, the resultant investment income is taxed at unearned rates and capital gains tax is payable on the profits you make from selling your holdings.

The convinced adherent of the DIY road may at this point say: 'Ah, but under my own provisions I can contribute as, when and how much I can afford and I am not obliged to make regular payments to a pension plan when it might be highly inconvenient for me to do so.' Pensions, however, are not like life insurance, though misguided salesmen sometimes try to make out that they are. You need not contribute a regular amount at all. You can pay a lump sum or a regular amount. In fact, you need not make a payment every year. There are even a number of plans now available under which you are entitled to borrow from your pension plan.

The only restriction that is put on you is imposed by the government and relates to tax benefits. In order for self-employed pensions not to become a vehicle for tax avoidance, the amount you can contribute to them is limited to 17.5 per cent of your income. You are, however, allowed to 'average out' your contributions over any six-year period to arrive at an overall percentage per year of 17.5 per cent.

There is also a further concession for older people making their own pension plans.

Age	Percentage of income qualifying for tax relief
36–45	20.0
46–50	25.0
51–55	30.0
56–60	35.0
61 and over	40.0

Since an increasing number of self-employed people – and their financial advisers – have come to recognise the merits of these schemes, a great many companies have moved into the market for self-employed pensions. Under a fair amount of jargon and an often confusing lineage of fine print, the plans they offer boil down to the following options.

1. *Pension policy with profits.* In essence this is a method of investing in a life assurance company, who then use your money to invest in stocks, shares, government securities or whatever. As we said earlier, the advantage from your point of view is that pension funds are tax exempt, so the profits from their investments build up more quickly. These profits are used to build up, in turn, the pension fund you stand to get at the end of the period over which you can contribute. There is no time limit on this period, though obviously the more you do contribute the greater your benefits will be and vice versa; also, you can elect to retire any time between 60 and 75.

At retirement you can choose to have part of your pension paid as a lump sum and use it to buy an annuity. This could in some circumstances have a tax advantage over an ordinary pension, but the situation on it is quite complicated and you should seek professional advice in making your decision. What happens with an annuity, however, is that you can use it to buy an additional pension, the provider of which takes the risk that if you live to a ripe old age he might be out of pocket. Equally, you might die within six months, in which case the reverse would be true. The statistical probabilities of either of these extremes have been calculated by actuaries and the annuities on offer are based on their conclusions.

One important point about a conventional with-profits pension that often confuses people is that it is not really a form of life insurance. If you die before pensionable age, your dependants and your estate will not usually get back more than the value of the premiums you have paid, plus interest. The best way of insuring your life is through term assurance, of which more later.

2. *Unit linked pensions.* Unit linked policies are a variant of unit trust investment, where you make a regular monthly payment (or one outright purchase) to buy stocks and shares across a variety of investments through a fund, the managers of which are supposed to have a special skill in investing in the stock market.

Combining investment with a pension plan sounds extremely attractive and much more exciting than a conventional with-profits policy, and it is true that in some instances unit linked policies have shown a better return than their more staid rivals. However, as unit trust managers are at pains to warn you (usually in the small print), units can go down as well as up and if you get into one of the less successful unit trust funds – and there are quite wide variances in their performance – you may do less well than with a conventional policy.

There are also, of course, fluctuations in the stock market itself which affect the value of your holdings. Over a period of time these fluctuations should even themselves out – you can get more units for your money when the market is down, and fewer when share prices are high. The only problem is that if your policy terminates at a time when share prices are low you will do worse than if you cash in on a boom. However, there is nothing to compel you to sell your holdings when they mature. Unless you desperately need the money you can keep it invested until times are better. Remember, though, since this policy is for your pension, you may not be able to delay using the funds for too long.

Most unit trust companies run a number of funds, invested in different types of shares and in different markets: for instance, there are funds that are invested in the US, Australia or Japan, or in specialist sectors such as mining or energy. If you find that the trust you are in is not performing as well as you had hoped (prices are quoted daily in the press) most trusts will allow you to switch from one fund to another at quite a modest administration charge.

3. *Term assurance.* While this is not a form of pension at all, it may be

attractive to add term assurance to your pension policy for tax purposes. Term assurance is a way of insuring your life for a given period by paying an annual premium. The more you pay, the more you (or rather your dependants) get. If you do not die before the end of the fixed term (eg 20 years) nothing is paid out. As with any other form of insurance, your premiums are simply, if you like, a bet against some untoward event occurring.

There is one indirect but useful connection between pensions and term assurance. The tax people allow you a scheme under which you pay term assurance premiums along with your pension premiums, both of them being relieved of tax at your top earned income rate.

The one thing that all types of pension scheme have in common is that their salesmen are all eagerly competing for the self-employed person's notional dollar. They will be anxious to extol the virtues of their own schemes, to withhold any unfavourable information about them and to make no comparisons, which could be odious, with other schemes. Your best plan in making your selection is to work through a broker and to let him or her make the recommendation, but that does not mean that you can abdicate responsibility altogether. For one thing, in order for a broker to make the right selection of pension plans appropriate to your circumstances, you have to describe what your needs and constraints are:

1. Can you afford to make regular payments?
2. Does the irregular nature of your earnings mean that the occasional lump sum payment would be better?
3. Do you have any existing pension arrangements – eg from previous employment?
4. When do you want to retire?
5. What provision do you want to make for dependants?

Very likely the broker will come up with a mix of solutions – for instance, a small regular payment to a pension scheme, topped up by single premium payments. The suggestion may also be made that you should split your arrangements between a conventional with-profits policy and some sort of unit linked scheme; certainly you will be recommended to review your arrangements periodically to take care of inflation and possible changes in your circumstances.

Brokers have to be registered nowadays, so it is unlikely that you will be unlucky enough to land up with someone dishonest. Check that the person you are dealing with really is a *registered* broker – not a consultant, because anyone can call themselves that. Some very big household names among brokers are not, in fact, registered but the majority are, although whoever you deal with, there are, as in other things in life, differences in the quality of what you get, which in this case is advice. It is as well to have a few checks at your elbow which will enable you to assess the value of the advice you are being given. For instance, national quality newspapers such as the *Daily Telegraph*, the *Guardian*, *The Independent* and the *Financial Times*, as well as some specialist publications such as *The Economist* and *Investors Chronicle*, publish occasional surveys of the pension business which include performance charts of the various unit funds, showing those at the top and bottom of the league table over one-, five- and ten-year periods. There are also tables of benefits offered by the various life companies showing what happens in each case if, for instance, you invest £500 a year over ten years. There are quite considerable differences between what you get for your money from the most to the least generous firms. If your broker is advising you to put your money in a scheme that appears to give you less than the best deal going, you should not commit yourself to it without talking to your accountant; but with brokers, as with many other professional advisers, the best recommendation is word of mouth from someone you can trust who can vouch for the ability of the person in question.

PART 2:
Businesses Requiring Capital

CHAPTER 2.1

Starting Your Business

Introduction

To buy and stock a shop, or start and run a hotel or restaurant, a building firm or a farm, is a sizeable investment – in your time, energy and, above all, money. True, if you buy premises for any type of business and the venture fails, you can cut your losses by selling the premises. You may avoid significant losses, provided you have bought at a *realistic* price, but losses there will be: on stock, on any refurbishing you carried out, and on the opportunity cost of your time and capital. So, do not rush into anything: consider the size of the investment and the possibility of failure and, conversely, recognise the personal sacrifices you must make to achieve success.

In considering the profit and loss account of a business you are thinking of acquiring, bear in mind the effect of the Uniform Business Rate. As the new occupier of business premises, you will have to bear the full cost of any increase in rates tabled from 1990.

Buying a business

All investments in business ventures are a risk, but they should not be too much of a risk. Do not overcommit yourself, and aim to finance your business as far as possible from your own resources. Of course, self-financing is often not feasible and you will probably depend on finance from a clearing bank, venture capital fund, insurance company or building society. In practice, clearing banks are by far the most usual source of finance for small businesses. Providers of 'venture' and 'development' capital have increased their role considerably in recent years. However, they will usually be looking for companies with

183

turnovers of £¼ million or more, and may require an equity stake in the company (ie part-ownership of the company) in return for finance. (See Chapter 1.3 for information on funding sources.) Insurance companies are important sources of *personal* finance, but are less willing to lend money to commercial ventures, as assurance policies rarely cover the size of the loan required by the aspiring businessman. And building societies are rarely prepared to give mortgages to commercial ventures.

It is usually to the high street bank that a small businessman will turn (though, with expert financial advice, good use can be made of the other sources of finance). Banks (and individual bank managers) sometimes vary in their willingness to lend to new enterprises and expanding businesses. Ask friends, people in other businesses and an accountant for advice on which bank(s) to approach. Your relationship with the bank manager is vital – both to the likelihood of your initial application for finance succeeding, and to the working of your business venture. If you have a long-standing relationship with a particular bank (and branch manager) as a *personal* customer, it may well be worth applying to that bank for *business* finance. A good record as a personal customer will go some way towards convincing the bank of your likely financial integrity as a business customer.

A more important consideration, however, is that the application you make to the bank should be clear and well thought through, and your cash flow estimates and business plans realistic and well structured. You must be clear about how much you need, for what purpose, for how long, etc. The onus is on you to prove your case. The following list covers points the bank manager will expect you to have thought through when you apply for funds in connection with buying a business; make notes on each point and be ready and *able* to cover each point objectively and fluently.

- What type of venture is it? Where will it be located?
- What is your experience of the trade, and how did you become involved in this particular project?
- What is the structure of your organisation, and who owns it? Is it a limited company, partnership or a sole trader?
- What business objectives have you set yourself: profitability or expansion, diversification or specialisation, etc?
- How will you handle marketing: advertising, representation, etc?
- What are your overheads: property, capital equipment, staff, running costs, etc?
- What is the value of its assets?
- What are your reasons for buying it at all (ie why not just start from scratch)?
- What sort of reputation does it have? With customers? Suppliers?
- Who are its competitors and where are they located?

- What unique selling points or similar advantages does it have?
- Are there any key people in it who you need to retain, and will they stay?
- Are you dependent on any key customers? How will you retain them?
- What is the state of the premises?
- How long do any leases have to run and what are the renewal terms?
- How old is the equipment?
- Can you estimate the amount of money you need, and the length of the period before you achieve profitability? Be realistic and thorough on this, as on all points.

You must be able to sell yourself and the project – a good test of *your* belief in the workability of the scheme.

A good relationship with your bank is invaluable. As well as a bank loan or overdraft agreement, your bank will offer a range of other loans for longer-term purposes, such as the acquisition of property and the funding of expansion.

Chapter 1.3 gives a more detailed treatment of the subject of raising capital, but some points have been reiterated here because this section is aimed at people who will be making a large investment in property and capital equipment. Subsequent chapters deal with major business areas in which property held on lease – or freehold – is central. Certain principles apply to all these areas:

- Pay a realistic price for whatever you purchase.
- Make all agreements you sign legally binding and use a solicitor to protect your investment.
- Do not underestimate the size of the investment that will be required.
- Do not overcommit yourself financially, and retain some funds or assets in case things go badly wrong.
- Consult an accountant before borrowing money from any source and make certain you know the provisions of all financial agreements.
- Have a watertight proposal to make to any potential lender.
- Use *bona fide* sources of finance.
- Your relationship with a lender must be based on mutual *trust* as well as mutual *interest*.
- Be realistic about your credit needs: buying the business is only the prelude to refurbishing and stocking it, insuring and perhaps fireproofing the premises, purchasing capital equipment and paying current expenses at a time when you are struggling to build a reputation and establish a business structure and clientele.
- Remember that you often have to give personal guarantees and/or

provide security on a business loan: thus default on the latter could lead to possession by your creditor(s) of personal goods.

☐ Know when (and how) to pull out if things go badly: where to sell stock, how to sell the premises, how to terminate long-term loans, etc.

☐ If things go well, know when (and how) to expand and diversify: do not over-extend your resources; ensure that your staff can cope with greater pressures.

CHAPTER 2.2

Farming and Market Gardening

The 'back to the land' movement has been quite fashionable in recent years, with all kinds of people giving up their jobs and homes in cities to live on smallholdings (communal or otherwise) where they try to be completely self-sufficient. Others, more commercially minded, may take up market gardening, which gives them a pleasant life in the country while they sell the fruits of their labours to others. Some more conventional souls may simply decide to buy a farm and rear cattle, grow corn or keep pigs or poultry.

In all cases, the romantic glow soon disappears. There are two essentials for any of these occupations, neither of them romantic: capital and the capacity for hard work. Take advice from professional bodies such as the Ministry of Agriculture's Advisory Service or the local county office of the National Farmers' Union. The local authority is responsible for agricultural education and you should make inquiries about courses that might be available in your area. The soaring costs of fuel and animal foodstuffs have already put many market gardeners and farmers out of business, so it is obviously essential to go into the finances of the operation very thoroughly before making a decision.

It is also essential to have the complete support of your family. This can be a very hard life, getting up early in all weathers to feed animals, breaking your back hoeing and weeding, and you have to be extremely keen and enthusiastic to take it on. If your nearest and dearest are not equally enthusiastic, forget it, for you are going to need their active help, since labour is both expensive and hard to come by.

Farming

Farming has become a technological occupation, requiring all kinds of special skills and knowledge. Unless you can convince a bank that you have this know-how (and some business experience) you are unlikely to get your money. Long-term loans for the purchase of land are available from the Agricultural Mortgage Corporation Ltd but, here again, properly prepared budgets and a realistic and comprehensive proposal will be required if the application is to be successful.

Now a highly risky occupation, farming gives only a 3 to 4 per cent return on the land. The failure rate is very high, and to take it up with little or no experience almost guarantees failure. Unless you know about fertilisers, pesticides, animal husbandry and farm machinery, you are likely to make some expensive mistakes, and remember that two bad years could wipe you out financially. The farmers who are most successful are those who start young, probably in a family-owned business. By the time they take over, they have acquired the necessary experience, usually backed up these days with a course at one of the agricultural colleges. You should not contemplate farming without some practical experience, or a degree or diploma from an agricultural college, or preferably both.

Another idea which is very popular with the 'get-away-from-it-all' brigade is to buy a smallholding and try to be entirely self-sufficient, perhaps even setting up a commune. It is an attractive idea, and the initial cost need not be great, but be warned: this is subsistence farming and you will find yourself working as hard as the American pioneers did. Also, even on a commune you may need a tractor and, for that, you are going to need money. You really need to be dedicated or rich (preferably both).

If the foregoing has not deterred you, get some professional advice, either from ADAS (the Agricultural Development Advisory Service of the Ministry of Agriculture) or from your local agricultural college or institute. There are also various farm management consultants and land agency firms who will (for a fee) give advice on what to do.

Even running a smallholding will demand considerable capital and expertise, as well as determination and immense hard work. Pat Burke, who runs one such smallholding, says: 'You must start with sufficient capital to carry you through the first year, since you will almost certainly make nothing at all until your second year. All the self-employed work long hours but running a smallholding involves particularly long hours – weekends don't exist.'

Market gardening

Unless you take over an established business, the main problems for the would-be market gardener are acquiring the necessary land and a greenhouse. You may be lucky enough to own a suitable piece of land already, or a garden big enough (two to three acres) to be worked commercially; otherwise you may have to pay anything upwards of £2800 an acre. A greenhouse is the other big expense. It is a vital piece of equipment, enabling you to grow tomatoes, bedding plants, pot plants for the winter months and seedlings for early vegetables. You can do without one, but you must then make enough money in the spring and summer to make up for the lean winter months when you have virtually nothing to offer except a few winter vegetables. You also have to make provision for the cost of heating a greenhouse: price increases in fuel have sent the cost sky-high, so you must make sure that every inch of space is working for you, if your profits are not going literally to disappear in smoke. Even the cheapest second-hand greenhouse is likely to cost at least £1600, while a new one costs five to six times as much.

If you are not a trained horticulturalist, it is a good idea to employ someone who is, or who has at least had practical experience of running a big garden and greenhouse. One full-time helper is probably all you will be able to afford in the early years. Seasonal help picking tomatoes, strawberries, beans, etc costs about £3.50 an hour, and is often difficult to find. You (and your family) must be prepared to work long hours and turn your hand to anything. On the other hand, there is a growing trend towards advertising 'pick your own' facilities during peak seasons. The amount people are willing to pay for the privilege of picking their own fruit compares favourably with the wholesale prices you would be able to obtain.

For general information, particularly on the economics of growing produce, contact the National Farmers' Union, which has a very good horticultural section. Another excellent source of information on what crops to grow, soil tests, etc is the Agricultural Development Advisory Service of the Ministry of Agriculture (ADAS).

One basic decision to be made, once you have decided on your crops, is how you are going to market your produce. If you are on a busy main road you may decide to rely heavily on local advertising and passing trade from tourists, etc, sending the surplus to the local market, or even taking a stall in the local market yourself. You can also send your produce to one of the big central markets, but you then have to pay a fee to the auctioneer, as well as transport costs.

CHAPTER 2.3

Retailing

Buying a shop

No book can answer all the questions or anticipate all the problems that buying a shop or starting a retail business entails, but it can warn you of the main reasons for failure:

☐ Paying an unrealistic price for the business.
☐ Lack of experience in the trade you enter.
☐ Cash flow problems caused by underestimating current costs.
☐ Failure to recognise the level of competition to the type of goods you sell or the service you offer (are you setting up a general food store next to a round-the-clock supermarket?).
☐ Choice of a bad location: away from the shopping centre, in a commercial area with little weekend trade, etc.

The character of areas and shopping precincts changes rapidly. The 'centre' of your town is perhaps moving, through lack of space, to an open-plan area with a multi-storey car park and a wide range of shopping units. Long-established shops in the 'older' part of town are often unable to survive, so be wary of being offered this type of business. There are wide variations in the desirability and potential profitability of even apparently similar retail businesses.

Ask where the business you have seen advertised is sited. Is it well positioned or far from the centre of trading activity? What is its reputation? Be sceptical of the seller's claims to a fund of 'goodwill' from long-standing customers. There is no guarantee that they exist or, if they do, that they will be as loyal to you. How much stock have you been offered as part of the purchase price? Does the shop need redecoration? What terms are you being offered: freehold or leasehold? What is the nature of the competition to your enterprise?

Such questions do not allow simple answers. These vary according to the type of business you intend to conduct. For example, a more specialised shop (selling, say, good quality hi-fi or photographic equipment at competitive prices) does not need to be as central as a grocer's, butcher's or general goods store. Customers will hear about it and seek it out and, having been satisfied once, will return for accessories, improved equipment and advice.

Think, too, about general location and the composition of the local population: is it predominantly young or old, middle class or working class, close to sports facilities or not, and so on? Is there a seasonal trade that you might capture? Are there shops nearby that may attract certain types of people, whose custom you might aim to tap? Would you have to work special hours to fit in with the habits of your potential customers (by, for example, staying open until 7 or 7.30 pm in suburban residential areas)? Would those habits affect your trade adversely at certain times (low 'traffic' at weekends in business areas, for instance)?

In short, you must consider a whole range of locational factors before choosing to buy an established business or deciding *where* to start a new shop. Four rules:

- ☐ Talk to people who know the trade and the locality.
- ☐ Take the advice of an accountant and solicitor who will, respectively, assess the financial worth of the purchase and the legal commitments you will enter into.
- ☐ Do not buy the first shop offered to you unless *everyone* thinks it is an unmissable opportunity (and, even then, think again!).
- ☐ Always assume the seller is asking too much.

This is not sophisticated business thinking; it is plain common sense. George Thorpe, a food retailer, stresses the need for forward planning. He says: 'Even if you have to borrow money, do not be under-capitalised. Keep your shelves full and well stocked since this will attract customers ... Apart from fruit and veg you will need to have five to seven times your weekly takings tied up in stock.'

You and your business

On a more personal level, can you and your family bear the strain of managing a shop: the hours of work, the tedium of filling in tax forms and keeping books, the problems of receiving early morning deliveries, the physical work that might be involved in taking and storing deliveries, the pressure of having always to be polite to the customers? (You might not wish to follow the dictum that the customer is always right, but would you survive? Small businesses depend on customers returning and on word-of-mouth promotion.)

Working hours are long, but made tolerable by a commitment to *your* business. You will grow to dislike VAT returns and difficult customers and you will encounter a host of petty day-to-day administrative difficulties, but if you are serious about the move in the first place, you should survive these. But ask yourself: is my immediate family as dedicated to the project as I am? What is a challenge to you may be a burden to them. So, be as sensitive to their needs as you are to your own.

Buying an established business

Shops for sale are sometimes advertised in the local and national press and in some trade journals,* or you can consult a firm of business valuers and transfer agents. It is a good idea to write down the specific requirements that you are looking for: this will not only help you to brief your agent and any other advisers such as your accountant and bank manager, but will also help you to clarify your ideas.

Shops are generally rented on a leasehold basis, and you should aim for a property with as long a lease as possible. In paying for the shop you will be buying the premises, fixtures and fittings, existing stock and 'goodwill'. How this price is arrived at depends on a number of factors, which you must analyse carefully before you commit yourself. *Stock* is generally valued for business sale purposes at current market cost price, and an independent valuation of the stock is desirable. *Fixtures and fittings* should also be independently valued, and an inventory of these should be made and attached to the contract of sale. *Goodwill* is a nebulous concept to which an exact value cannot be attached. Obviously, the more the shop relies on regular, established customers, the higher the value of the goodwill; conversely, the more it relies on casual, passing trade, the lower the goodwill value. The price of a shop will also to a large extent depend on the potential of the local area. You will need to make a careful assessment of factors such as:

1. Competition. Do not make the mistake of thinking that the absence of a nearby competitor *necessarily* guarantees success. A shop that has done reasonably well in the face of nearby competition is a safer bet than a shop with a similar record which has had a virtual monopoly of local trade. There is always a danger that if there is no competition, someone else may move in after you. Another common mistake is to see only shops of the same trade as competition. Indirectly, all other traders in the area are competition, since all are competing for a share of the consumers' spending power.

---

* A full list of these is contained in *British Rate & Data (BRAD)*, a monthly listing of all commercial periodical publications and newspapers, which should be available in any reasonable business reference library.

2. Nearness to railway stations, bus stops, etc: this may substantially increase the flow of passing trade. A map may help to clarify the exact potential of the location.
3. Any further local development plans – check with the local authority.

It is important that you and your accountant study the books thoroughly. In particular, examine the trend of the profit and loss account over the past few years to determine whether the business is improving. Another important point to note is whether the previous trader has been paying himself a salary, or whether this has to be deducted from the net profit figure. An excellent guide to what is involved in buying a shop is another *Daily Telegraph/*Kogan Page guide which is actually called *Buying a Shop*, by A St J Price. The chapter on negotiating with a vendor is particularly clear and useful.

We spoke to the owner of a general goods shop who makes these points strongly. 'Location, potential competition and overheads are the three key points to watch. If you're buying an existing store scrutinise the accounts minutely. Is it possible to run it with one less member of staff, for example? Are home deliveries being made? These can be very, very expensive. Don't try to compete on prices with the big boys – you'll lose! Stock lots of lines and if need be sell, say, sugar at a loss knowing you've got a good margin on shampoo. There's no guarantee that goodwill will pass over to you on completion of the sale – your face might not fit and there's little allegiance nowadays from customers.'

Starting from scratch

You may want to take over premises which have previously been used for other purposes, in which case you should look closely at the previous owner's reasons for closing down and determine to what extent the same factors will affect you, even though you are engaged in a different trade. If you are going to use them for another type of business, you must get planning permission first. Or you may want to rent newly built premises, in which case you will probably have to pay a premium. The premium is based on the potential of the area, but try to get an *exact* idea of what that potential is: the number of new flats being built nearby, for example. In general, the premium should be lower than the goodwill price you would pay for a going concern, since it only indicates potential, not a record of success.

Legal obligations

The most important Acts* affecting shops are:

- ☐ Contracts of Employment Act
- ☐ Offices, Shops and Railway Premises Act
- ☐ Shops Act
- ☐ Trade Descriptions Act
- ☐ Weights and Measures Act
- ☐ Sale of Goods Acts
- ☐ Local Authority By-laws
- ☐ Consumer Credit Act
- ☐ Redundancy Payment Act
- ☐ Payment of Wages Act
- ☐ Employment Protection Act
- ☐ Sex Discrimination Act
- ☐ Health and Safety at Work Act
- ☐ Unfair Contracts Act
- ☐ Prices Act
- ☐ Supply of Goods and Services Act.

These fall into four categories. First, employment legislation (see Chapter 1.11). Check the ages of your employees; ensure that they are taxed, and that you pay your share of their National Insurance contributions; cover them regarding pensions and superannuation; know where they stand in relation to the Employment Protection Act. (If they work more than 16 hours a week and more than 104 weeks continuously, they will be covered by its provisions and are eligible to claim against wrongful dismissal, etc. Similarly, if they work full-time and have been employed for more than 104 weeks they are eligible for redundancy payments if you make them redundant.)

Second, safety, security and planning. You should insure your premises and stock, and cover yourself against liability, including liability for defective goods (potentially liability will vary widely depending on the goods you sell and the services you offer). In the case of a food shop you must satisfy a health inspector, and other types of premises will have to be passed fit by a fire officer. Check these and local planning laws before you start trading. The quickest way to find out which of these laws apply to you is to contact your local Shops Act Inspector. He will also provide details of by-laws on opening hours, Sunday trading, pavement displays, etc.

Third, fair trading. Know and follow the provisions of the Consumer Credit Act and the Trade Descriptions Act. There are strict rules on how you display prices, on recommended prices and 'special' offers, on

---

*Other Acts, such as the Pet Animals Act, affect specific types of shops.

the giving of guarantees, on the rates of hire-purchase you can offer and the other types of credit you make available, and so on. Again, cover yourself against expensive litigation by going through existing legislation with a solicitor, looking at standard practice in businesses similar to your own, and taking advice from the local Weights and Measures Inspector.

Finally, be aware of your standing under the Sale of Goods Act. When you sell something, the merchandise you sell should be in good condition and fit for its stated purpose. If it is not, your customer is entitled to a suitable replacement or a refund. When you provide a service, under contract law it should be up to the required standard; if it is not, the customer can claim compensation. The Supply of Goods and Services Act 1982 brings the sale of goods and the provision of services into line and makes all retailers responsible for the product or service they provide.

Keeping accounts

A great deal of bookwork will be inevitable: keeping count of stock levels and daily sales (for personal use and for VAT purposes); an elementary statistical breakdown of what is selling; keeping tabs on credit customers, orders, returned goods, etc. Your accountant and bank manager will wish to see comprehensive and up-to-date accounts to check your progress. See Chapter 1.5 for an introduction to simple accounting, but be warned: for anything more than day-to-day bookkeeping it is worth using a qualified accountant.

Leasing

Leases are written in legal jargon and for that reason the vendor is sometimes apt to sign without really understanding what the lease says. This is a great mistake, and if you cannot follow the wording or are unclear about anything, you should ask your solicitor to explain it to you. Look out particularly for restrictive covenants that prevent you from transferring the lease to a third party or from carrying on certain trades and professions at those premises.

Security

Never leave cash lying about. If there is a lot of money in the till, take out a round sum in notes and leave a chit in the till to remind yourself where it is. Watch out for shoplifters, and ensure against them as far as possible by not leaving small, valuable items in easily accessible positions. Do not leave customers or visitors unattended. Remember that you must be insured right from the start, even before you have opened up for business. The Home Office produces a pamphlet on theft by staff, a danger which must not be overlooked. Consult your local crime prevention officer, who will advise you on ways to combat both dangers.

Stock

It is sensible to buy stock from a wholesaler, or cash and carry, or from a manufacturer's agent, since you will generally need frequent deliveries of small quantities of goods. Have as few sources of supply as possible, to cut down your workload. There are a few exceptions to this. In the case of cigarettes, for example, it is better to deal direct with the manufacturer.

Make sure you know at all times what your stock levels are, and devise a system whereby you know when to reorder, before stocks run too low. The stock should be cleaned and dusted regularly and any stock that remains unsold over a long period should be discarded. Stock-taking should be carried out regularly, depending on the type of business in which you are engaged.

Layout and display

Cleanliness and hygiene are, of course, absolute musts. Layout, too, will be important. Make the interior of the shop as attractive as you can: displays, however small, should have a focal point, and should be changed frequently. Allow space for your customers to move and, if necessary, push prams, and make sure that they have access to all the goods on your shelves. Think, also, about your window displays: manufacturers will often supply signs and special display items which may improve the look of your shop.

Case studies

It would be impossible to cover the whole range of shops: general and specialist, selling goods and offering services, urban and rural, central and suburban, business and consumer orientated, and so on. A few case studies are included here only for illustration, and a note is added on sub post offices, which are a rather special case. But no one *type* of shop or method of operation will necessarily work. Find something that suits you, and let what you do and the style you adopt reflect your personality.

Antique shops

This is a prime example of an area where you must be experienced: you must have a thorough knowledge of antiques, of the business and of other dealers. Whether you are starting from scratch or buying an established business, you will need funds to buy stock. If you buy a going concern, you may find that the stock consists of all the duds and non-sellers of the previous owners, and you will have to get rid of it all and start again.

You will learn the technique of buying things at auctions: always go to the preview first and mark on your catalogue the items you are interested in and the price you are prepared to pay. Beware of being 'trotted' – other dealers running up the bidding and then dropping out at the end, leaving you to pay an unrealistic price. Country auctions are usually widely advertised in local papers and you will soon get to know local dealers and their specialities. You must then build up a body of reliable clients, who will form the backbone of your business. These may include other dealers and foreign buyers.

You are most likely to make a success if you specialise, and learn as much as you can about your speciality whether it is pictures, brass and copper, china or furniture. Use *The Lyle Official Antiques Review* if at all in doubt about the auction value of any item.

One main drawback is the hours you will be expected to keep – this is *not* a 9 to 5 job! Evenings will probably be spent entering up sales, pricing new acquisitions, etc, and then foreign dealers have a nasty habit of travelling overnight and arriving on the doorstep at 8 am ready to do business.

Robert O'Connor, an antique dealer, gives would-be dealers some advice: 'Buying is the key to success – you can't ring up a wholesaler and order 12 dozen. Selling is not as difficult as long as it's the right piece and the right price. You have to know and love your subject and not be motivated by profit. Work hard at developing lines of supply and specialise in an area that particularly interests you. Go to sale rooms, visit other dealers, study, read and handle the items and your instincts will develop.'

Travel agency

Anyone can buy a shop and set up a business as a travel agent – you do not need any special licence or authorisation. On the other hand, if you want to become an authorised agent for British Rail, or any of the major airline companies, or any of the big shipping companies, there is rather more involved. Before you can earn commission on the sale of tickets from these various bodies you have to satisfy them that you are a reputable company, and their requirements can be fairly stringent.

Two essential requirements if you are setting up on your own are contacts inside the business and sufficient capital. Most people will acquire the necessary experience *and* the contacts by working in an agency for a year or two until they have learned the ropes. At the same time they will probably work part-time for the examination of the Association of British Travel Agents.

It is essential to belong to the Association of British Travel Agents, who also have to be satisfied that you are a reputable firm. The validation process takes at least four months. If you are a limited company, they require you to have an issued share capital or capital account balance of at least £30,000 and also to put up another £30,000 as a bond for your bank or insurance company. To gain approval by IATA (International Air Transport Association) and British Rail (who do all their own, very thorough, investigations), you have to prove that you are a reputable firm with sufficient financial backing, that you are generating sufficient business to warrant selling their tickets (the financial requirements vary according to the locality), that your staff are sufficiently trained and knowledgeable, that your premises are of a sufficiently high standard and promote the right image. Then, and only then, will you be able to advertise that you are an authorised agent.

It will take at least one or two years to work up the necessary volume of business. In the meantime, most people concentrate on hotel bookings and package tours. You can deal in air and rail tickets, but only through another friendly agency, and of course *you* do not then earn the commission (it is illegal).

Choosing the right area is obviously important – centre of town, busy suburb, prosperous market town, for example. There is a great deal of competition and you will survive and prosper only if you provide a friendly and *reliable* service which is also competitively priced. Remember, too, that the most lucrative business is done with firms: you should cultivate every contact you can find in the hope of becoming *the* company agency for nearby business firms.

Newsagents and tobacconists

Extremely hard work and long hours are involved in running this type of shop, and it is not a particularly profitable area. You will probably need to organise a daily delivery service for newspapers, which will involve getting up very early, marking newspapers, paying delivery agents, keeping books of customers' credit, etc. You will have to deal with a large number of suppliers, whose representatives will call regularly. You will have all the headaches of VAT and the constant small price rises which particularly affect cigarettes and confectionery. Moreover, you will have to keep the shop open for as many hours as possible – most newsagents close only on the days when newspapers are not printed. If a member of your family is available to work in the shop, the extra help will be invaluable and you can avoid the problems which taking on staff might entail.

Ironmonger's/DIY shop

The principles for this type of retail outlet differ from those which apply to a newsagent's in several important respects: trade will often be more specialised, so location is likely to be less important; stock will often be expensive and heavy initial capitalisation may be necessary and, because some items will be bulky and a wide range of stock must be held, relatively large premises will be required.

Russ Morgan, who runs a DIY shop, also emphasises the degree of expertise you need to have: 'You must know the tools you stock and the jobs they're capable of doing so that you can advise your customers correctly. You are not merely selling products, you are also a key source of advice, and if your advice is good and your products are right, then people will return again and again.' He is also aware of the high cost and the importance of stock control. 'Get your stock level right. Too little and word gets around that you can never get anything there. Too much and the cost of keeping your stock on your shelves eats into profits. If you are taking £1000 a week then your stock should be about £8000. But do remember if someone buys a very expensive plane to reorder immediately – if you don't someone is bound to come in next week asking for it and you won't be able to help him.'

Sub post offices

As a sub postmaster you are effectively a 'franchisee' of the Post Office. You offer its services and sell its products at prices which it dictates and for which you receive payment. The postal services you provide will often be only part of the overall service, and the Post Office will not usually restrict other sales. But it will be an important part of the business, attracting a steady stream of customers who, once inside the shop, may be tempted to buy other things.

A sub postmastership is not *automatically* transferred from seller to buyer and the change has to be ratified by the Post Office. You should realise this when purchasing any business that includes postal services.

Owing to the decline in the number of rural and sub post offices and the demand for such businesses, competition is fierce and it is becoming increasingly difficult to obtain a sub postmastership.

CHAPTER 2.4

Franchising

The best-known UK franchises are Body Shop and McDonalds, though in fact quite a number of familiar high street shops, restaurant chains and a great many kinds of home and business services are operated as franchises. This means that the person operating the franchise – the franchisee – has bought from the franchisor the right to trade under an established name, rather than establishing his or her credentials from scratch.

That in itself can be a great advantage, but taking up a franchise goes further than that. The franchisee is buying a working business blueprint that has previously been tried, tested and de-bugged by the franchise owner – the franchisor – and by his other franchisees. With it he buys training, start-up support, an operating manual and a helpdesk for day-to-day problems, at least in the early stages. He also buys the exclusive right to operate that franchise in a given territory.

The format for operating the business is laid down very precisely, down to the stationery headings, the uniform you wear when on duty, the layout of your premises and how much you charge your customer for goods or services. The idea is that if you follow the format, you cannot fail because it has been tested and found to work. If you put in the hours, you will generate a predicted level of turnover and predicted net profit margins. These will enable you to recoup your initial investment – the start-up costs and the upfront fee you buy for the right to operate the franchise and to be trained in running it as a business – within two to three years.

The net margin is calculated to allow not only the usual overheads, but also a royalty to the franchisor. That varies between five and ten per cent, depending on whether or not the franchisee involved is buying goods from the franchisor on which the franchisor himself makes a profit as a supplier or wholesaler.

It sounds like a wonderful idea. Where's the catch? First of all let us say that franchising has proved itself to be a very good way of starting a business of your own. Failure rates are low and because of this, the banks have been more ready to lend money to franchisees than for many other forms of small business, especially in the start-up phase. In fact the franchising department of your bank is the best place to start investigating a franchise proposition, because there are quite a number of snags to watch out for.

Choosing a franchise

One unscrupulous operator confessed to me in an expansive post-lunch mood, 'There's two born every minute – in case one of them dies'. There is very little legislation in the franchising field and there have been plenty of instances where franchisees have been induced into parting with their upfront fee and have seen very little in return for their money. The bank may not say outright that this or that franchise proposition should not be touched with a bargepole, but if several banks refuse to lend you money on it, don't go further. Either you are wrong for the business or the business is wrong for you. Or it is just plain wrong, full stop, probably because the pilot stage when the format is tested has not been carried out properly, or not at all, or because the upfront fee and/or royalties are regarded as too high or because the thing is simply known to be badly run.

There are also businesses that call themselves franchises but are really variants of pyramid selling, where you get paid for recruiting other members to a chain of people, each one selling stuff, often of very little intrinsic value, to the next link down. Strictly speaking, this form of trading is illegal, but there are ways around it which sail very close to the borders of the law without actually breaking it.

Even if you don't actually need the money, a check with the bank is worth making. It will cost you nothing and it could save you a great deal of money. Indeed, if the franchisor tries to pressurise you out of taking sensible precautions, walk away immediately.

In addition to the bank check, you should ask to talk to existing franchisees, even of a reputable franchise, chosen by you at random, not ones nominated by the franchisor. Things can change. Ask whether they are achieving the income levels and profit margins forecast and how many hours a week it takes to do that; whether, given the chance, they would make the decision to take up that franchise again; and if there is anything they would like to change. That could be a negotiating point if and when you come to signing a contract.

A final check is to ask whether the franchisor is a member of the British Franchise Association (BFA). Not all of them are, but many of the good ones have membership. The BFA is a franchisor body but it

INTERNATIONAL FRANCHISES

TeleConnection also offer
Voice Mail Bureau Services
for franchising
on an international basis.

For further information
please contact us on:

TELECONNECTION
44 (0) 71 957 7000

lays down standards and conditions which also protect franchisees.

One of the problems in franchising is that not all good ideas work well everywhere. That is certainly true of franchises that have been a great success in other countries, notably the USA, but it is also true within the UK. In the eighties there was a household name health food franchise which did extremely well in the south-east of England, but turned out to be a terrible flop in the meat and two veg belt north of the Wash. A tremendous amount depends on the area, even within the same town.

Franchisors make great play with the notion of an 'exclusive territory' but it doesn't mean all that much. There is nothing to stop a franchisee from a different franchisor opening up a similar business in your exclusive territory, or indeed a similar, non-franchised business doing this. Think how many fast print shops and fast food outlets there are around, for instance.

At the same time, there is no doubt that those who get into a good franchise at an early stage, before all the plum territories are assigned, can make a lot of money. Some of the early Body Shop franchisees are now very wealthy. It shows that franchising, format though it is, still calls for the exercise of some commercial judgement.

The average length of a franchise agreement is seven to ten years, but these days very few products or services hold their competitive advantage for as long as that. You need to be sure that the franchisor is sufficiently resourceful to keep coming up with new ideas and sufficiently resourced to develop them. In the recession of the nineties it was noticed that some franchisees got into difficulties because the franchisors were themselves under pressure. They could not give the franchisees enough support.

Not everyone is temperamentally suited to be being a franchisee. Though to a large extent it is your own business, you are still tied to the franchisor's apron strings in regard to what you can and cannot do – for instance, you may be limited as to the range of services you can offer or the goods you stock. That condition may become very irksome if you think you see business opportunities that your contract prevents you from exploiting.

The franchise agreement is a long and complicated document which sets out what your obligations are to the franchisor, and vice versa during the term of the contract. Do not sign it without making sure that you understand it fully and that it neither omits nor adds anything different from that which you agreed or assumed verbally. In fact, you should also show it to a lawyer who knows about franchising. That may not necessarily be your usual lawyer. If he is not confident of his knowledge in this field ask him, or the bank, to recommend someone that is.

A fuller account of this topic is given in *Taking Up A Franchise: the Daily Telegraph Guide* by Colin Barrow and Godfrey Golzen, also published annually by Kogan Page.

Management Buy-outs

Management buy-outs are at the more expensive end of the spectrum of self-employment opportunities discussed in this book, but they are becoming more common and, at the lower end of the cost range, are comparable to setting-up costs of franchises in the medium to upper price field: £100,000–£250,000.

The opportunity for a buy-out occurs when the owners of a business decide to dispose of all or a part of it. That may give the existing management the chance to become bidders for it themselves. Indeed, there have been cases where the entire workforce became bidders, with the existing management becoming their spearhead. A notable example was the management buy-out of the National Freight Corporation, which received a great deal of publicity when, on a subsequent flotation, large capital gains were made by those members of the workforce who had participated in the buy-out.

The NFC buy-out was a large one which occurred in consequence of a privatisation measure. More commonly, buy-out opportunities occur because the owners:

□ Want to sell out to raise cash
□ Decide that the business is not a core activity
□ Feel the business is not sufficiently profitable
□ Feel the business needs investment which they are unable or unwilling to make.

Another cause can be the business going into receivership.

In recent years finance for buy-outs that look as though they stand a chance has been readily available from sources of venture capital, though the bidders are expected to shoulder a considerable part of the risk. As with other kinds of business loan, the providers of finance expect to see a business plan. Where larger sums are required, it has to go into a lot of detail. Among the points to be covered are:

- Descriptions of the assets and liabilities of the company
- The nature and value of work in progress
- Detailed cash flow projections
- The background and qualifications of the buy-out leaders.

However, there is another equally important set of conditions that have to be fulfilled. By law the owners have to satisfy their shareholders that the buy-out represents the best deal for them, though that need not necessarily mean that they are the ones that have come up with the best offer financially. But if that is not the case, they do have to demonstrate that a sale to them is the best solution, either because it is the quickest or because, if the buy-out participants left the company, its saleability would be diminished. The latter is often particularly true of service-based companies with few tangible assets.

Buy-out negotiations are complex and can be fairly long drawn out: four to six months is about the minimum. Good (and therefore expensive) legal and financial advice is essential and should be costed into the total financial requirements.

The question is, though, whether the owners should be approached with an offer or be asked to name a price. Some financial institutions like to have a clear idea from the start about how much money they are being asked to put up – in other words, they prefer the owners to name a price. On the other hand, a cash bid can sometimes surprise the owners into parting with the business for a modest price. This is where commercial judgement about how to structure the bid is called for.

It also requires a lot of preparation in assessing the value of what the buy-out team is acquiring. That should be clearly specified in the bid document; otherwise you may find that the owners are excluding a particularly promising development or valuable asset. However, the advice given by the experts is that having fixed a maximum price for the buy-out related to a sum that will enable you to repay the loan and its interest charges (and also make a living) within a reasonable period of time, you should not go beyond that figure.

Hotels, Catering and Entertainment

Hotels, pubs, clubs and the range of independently owned eating places, from simple corner shop cafés to long-established, expensive restaurants, constitute a vast business. There are over 30,000 hotels and large guest houses and a vast number of pubs and clubs. And in employment terms, catering is one of the biggest industries in the UK. The range of opportunities and business options is so wide that we can barely scratch the surface, but an outline of each area will be given and some general conclusions drawn.

The business

What is true of running a shop, that you need unstinting energy and commitment, is even truer in this field. Your hours will be long and irregular. You are likely to have to work 365 days a year. You may have to deal with dissatisfied and difficult customers. There is a mountain of paperwork to monitor and national and local regulations to understand and abide by. Your family, which is in any case likely to be directly involved in the running of your hotel, restaurant or café, should be as committed to succeeding as you are.

Offsetting these disadvantages, these areas, particularly owning a restaurant or hotel on which you can stamp your personality and deal very closely with your customers, have many attractions. Indeed, perhaps too many: new restaurants open with great frequency but often quickly collapse because of poor planning, bad management, lack of finance, or a simple lack of realism about the scope for *that* type of restaurant in *that* locality.

Location

As in retailing, location is crucial. Decide what sort of operation you wish to conduct and then look for the premises. If you want to start a hotel or guest house, look for an expanding inland tourist spot or popular seaside resort. In the latter think about the problems of surviving the winter, with only limited and erratic custom. Ask yourself what type of visitor the place attracts and who might be attracted by price reductions out of season (pensioners or disabled people perhaps). Understand the character of the area in which your business will be sited, and have some idea *whose* needs you will cater for. This applies as much to services as to manufacturing firms, and is crucial when you decide how to market that service.

Getting planning permission

This is more difficult than you might think. Local authorities will want details not only of what you intend to do with the premises but of structural changes you intend to make, of the effect the development will have on other properties, of the safety factors involved, of the parking facilities available for your customers, and so on. You will have to submit detailed plans, and will probably need to consult a lawyer and a surveyor. Even then your application may not succeed, and you will have bought a good deal of expensive legal advice with no return. Remember that restaurants and clubs may be noisy, keep long hours and attract a large number of patrons – local authorities are naturally anxious to regulate these developments, and your application may therefore be lengthy and will need to be well planned and properly researched.

Restaurants

New restaurants open every week, particularly in the London area. But almost as many close, and only the gifted and the adaptable survive. Establishing a restaurant is extremely expensive, particularly when you have to convert premises (as is usually the case). A good idea is not sufficient; you also need diligence and, above all, *money*. In a period of tight money and high interest rates, financial backing for enterprises as doubtful as restaurants is in short supply.

There are basically two kinds of people who open a restaurant – the gifted amateur or professional cook, and the 'ideas man' who knows how to fulfil a taste and buys premises and finds the staff to meet that need (many of the 'in places' in London are now more rated for décor, music and clientele than for their cuisine). The main problem for the amateur or professional is likely to be how to maintain standards without wasting an enormous amount of food and losing money. One answer is to have a *small* choice of dishes which are changed regularly. He will have to spend quite a lot of time finding the best sources locally for fresh meat, fish and vegetables since his reputation depends on it. The restaurateur who has a speciality (such as steaks) and sticks to it will find life a lot simpler.

Where your restaurant is located is obviously essential. If it is in the centre of town, well and good. If not, you must set about advertising, make sure your friends spread the word around, find an eye-catching décor and try to get yourself written up in the local paper. If you are sufficiently confident, you could try writing to the restaurant critics on some of the big magazines (such as *Harpers & Queen*) or newspapers.

If your restaurant is quite small, you will probably find it more economical in the long run to be as mechanised as possible with chip machines, dishwashers, freezers, etc, rather than hiring a lot of expensive, possibly unreliable, staff. Costing can be quite difficult, with the rising price of food, but beware of undercharging. There is a temptation to court trade with low prices, but you will soon find it impossible to keep up standards. Moreover, do not undercharge when you first open simply to attract customers; when your prices rise they will see through your scheme and look elsewhere. Charge the going rate: decent food, pleasant surroundings, efficient and friendly service and a reasonable location should guarantee some degree of success.

It is a good idea, too, to realise your limitations and not try to be grander than you are – if you are basically steak and chips there is no point in trying to produce cordon bleu menus: you will soon be found out!

We spoke to a restaurateur who points to seven problem areas:

1. Wastage.
2. Overheads – heating and lighting cost £80 per week for a 30-seat restaurant!
3. Payment of VAT.
4. Establishing good and appropriate décor.
5. The need to change the menu – don't let yourself or your customers get bored with it.
6. Maintaining your profit margins.
7. Coping with fluctuations in demand – no customers one night, 50 the next!

Recommended reading from Kogan Page: *The Catering Management Handbook* and *How to Run Your Own Restaurant*, both 1994.

Cafés, snack bars, etc

The large restaurant has very different problems from the small, unpretentious café. The former provides particular foods with (one hopes) a distinctive touch, and will seek to build up a clientele. It may encounter problems in employing staff, dealing with alcohol licensing, regulations on opening hours, fire precautions, and so on. Moreover, it may be vulnerable to economic downturns and changing consumer tastes. By contrast, the café offers a simple service to the local workforce and others at a reasonable price. Fads of taste and the vagaries of economics count for little.

Owning a café is more closely allied to general retailing than to being a restaurateur. True, you must be able to prepare a reasonably wide range of good food cheaply, quickly, efficiently and hygienically. But this should not be beyond the capabilities of the average person.

Reread the retailing section: location will be important and your business must be located in heavy 'traffic' areas. Recognise that each day will have peaks and troughs – a rush at noon to 2 pm perhaps? Can you cope and, if you can, will you then be overstaffed for the rest of the day?

Your business must be covered by health and safety regulations and must be passed by a food inspector and a fire officer. Regulations on bookkeeping and VAT returns apply to you with equal force as to any other retail business.

The hotel business

You must choose your hotel or guest-house with great care. It is a big investment to make, so be sure to examine the following points:

The area
What is the competition like? Are there any plans for redevelopment locally which might involve one of the big hotel groups? Is it on a main road or tourist route, or is it hidden in the back streets or down a country lane? Does the area as a whole seem to be coming up in the world, or going down?

The customers
Ideally, you want to attract a variety of clientele, so that you are fairly busy all year round. Seaside hotels are full up for most of the summer, but virtually deserted in the winter: are you going to make enough profit to cover those lean winter months? Other hotels in industrial or commercial areas will find that they are full of businessmen during the week, but that the weekends are very quiet. The most successful hotels are those which have a good mix of commercial, holiday, conference and banqueting business. Study the accounts if you can and see what the pattern of business is.

The fabric
What state is your hotel in? You must find out how much renovating or decorating needs to be done and how much this is going to cost. What are the maintenance costs likely to be?

The law
There are a number of laws that the hotelier is subject to, particularly health and safety legislation. Insure your property and protect yourself against liability; make sure you meet the necessary safety levels for fireproofing and hygiene, or your insurance may be worthless. Another important set of regulations, if you are opening a new hotel, covers licensing. There are various guides to the licensing laws, but if you have to apply for a new licence it is wise to do it through a solicitor.

Also very important is the Fire Precautions Act of 1971. Every hotel, if it sleeps more than six people, must have a fire certificate from the local fire authority. When buying a going concern, find out if it has a fire certificate, or if an application for one has been made (if not, the hotel is being run illegally). If the fire authority has already inspected the building, check on the cost of any alterations required to bring the premises into line with the Act.

Staff
Good staff are obviously essential for the smooth and efficient running of a hotel, but they are very difficult to come by. This is an industry with a very high staff turnover, especially among unskilled staff, and you must expect to spend a lot of time interviewing, supervising and training. Everyone in the business agrees that it pays to take your time (however inconvenient) and select staff very carefully, rather than always employing the first person you see because you are busy.

Goodwill
Does the hotel you are considering buying have a good reputation? Will regular visitors return even though the hotel has changed ownership?

Past performance and potential
How has it operated in the past: could you improve on it? What is the sleeping capacity? Could it be increased without reducing standards? Can seasonal fluctuations be reduced by good marketing? How great are staff expenses and other overheads as a proportion of turnover? What is the hotel's net profit as a percentage of turnover?

Pubs

The following section refers to brewery tenants, not to pub managers (who are not self-employed) or to the owners of free houses, which are now so few and far between as to make the possibility of finding a vacant one very unlikely.

Tenants rent their pubs from the brewery company, paying an agreed sum to the outgoing tenant for fittings, equipment and stock. They agree to buy their beer from the brewery, and generally cannot buy stock (even of items other than liquor) from any other source without the brewery's permission. They keep their own profits and are responsible for their own losses, the brewery receiving only the rent on the premises and the guaranteed outlet for its product.

There are more applications from prospective tenants than there are tenancies available, so the breweries are able to 'pick and choose' to some extent. The qualities they look for in a prospective tenant are:

1. Sufficient capital resources to purchase fittings, equipment and stock in hand, to cover immediate running expenses, and to provide a sufficient reserve to cover the tenant in the event of a temporary reduction in trade.
2. A preference for married tenants. Running a pub is very much a family affair, and your spouse's experience and attitude can be a decisive factor.
3. Good health, since running a pub involves hard physical work and long hours.
4. Some managerial experience, in any trade – this would count in the applicant's favour, though it is not strictly necessary. Similarly, experience or training in the liquor trade would be useful, and though not a mandatory requirement it would be useful from your point of view to have experienced the trade in various capacities first.

We spoke to one publican who offered this advice: 'Watch the optics, the fiddles and the free drinks to friends. Watch that the brewers don't send you lines you don't want. Don't commit yourself to loans and brewers' discounts – there'll be conditions in the fine print you won't like. The Weights and Measures boys will be calling often to check your measures and make sure you have price notices and age warnings up.'

Detailed information is given in *Running Your Own Pub*, published by Kogan Page, 1992.

Tenancy agreements

Most breweries have a standard form of agreement to be signed by the tenant. The procedure for taking over the fittings, furniture and equipment is the only area in which there may be a substantial difference between breweries: some require the new tenant to buy these items from the outgoing tenant, while in other cases they remain the property of the brewery, and the tenant lodges a deposit, returnable when he gives up the tenancy. Other items covered in the tenancy agreement include rent (usually paid quarterly), the term of the tenancy, responsibility for repairs, a requirement that the tenant must take out employer's and public liability insurance, the terms on which the stock is purchased, the brewery company's right of access to the premises, requirements connected with transfer of the licence, and terms on which the tenancy can be terminated.

Licences

The tenant usually takes over premises that are already licensed, so he has to negotiate the transfer of the licence from the outgoing tenant to himself. It is advisable to be represented by a solicitor in your application for transfer of the licence.

Training

If you are accepted by a brewery for a tenancy, and neither you nor your spouse has any experience of the trade, it is likely that both of you will be asked to attend a short residential course, run by the brewery company and lasting from one to two weeks. While you are waiting for a suitable tenancy, or applying to different breweries, it is advisable, if you have no experience, to work part-time in a pub. This will give you some experience, and will help you to decide whether you are really suited to what is in fact a very arduous job.

Other opportunities

It is possible to run clubs, cinemas, theatres and so on independently. Indeed, the attractions for the music lover or cinema buff are considerable as it seems to be possible to mix business with pleasure. But base any decision on *business* sense, not on a romantic notion of making your leisure interest pay. Can the town support another cinema, particularly if you intend to show nothing but *avant garde* and experimental films? (Whether you want to show more obscure films or not, if the major companies have tied up the distribution of the money-spinning movies you may have no option!)

You will face the same problems as the hotelier and restaurateur in choosing the right location, employing staff, perhaps getting restrictions on opening hours lifted, obtaining a licence to serve alcohol and meeting fire regulations.* (Some of these problems can be circumvented if you make your institution a private club, admitting members only at some sort of fee, though future legislation may close this loophole.) And do not forget the less well-known legislation on health, hygiene, noise abatement, etc, which may involve you in short-term inconvenience or, worse, long-term and expensive rounds of litigation.

---

* This could be extremely expensive if alterations to a club or cinema have to be made to comply with regulations. Consider this when you buy a property which you hope to convert, and check that an established business has a fire certificate.

Which business?

Whatever type of service you provide, you will need sound financial backing, commercial acumen, the ability to offer something distinctive and market it accordingly, and patience in choosing the right opening. Fix on a 'target' population: advertise in newspapers and periodicals which they are likely to read, and be prepared for an initial struggle while you attempt to build up the business. The business field you choose to enter should be one in which you have some expertise, something distinctive to offer and a practical marketing strategy. But, even then, you will need resilience and the ability to work hard for long periods.

CHAPTER 2.7

Construction, Building and Maintenance Services

Builders, carpenters, plumbers and electricians are in constant demand. Established firms charge high labour rates, and people qualified in these trades can obtain a steady income by taking on extra work at reasonable rates. Alternatively, if you are more ambitious, you may start a building or redecoration company. You will need some capital, the necessary equipment, some means of transport, and a rudimentary administrative system – to take commissions for work, send invoices, check payments, keep tabs on costs, etc.

You may also need a tax exemption certificate, which customers (such as the local authorities) will require to ensure that you are a Schedule D taxpayer. If you work solely for private householders, small shops, etc, you will not need this certificate. But if you work for a main contractor, local authority or government department, you will have 30 per cent of all bills (except the cost of materials and VAT) automatically deducted by them, unless you have this certificate.

The Inland Revenue publishes a guide on how to apply for and use these certificates. If you are refused a certificate – and without one you will find work difficult to get – you can appeal within 28 days to the local General Commissioners.

Training

The orthodox training for these trades is by entering into apprenticeship after leaving school, but it is now sometimes possible for older people to learn these skills at government training centres (details from your local employment office).

Much of the work available in private households consists either of

216

very small jobs, such as putting up shelves or wallpapering, or conversion work, for which you must take into account building regulations and you or the house owner should get planning permission if applicable. You will find that the wider the range of skills you can offer, the more you will be in demand, since one job might involve both carpentry and decorating, for example.

It is advisable to work with a partner, since you will often need help with lifting, measurement, etc. You will also find that it is invaluable to have contacts who specialise in other, related trades, since you will often find that you cannot complete a job without the help of, say, an electrician. Contacts will also help you to find work since they will get in touch with you to finish jobs that they themselves cannot complete.

The building regulations

Major structural changes must conform with national and local building regulations. If in doubt, consult your local authority (ask for the District Surveyor or Building Inspector).

Planning permission needs to be granted for external extensions exceeding 1300 cubic feet. If the building you are working on is listed as being of historic interest there may be regulations against changing its external appearance – again, check with the local authority. These problems concern the person who commissioned the work more than they affect you, but it is as well to guard yourself against liability.

How to get work

As explained above, contacts in related trades are invaluable. You might also obtain subcontracted work from small building firms. Landlords and property agents are useful people to cultivate, as they often provide a great deal of maintenance and conversion work. You may also wish to advertise in the local press. But beware of making claims which you cannot support: do not, for example, say that you are a master builder if you hold no such certificate.

Sources of information

1. The Department of the Environment publishes a leaflet called 'How To Find Out: Getting the Best from Building Information Services', listing 80 important information sources for the construction industry. They also publish a large number of advisory leaflets on subjects such as 'Emulsion Paints', 'Frost Precautions in Household Water Supply', 'Sands for Plasters, Mortars and Renderings', etc. These are available

217

from HMSO bookshops or from the Building Centre and other booksellers.

2. The Building Centre is at 26 Store Street, London WC1E 7BS (tel: 071-637 1022). There is a bookshop and displays.

3. The Building Research Establishment is the largest and most comprehensive source of technical advice available to the construction industry. It operates from Watford.

Painting, decorating, plumbing and electrical work

These are areas which attract numerous 'cowboys' offering little or no expertise and a generally poor service. Fortunately, because continued custom depends so much on word of mouth, the rogues tend to fall by the wayside and only those offering a professional service survive. If you are experienced in one of these areas, try it for a while on a part-time basis and, if you have a steady stream of jobs and apparently satisfied customers, enter the profession full-time.

You will probably have been employed with a firm in this capacity and may at first worry about days (or weeks) without work and a long-term shortage of orders. But you must learn to live with the downturns, and price your work for jobs accordingly. These services are always in demand, and if you do a competent job at a competitive price you will survive. Word of mouth will win you most orders but, if you can cope with additional work, go out and look for it: put ads in the windows of local shops, in local newspapers and in the Yellow Pages.

We spoke to a painter and decorator who offered this advice: 'It's silly to start with no work in hand so make sure you have sufficient work before you take the plunge. By "sufficient" I don't mean bits and pieces but solid full-time jobs. Recommendation is better than advertising and do a good job for a fair price.'

PART 3:
Directory of Low Investment, Part-time Opportunities for the Self-employed

CHAPTER 3.1

Part-time Work

Part-time work has become a significant part of the UK economy. Official figures show that 22 per cent of the workforce are employed on this basis, and the indications are that by the end of the century it could be as much as a quarter.

The range of ways in which people work part-time is also wide.

- ❑ 'Portfolio' part-time work – doing part-time jobs for several different employers on a regular basis
- ❑ Working part-time for a single employer – for instance, the human resource strategy director for the employment agency, Reed Executive, only works there three days a week
- ❑ Doing a part-time job as a spare-time activity, usually to earn extra money. Sometimes this takes the form of extending the job you do for your employer into private work in your spare time – a matter we will cover in a little more detail shortly
- ❑ Casual work – occasionally taking on work to help out a friend or to augment one's income.

The Inland Revenue suspects that a significant part of the black economy, through which some £10 million a year is lost to the Exchequer, flourishes through casual and spare-time work. Anecdotal evidence suggests they are probably right. A great many tradesmen express a strong preference to be paid in ready cash by private customers. Such payments are extremely difficult for tax inspectors to trace.

It is likely, however, that people who fail to declare their income from part-time work are more concerned to conceal their activities from the DSS than from the Inland Revenue. It is very easy to cease to be eligible for unemployment benefit by earning income of more than the basic unemployment benefit for any given six-day period. If this source of earned income does not continue and you wish to sign on again, there can be considerable delays before you receive unemployment benefit. There is a strong temptation, therefore, if you do something that brings in a few pounds a week while you are unemployed, not to declare it.

The government recognises the fact that income from a new business is usually less than the dole and the Business Start-Up scheme (see page 59) helps to bridge the gap.

Tax advantages of part-time employment

If you are married with another source of income, not declaring your earnings from part-time work might be a very unwise move – apart from being illegal. In the first place it is usually unlikely that you would have to pay tax on it at all because of the single person's earned income allowance of £3445. This means that the first £3445 of everyone's earnings is free of tax; so if you can arrange for your spouse to earn that amount of money from your source of extra income, you will not pay any tax on it – assuming he or she does not already have a job. Remember, it is the profit that is taxed, not the total earnings. If you cannot get that figure close to £3445 by setting off against gross earnings all the allowances described in Chapter 1.12, then you are either doing so well as to make it worth considering turning your spare-time occupation into a full-time activity, or you should get an accountant, or you should change the accountant you have. However, you do have to prove, to the satisfaction of the tax inspector, that your spouse really is working in the business – taking messages, typing invoices, bookkeeping, or whatever. Holding the fort by looking after the kids and doing the shopping so that you can get on with it does not count.

All this is reinforced by the fact that even if you do not pay tax on them, there are definite advantages in earnings that are taxed under Schedule D. You will be able to claim allowances on services (gas, electricity and water) for the use of part of your house, plus a proportion of your bill for the telephone, stamps and stationery – whatever, in fact, can be shown to be reasonably related to the nature of the activity you are carrying on. Small is beautiful, provided you declare it.

Planning and other permissions; insurance

Strictly speaking, if you carry on a business from home you have to apply for planning permission, as indicated in Chapter 1.2. In practice, very few people bother when it comes to part-time work, though if what you are intending to do creates a noise, a nuisance or a smell (and some crafts and home repair activities do some or all of these things even when carried on in quite a small way) you should inform the local authority of your intentions. Complaints from neighbours not only cause embarrassment but can also result in your being required to find proper premises, the cost of which may invalidate your whole idea. Applying for planning permission will highlight such potential problems, and forewarned is forearmed. By the same token, if planning permission has been granted you will be able to face most complaints with equanimity.

If you are doing anything with food – making pâtés for your local delicatessen, for instance – you should inform the environmental health inspector. Here again, very few people bother and, in fact, the health officials are more concerned with commercial kitchens than domestic ones, which are generally cleaner; on the other hand, you could be liable for prosecution if it turns out, for instance, that the cause of someone being made ill by your pâté was a breach of the health regulations.

One important precaution you should not neglect if you are planning to work from home, whatever that work is, is to tell your insurance company. This is because your normal house and contents policy covers domestic use only and if you change the circumstances without telling the insurers they could fail to pay you in the event of a claim – and would probably do so if the loss was caused by the undeclared activity. Additional insurance cover will not normally cost you much, which is often more than could be said for any loss that occurs.

Assessing the market

From the point of view of anyone contemplating full-time self-employment, the principal advantage of part-time work is not really that it is a source of extra income, however valuable an incidental that may be, but that it serves as a trial run for the real thing. Opinions may differ as to what the prime factors here are in order of priority, but few would disagree that the most important thing is to assess whether there is a market for the goods or services you are proposing to offer, at a price that will bring you a worthwhile profit. Working part-time at something will give you an idea whether the demand and the competition will enable you to do that.

For instance, if working 12 hours a week, evenings and weekends, produces a gross £100 a week – £4800 a year, allowing for four weeks' holiday – and your present income is, say, £22,000, there is a marginal case for considering full-time self-employment. By working 48 hours a week you could, on that evidence, gross about £19,000 in a 48-week year. Of course, it would depend on what your costs were, but some of the fixed ones – tools, for instance – would not change if you expanded your activities. If there was evidence for a very strong demand you might even consider raising your prices, especially if the experience you have gained about the market indicates that you are appreciably cheaper than the competition. Alternatively, you might discover that by making one or two modifications you could either charge more than the competition or create a stronger demand for your original concept. It is much easier to make these adaptations to market conditions while still operating at a modest level and with a main income from another source.

Objectives

Whether the person in a £22,000-a-year secure job throws his hand in for £19,000-worth of insecurity depends not only on financial factors but on personal objectives. Here again, working part-time before making the commitment to full-time self-employment will help you to shape your thinking about what those objectives are and what they are worth to you. If independence is the overriding factor you might feel that even a sizeable financial sacrifice is worth making. On the other hand, if money is the main objective and you are secure in your main job, then clearly, in the instance we have given, you are much better off earning an extra £4800 a year from your part-time job, plus £22,000 a year from your main one, than giving up the latter altogether – unless you could see a way of doing better than £4800 pro rated over a 48-hour week.

Another objective that could be tried out is whether you can work with an intended partner. Some very successful businesses are run by people who have little in common except a respect for each other's abilities, but it is usually difficult to test such qualities unless you have actually worked closely with someone. Trying out a partnership arrangement on a part-time basis is a good way of doing this.

Assessing yourself

There is also the question of assessing your own suitability because there is a big gap between pipe dreams of independence and the reality, even when it comes to working full-time at something you have previously enjoyed doing as a hobby. Apart from the fact that what is fun as a hobby can sometimes be quite another proposition done hour after hour and day after day, there is often a huge difference between amateur and professional standards. For instance, it may take you all day to turn out a widget – that mythical, all-purpose British unit of manufacture – whereas a professional can do it in a couple of hours. That is fine when you are doing it more or less for fun, but fatal if you are trying to earn a living, unless you are confident you can get to professional standards fairly quickly.

Whether you can actually do so usually depends on how good you are at working for very long hours, initially for not much money and spending a great deal of your 'spare time' on administration: keeping records, writing letters and preparing quotes. You will not know your capacities in this respect until you try, but working part-time will give you an inkling.

It will also give you some indication of your family's attitudes to your work. If you are working part-time on top of a full-time job, you are probably reasonably close to putting in the sort of hours that are needed to make a success of self-employment at least for an initial – and usually prolonged – period of time. In other words, your family will not see a great deal of you unless they are able and willing to pitch in as well. They may view this prospect with equanimity; on the other hand, workaholism can be as great a source of family tension as alcoholism. When working part-time it is quite easy to cut down the hours you are putting in, or even to stop altogether. If your living depends on it, the case is altered completely.

Financial commitment

One of the advantages of part-time work is that you are keeping your overheads, or fixed costs, low. You can work from home instead of renting premises or offices. You can hire equipment instead of buying it. You may even be able to use facilities available at your place of work – photocopying, for instance – though to what extent that is a wise move depends on the attitude of your employer. Some take it as a sign of initiative, provided that it does not interfere with your regular job. Others hate it, in which case you will have to be very careful how you go about it, and at least account for everything you use. The point is, though, that for part-time work you will not have to 'tool up' expensively and, indeed, you should avoid irreversible financial commitments as much as possible. Do not, for instance, buy a van until you are sure you are going to get profitable use out of it, or unless you want one anyway. Do not, to take another case, buy a knitting machine – hire it and see whether you really can make knitting pay.

The principle can be extended to any given activity. Earlier in this book we stated that you should never buy anything unless you have to and until you have established an ongoing need for it. That was in reference to full-time activities. It is even more the case with part-time work, because by definition the number of hours you have in which to amortise the cost – to make a profit and get your money back – are far fewer.

Opportunities

Extension of full-time employment

In the previous section we referred to the situation where someone is carrying on into evenings and weekends private work normally done for an employer in the daytime: typical examples might be repair and building work, some forms of design, and teaching extended into exam coaching. The great advantage of this type of work is that it can give you a direct access to the market. Everybody who walks through the door at your place of employment is a potential private customer, whereas in other forms of part-time work, finding the market is an important but difficult part of the total concept. Furthermore, private part-time clients can later be turned into sources of work on a larger scale, either directly or as leads to other work. Even suppliers can be useful people to get to know, both in terms of establishing your credibility when it comes to asking for credit and in the matter of sorting out good and reliable suppliers from the many other varieties.

The principal disadvantage of this type of work is that it can lead to a conflict of interests. The temptation to steer work your way rather than towards your employer can be very strong. It need not be anything as blatant as buttonholing your employer's customers at the door. There are subtler ways of bending the rules. The best way to avoid such temptations is to develop your own clients and contacts as soon as possible.

Turning a hobby into a source of income

This is usually the most satisfying form of part-time work because people generally perform best at what they most enjoy doing. Furthermore, many people, especially the over-30s, find that they have gone or been pushed into careers that do not reflect their real interests or skills, or that they have simply developed new ones that they find more satisfying than what they do for a living. Practising crafts of various kinds is a case in point.

The trap here is the one that we have referred to earlier – that there is a world of difference between doing something for fun and working at it full-time. Professional craftsmen have years of experience which enable them to turn out work quickly and economically. They also know the market: who buys what, at which price; what sells and what does not. In the case of photography, to take another instance, the good amateur turned professional is competing in a field where contacts are all-important and where high standards of work depend not only on individual skill, but on having the latest equipment.

Learning a new skill

Sometimes people learn a new skill, perhaps at an evening class, which is capable of being turned to commercial use – particularly these days when the range of services available from shops and manufacturers has become increasingly scarce and expensive. Popular examples are picture framing and upholstery.

There are also non-manual skills, which can be turned to good account, such as selling; quite a number of people, especially women, are engaged in party plan or catalogue selling. The problem there, however, is that it is difficult to go into a higher, full-time gear to make a living from that type of work, because commissions are fixed percentages and, in the case of catalogue selling, quite small ones.

Reviving an unused skill

This is also very popular, especially with women thinking of returning to work. The most frequently cited example is typing, but as it happens this one neatly illustrates the importance of observing the laws of supply and demand in choosing even a part-time source of income. Because there are many women available for such work, the rates are not particularly good. The only way you can lift yourself into a higher bracket is by identifying a service which few other typists offer and for which there is also a demand: in a university town, for instance, there might be a call for someone who can type theses quickly and accurately. An exporter, to take another example, might have a demand for someone who can type accurately in another language.

The same supply-and-demand principle also applies to translating. There are many graduates around who can translate from one of the main European languages into English, but rather fewer who can do the more difficult, reverse kind of translation: from English into idiomatic French, German or Spanish. Even rarer, and therefore more marketable, is fluency in another language *plus* a qualification in a specialist subject such as law or science.

Using an existing asset as a source of income: accommodation

By far the biggest asset that most people own is their house. When there is a need for more money, or as members of the family grow up or move away, that asset can be a source of income: rooms can be let, the house can be subdivided into flats or even – ultimately – the whole place can be turned into a guest-house. The advantage of these courses of action is that little skill or training is required to turn them into money-making activities. The disadvantage is that they are full of legal pitfalls which deter a great many people. The common option is to circumvent the law by moving into a cash only, black economy relationship with tenants, but by that token you also lose much legal protection that would be available if there was a dispute. By getting a tenancy agreement drawn up you can protect yourself to a large degree, especially if you are also the kind of student of human nature who can spot a potential troublemaker before he or she crosses your threshold.

The best kind of asset to have is a country house grand enough to attract paying sightseers rather than tenants. But in that case you would have an army of legal and financial advisers at your elbow and perhaps would not be reading a book like this!

Letting rooms

In recent years, and especially since the 1980 Housing Act, there have been many horror stories about the difficulty of getting rid of unwanted tenants, even, on occasion, when they have been well behind with the rent. For this reason it is very unwise to let rooms without having an agreement drawn up by a solicitor; even the Citizens' Advice Bureau staffed, in general, by people whose natural sympathies lie with the tenant, recommend this. It is usually unwise, incidentally, to have a room-letting agreement which runs much longer than on a month-to-month basis because, except in extreme circumstances, the courts are likely to take the view that an agreement will have to run its full course before being terminated.

The other piece of legislation to beware of is the Rent Act of 1977 which gives the tenant the right to go to a tribunal and ask for a 'reasonable' rent to be applied if he or she thinks you are asking too much. A register of reasonable rents is kept at your local authority's Rent Assessment Panel office, if you want to check what these are, but you will often find that these do not allow for subtle shades of amenity – the social difference between nearby streets, for instance.

The best way to get good tenants is to select them – not by race or sex, which is illegal – but by asking for references from their previous landlord.

CHAPTER 3.2

Crafts and Domestic Skills

Cooking

With restaurant prices as they are, taking people out for a meal – even on an expense account – can be an alarming prospect. It is quite easy, for instance, to run up a bill in excess of £200 for wining and dining four people. You can do the same thing infinitely more cheaply at home, but not everyone has the skill, the inclination, or the time to do it and this is where the private caterer comes into the picture. Even firms trying to cut down on lavish entertainment are tending to invite customers to lunch or dinner in private dining rooms rather than taking them out to what is often an indifferent, though expensive meal.

If you are a good cook and interested in applying your skills in order to earn money, it is worth putting the word around to firms in your area. You can do it indirectly by letting it be known you are available, through friends or quality food shops, who are sometimes asked to recommend cooks; directly by letters to the chief executive of local firms; or by advertising.

Generally speaking, you do not have to be up to cordon bleu standards. The average businessman is reported to prefer good, orthodox, well-cooked food to anything exotic. You present your customers with a range of possible dishes from a menu – which is in fact your repertoire – and then let them order in advance the meal they want you to cook.

They may have a kitchen on the premises, in which case you will have to make sure that the equipment, crockery and cutlery are adequate. Otherwise you will have to cook the meal at home and bring the necessary adjuncts with you, or buy them. If you have to cook at home, you will either have to stick to cold buffets or make sure that suitable facilities are available for warming up the dishes on the spot. In other words, a gift for efficient administration and organisation is almost as important as cooking skills.

This also extends to doing your costings. If you cook at home, you will have to take account of the use of gas and electricity; indeed the agreement you make with your customers should specify clearly who pays for what. Do you buy the food on their account or do you buy it and put it on the bill? What happens to food that is left over? And who does the washing up or indeed serving at table?

The simplest way to keep matters straight is to charge an hourly rate to include shopping time, preparation of food and cleaning up afterwards. It is generally reckoned that you should aim to clear £45 from the average meal prepared for six people.

The trend towards home cooking and baking also opens up opportunities to supply the growing number of wine bars and speciality food shops. They are often interested in buying from private individuals who can make pies, pâtés and other forms of cooked food. Looking at what they have on offer will give you an indication of demand and going rates. The prices shown will reflect a mark-up of 30 to 40 per cent of the price at which they are bought.

Dressmaking

There are various types of dressmaking that can be done at home: outwork for the garment trade; running up made-to-measure clothes, repairs and alterations, and specialised work such as leather work, embroidery or crochet, which can be sold to boutiques or through mail order. Outwork is repetitive and the pay is low: it is not recommended. Making clothes for friends and for customers brought in by advertisements and recommendations is much more interesting, though even here the rewards may not be high. The easiest type of work is when the customer presents you with a commercially produced pattern and fabric for it, so all you have to do is cut it out and sew it together. Making your own patterns, on the other hand, requires a fair amount of skill, as translating a flat piece of paper into a three-dimensional garment is quite a complicated business. If you *do* know how to make your own patterns, then the customer can present you with a rough sketch, or even just a description, and you work from there.

If the customer does not present you with the fabric for the garment she may give you vague instructions and then be unhappy with your interpretation of them. A compromise could be for you to go shopping with her, to ensure that the chosen fabric is suitable and that sufficient quantities are bought. Thread, zips and trimmings can be bought at the same time. Alternatively, you could build up your own stock, by buying remnants and reduced lines, and offer the customer a choice from these.

It is important to have a fitting as soon as the garment is in one piece, and a second fitting may be needed to check on details such as the hang of a sleeve or to make sure that the collar lies flat.

Alterations (zips, hems, etc) form quite a high proportion of the work of many home dressmakers and these jobs can be fiddly and time-consuming. It is not possible to charge much for this type of work, so if you advertise your services you may find it worth your while to emphasise the fact that you do not do alterations.

Embroidered, leather or crochet garments and knitwear can be sold to boutiques or by mail order (most women's magazines carry small ads for clothes). You must make sure that you have sufficient stock to cover any bulk orders you may receive. You also need a talent for sensing fashion trends almost before they happen, as it will take several months before your garments appear in the shops.

You really need an electric sewing machine: a swing-needle one will enable you to do zigzag stitches – useful for buttonholes, neatening off raw edges and simple embroidery. A zip foot for the machine is also desirable. Other pieces of equipment you will need are pins, shears, needles, thread (keep two or three reels of black and white in stock, and buy other colours when you need them), french chalk, a buttonhole cutter, a tape measure and a steam iron.

Jewellery

The designing and making of jewellery is a highly competitive business. Before investing in expensive materials and equipment, you must prove to yourself that you have some flair for design and are suitably skilful with your hands. Starting off with lapidary work is a good way of finding out if you have the necessary artistic ability and, most important, if anyone wants to buy your designs. From there, the best plan is to take an art college or City and Guilds course in jewellery, and sell the results while you develop some expertise. The great advantage of doing this is that you can use college equipment while you gradually build up your own collection of tools.

The most successful students find that they have no difficulty in selling their work while they are still at college. Start by showing off your handiwork to friends; if your work is good enough your reputation will spread by word of mouth and you will soon find the orders coming in. From there you can progress to taking samples of your work to various jewellers and department stores in the hope of getting orders. You can also hire a stall in a street market on Saturdays and see how successful you are.

The initial outlay on tools can be quite small, especially if you are able to use college equipment as well. Eventually, of course, you will need your own equipment and this can be expensive, so you would be wise to save some of your initial profits towards buying equipment. Materials are also expensive, and it is important to get the pricing right if you are going to make a reasonable profit. Here your best plan is simply to show samples to a well-established jeweller. He will soon tell you how much he would charge, since he obviously does not want to be undercut by a newcomer.

Lapidary work

Lapidary is the art of working in gemstones or pebbles and it forms an excellent introduction to the art of making jewellery, since the basic materials are not as expensive as in jewellery proper.

Learning the techniques of lapidary work is quite simple: there are many books on the subject, as well as clubs and societies. *Gems* is a monthly magazine which lists suppliers, as well as clubs and organisations. Most books will also give you a list of the tools and equipment required. The main item of equipment for lapidary work at home is a tumbler, which is used for grinding and polishing the stones (obtained from craft shops), which are then set in silver, copper, steel, etc to make rings, pendants or brooches.

You will have to be patient; it can take up to 12 weeks to polish a consignment of stones. But you should then have no trouble selling your pieces via local shops, stalls in the local market, department stores, even coffee mornings. Do not undersell your work; look round the shops and see what comparable pieces fetch before offering your work to a shop.

Making loose covers and curtains

To make a living sewing, you must be an experienced and fast worker. Loose covers in particular involve far more work than the inexperienced would ever imagine, so do not gaily undertake to re-cover someone's sofa over the weekend. There are plenty of good handicraft books that give step-by-step directions, and provided you follow them accurately you should not have any problems, even as a beginner. The most important point with loose covers is to know how to measure up accurately, and this is essential when dealing with expensive fabrics.

You will need a sewing machine with a piping foot, enough room to lay the material out properly for cutting and measuring, a really good pair of dressmaking scissors, and a good deal of patience.

You will soon find work by advertising in the local papers, and by word of mouth, once you have done a few jobs. To find out what to charge, ring up one of the big department stores that offers this service and ask them for a quote: make sure your quoted price is then a few pounds cheaper and you will have no trouble finding more work.

Beware of taking on too much and so failing to deliver the goods in time. Take on one job at a time, until you know exactly how long it takes you to do a pair of curtains, or a chair cover, etc. Otherwise, you will end up with a lot of irate clients and a bad reputation for being unreliable.

Picture framing

Some local authorities run evening courses in picture framing. It is also possible to learn the craft by working in a gallery, though usually galleries are rather a 'closed shop'. Basically, as with all crafts, it is best to experiment as much as possible before you undertake commercial work. You need a good worktable and some large shelves on which to store your work. Basic tools are a mitre saw for the corners; clamps, to hold the corners together while they are being glued; accurate rulers and a set square. Hammer and nails, and a vice and mount cutter are useful, though not strictly necessary.

You will also need mouldings, a backing board, which can be either card or hardboard, and glass. Your local glass merchant will cut glass to the right size for you; this is easier than doing it yourself.

Suppliers are often unwilling to supply materials in small quantities, but if you look around, you should be able to find some small firms who are willing to do so. If you are keen on jumble sales, you will find that you can often pick up old picture frames for next to nothing, and these can be revamped.

For making the actual frames, great care and accuracy are needed in order to get the mitred edges to fit exactly. Compare prices by asking galleries and picture-framing shops for quotations.

Pottery

It is possible to 'teach yourself' by reading and experimentation, but if you want to take a course many local authorities run evening classes in pottery (they are popular so book as early as you can).

Unless you are going in for pottery in a small way, you will need plenty of space for working and storage. It is a good idea to convert your garage, or an outside shed, into a workroom since it then won't matter if you make a mess. Your workroom should ideally be equipped with a decent-sized sink, a solid work-surface, preferably with a plain wooden top, plenty of shelves, a damp cupboard (which can be a wooden cupboard lined with plastic sheeting or with slabs of plaster which are periodically soaked in water) and a waterproof container for storing clay. Other basic requirements are the kiln (if you are eventually planning on a high turnover of work, you will need to buy the largest kiln you can afford); the potter's wheel (though this is not absolutely necessary for a beginner, since you can do mould, slab and coil pottery without one); an assortment of bowls, buckets, basins, sieves, etc; and a set of small tools – cutting wire, a knife, scrapers, 'bats' (squares of hardboard used for carrying and drying pottery), sponges, brushes and modelling tools.

You may prefer to use your own local clay, in which case you will have to devote time to its preparation, or you can buy it ready-prepared from a potter's merchant or pottery supply house. Local brickworks will often supply clay cheaply, though it may need some extra preparation. It is usually supplied by the hundredweight, and smaller amounts are proportionately more expensive. It is important that it should be kept in a cool, damp place.

You can buy ready-made glazes, though it is possible to mix your own. You will also need sand, slow-setting potter's plaster, grog, oxides, slips (engobes) and wax.

If you visit craft shops with samples of your work, you will find that some will take pots on a sale or return basis, while others will buy a small quantity of your work outright and order more if it sells. Alternatively, you may want to sell your work direct to the customer, in which case you could start off by hiring a market stall, with the eventual aim of owning your own shop.

Upholstery

This is an area where it really pays not to price yourself out of the market. The real dyed-in-the-wool professional is so expensive that many people cannot afford the prices. If you have served a long apprenticeship you are of course entitled to charge the top rate, but if you are planning to work as you learn, set your sights a bit lower financially and you will find far more work. You can either buy junk furniture to do up yourself, or advertise to do up other people's furniture. Until you have had some experience, it is probably best not to invest too much money in buying furniture, unless you have lots of storage room and no immediate need for the cash.

You can start out via evening classes, or inquire at your local public library. There are plenty of good books on the subject, and you should soon be able to tackle bedroom or dining room chairs, footstools, etc, without any trouble, but do not attempt buttoning, springs, chaises longues, etc until you have had a bit more experience.

There is a tremendous demand for reasonably priced upholsterers, so you should not have much trouble finding work. Advertise in your local paper or even in the national press, once your work is good enough to tackle big pieces. It is also worth visiting a few antique shops, since they often have upholstery jobs to be done.

The right tools are very important and not too expensive. You will need a webbing stretcher, tack hammer, set of upholstery needles and a regulator. You can buy the tools and materials from specialist suppliers, which are listed in the Yellow Pages.

Trevor Constable, a furniture restorer, mentioned some of the pitfalls to beware of: 'You can't go for work like a bull at a gate. Antique dealers will promise you lots but little will materialise. If you've got the skill, word will get around and work will come in. Don't put all your eggs in one basket. Get a range of customers and don't rely on one source for more than, say, a third of your total work. If you are totally committed to one source and it dries up . . . you're out of business.'

A comprehensive programme of training in a wide variety of crafts and skills is given at West Dean College, West Dean, Chichester, West Sussex PO18 0QZ.

CHAPTER 3.3

Driving

Apart from orthodox taxi firms, which employ full-time drivers 'plying for hire' (ie to a large extent picking up fares on a casual basis in the street), there are also cab hire firms which supply cars with drivers on demand, in response to a telephone call or some other kind of prior arrangement. These firms do not maintain a vehicle fleet of their own but employ outside people, generally part-timers, who drive their own cars, picking up the cab hire firm's clients. The cab hire firm thus acts in somewhat the same way as an employment agency; they supply the leads for drivers on their books.

To get this type of work you should have a clean driving licence and you must take out a special 'hire and reward' insurance. Remuneration varies from place to place and firm to firm, but like ordinary taxi fares it is based on the mileage, the time the job takes and the hour at which it is carried out. The cab hire firm lays down the rates, and a percentage of the fare has to be paid to them on each job though there are some firms that make a flat weekly charge to drivers on their books.

Work is obtained initially by phoning in to base, which is obviously chancy. However, once you have established your status as a regular, many cab hire firms will offer to lease to you or otherwise supply you with a two-way radio and this is a much more reliable way of keeping up the flow of jobs.

Cab driving involves working long hours in order to make an adequate income, and remember that you must allow for petrol, depreciation and insurance. However, the casual nature of cab driving makes this a suitable occupation for those who are filling in time between salaried work.

Cab hire firms are to be found in Yellow Pages. Alternatively, your local garage may be able to advise you of good firms which are looking for drivers with their own cars.

In London, all taxicab drivers must be qualified with the Metropolitan Police Vehicle Carriage Centre and must have passed the so-called 'knowledge'. This is an arduous process, requiring considerable driving skill and an intimate knowledge of routes throughout London. Even if you pass successfully, getting your own cab will be difficult, and self-employment proper may have to be preceded by a period spent driving for one of the many London cab companies, which provide and service the cab and take a substantial cut of the total 'take'.

CHAPTER 3.4

Entertainment

Disc jockeying

Most people start doing DJ work because they enjoy entertaining people and listening to music. Essential requirements for the DJ are a lively, outgoing personality, a good knowledge of pop music (some DJs specialise in one particular type of music) and as large a selection of records as possible. Disc jockeys are engaged by clubs, pubs, etc, either on a regular basis or for one-off sessions. They are generally expected to bring their own records, but equipment may be provided.

The minimum equipment needed to run a mobile disco is a pair of turntables, an amplifier of about 50 watts – more if you think you will play at outdoor gigs or bigger venues – at least two 20-watt speakers, and some form of transport, preferably a van rather than a car. Shop around and find out what discounts are available through the Disc Jockey Federation. Above all, sound quality must be high; no amount of 'extras' will compensate for poor sound.

For the more ambitious, and those with more money to invest, a magnetic cartridge, which improves the quality of the sound, is recommended, and this involves the use of a pre-amplifier and a mixer. You will probably want to use more than two speakers, and a more high-powered amplifier. You may want to invest in stereo equipment, although you will find that this can create problems caused by the many different kinds of room in which you will want to use the equipment. Beyond basic equipment, you will decide whether to provide 'extras' such as a light show, a microphone for the DJ, a strobe, all of which can push up your costs considerably.

If you are going to operate a mobile discotheque as part of a public performance, which is defined as one which takes place 'outside the domestic or home life of the participants', it is necessary to obtain a licence from Phonographic Performance Ltd, 14–22 Ganton Street,

London W1V 1LB. A licence is needed for *any* kind of public performance: even a performance at a firm's dinner dance, for example, would need to be covered. The fees for a licence are on a sliding scale, depending on the amount of time and size of audience for which it is granted.

Playing a record involves two copyrights: that of the record company, which is covered by the licence from Phonographic Performance, and that of the music publisher and composer, which is covered by the Performing Right Society Ltd, 29–33 Berners Street, London W1P 4AA. Most public halls are covered by a licence from the Performing Right Society, but you should check up on this before operating in a public place.

There are a large number of mobile discotheques operating, particularly in London and the Home Counties, so you will find that competition is keen. Demand tends to fluctuate seasonally, with November and December being the best months for bookings.

Advertising in local papers and magazines and the distribution of printed leaflets or business cards are recommended ways of getting bookings.

Pay is variable, according to the type of function and equipment used. Mobile discotheques charge between £50 and £80 a night for private parties, more for weddings and public functions. You must 'cost' your time to a certain extent: if you are playing at a private party, for example, it is likely that you will have to carry on well after midnight, and you should allow for this.

CHAPTER 3.5

Media and Communications

Indexing

Publishers have a constant need for indexers whom they can trust to work quickly, efficiently and thoroughly. Indexing requires the ability to understand the arguments and principal themes of a book and organise the material by key words, often to a brief given by the author or publisher.

Various professional qualifications are obtainable in indexing, and the Society of Indexers (38 Rochester Road, London NW1 9JJ; 071-916 7809) operates a scheme of registered indexers for those with experience. Indexing is a skilled task and the hourly rate for a qualified indexer is about £10.50. As in many other areas, freelance indexers will tend to develop relationships with particular publishers, perhaps even with individual editors, especially if the indexer concentrates on a specific subject area.

Market research interviewing

Market research interviewing mainly involves either visiting people in their own homes to ask them their views about commercial products (or possibly about social issues) or stopping people in the street to ask them a series of questions about a particular subject.

Basic requirements for the job are patience, perseverance, and the ability to relate to a wide variety of different types of people. You must be available to work some evenings and weekends, and possibly to spend the occasional night away from home. A car is not absolutely necessary although it does help, and you must be on the telephone.

A short training course is provided by the large, reputable market research companies. It is fairly easy to be accepted for a training course, as interviewers are generally in short supply, but it is important to show that you are going to be available for work on a long-term basis, as the company sees your training as an investment.

Most interviewers put their names down with several market research companies. They can expect a steady flow of work, particularly in London though probably less in the rest of the country.

Opportunities exist for promotion from interviewing to supervisory and managerial posts, but after promotion one would no longer be working on a freelance basis. Other types of freelance work, besides interviewing, are sometimes available from market research firms: clerical work, for example, or the coding of questionnaires.

If you are interested in working as a market research interviewer, write to the Market Research Society, who will supply on request a list of research companies employing interviewers. Or you can contact one of the bigger, more reputable market research agencies such as BMRB International Ltd, Hadley House, 79–81 Uxbridge Road, London W5 5SU; 081-567 3060.

Pay rates are about £35 for a six-hour day or £6 an hour on the street, plus expenses. Pay can be higher for experienced interviewers.

There are also a surprisingly large number of small market research companies – one- or two-man bands who compete with the larger market research organisations. They have often left the latter to set up on their own, perhaps specialising in a particular area and using the contacts drawn from their previous commissions.

Teaching and tutoring

If you have a degree, teacher's diploma or some other qualification, it is worth thinking about private coaching, especially if you have children of your own and perhaps find it difficult to work normal school hours. Try advertising in your local paper or, better still, in the personal columns of *The Times*, the *Daily Telegraph*, *The Independent* or *The Times Educational Supplement*. State the subjects and the level to which you are prepared to teach. Demand will depend a lot on the area in which you live: you might do better in the 'smarter' areas where parents tend to worry more about their children's chances of winning scholarships, achieving university entrance, etc. There is a particular demand for tutors in mathematics and science subjects. As well as normal school subjects, there is also a demand for people who can teach piano and other musical instruments or give extra coaching in various languages. The average rate for private tuition is £7 to £15 an hour, depending on your personal qualifications and the level to which you are teaching.

You can register with a local or national educational agency such as

Gabbitas, Truman & Thring. It is also worth contacting your local education authority, which may have received an inquiry from parents or students. They might also put you on their books as someone who can do supply teaching in an emergency, which is also paid by the hour.

Translating/interpreting

The growing emphasis on exports and on our links with the Continent means that this is an expanding field. It is also a highly competitive one, though, and you need to have quite a lot to offer to make a successful living. Most translators work in French and German, for example, so it helps if you are an expert in one of the more unusual languages: there is a great demand at the moment for specialists in Eastern European languages, as well as Chinese, Japanese and Arabic.

As well as having a language qualification – either a degree or college diploma (such as the Institute of Linguists qualification) – you should also have some other skill or professional qualification to offer. Few firms employ translators for their knowledge of the language alone. They want people who can deal with business correspondence, translate engineering and computer manuals, medical textbooks, technical leaflets, advertising brochures for all kinds of products, etc. It always pays to cultivate a special subject and become known as the expert in that field.

To get started, try writing to all the translating agencies in the Yellow Pages. Business firms tend to put their work through these agencies, so unless you already have good contacts with a few firms it is a good idea to get on to the books of an agency. If you fancy literary translating, the best idea again is simply to write round to the agencies and to publishing firms noted for their foreign literature back lists.

Rates of pay vary considerably, depending on the quality of your work, the degree of difficulty and the quality sought by the employer. Chinese and Japanese translators are the best paid, and European language translators the worst, with Arabic and Russian specialists somewhere in the middle. If you work for a company direct, without going through an agency, you can charge more. You *can* take on work for private individuals – letters, etc – but it is unlikely to be worthwhile financially, since you can't charge so much.

Translation work requires a complete knowledge of at least one language other than your own, a broad education and a wide range of interests. You will also need a well-stocked personal reference library: translating is a highly skilled technical task which will need back-up from all manner of dictionaries and reference works.

Similarly, work as an interpreter requires rapid intelligence, great stamina and complete fluency in two (and probably more) languages.

These qualities are especially needed for conference work – very few people are good enough, and there are only about 50 conference interpreters in the country, but you can also find work at exhibitions, business meetings, as couriers for travel agencies and guides for the London Tourist Board or the British Tourist Authority.

The relevant professional body for translators and interpreters is the Institute of Translation & Interpreting, 377 City Road, London EC1V 1NA; 071-713 7600.

Writing

Freelance writing is a profession to which many are called but comparatively few are published, and from the outset it should be said that unless one is working or has worked on the staff of a newspaper or magazine of some standing, by which a network of professional contacts has been built up, it is a very difficult field for the total newcomer to break into. The best policy, then, is initially to consider freelance writing as a means of earning extra money over and above that earned from a regular job, which will provide the safety net of a dependable income. If the job is in a related field, such as public relations, advertising or book publishing, so much the better from the point of view of giving the potential writer constant practice at the basics of wordcraft as well as the opportunity to make new and helpful personal contacts. For the purpose of this section it is assumed that the would-be freelance writer is considering producing articles and short fiction for newspapers or magazines, since first novels, always a favourite with new writers, are notoriously hard to place.

The basic requirements of the journalist's craft and the key to success in placing articles are:

1. The choice of a subject to write about.
2. Ensuring that the subject is presented in such a way that it can be readily assimilated into the publication to which you submit it.

The choice of a subject to write about is a more subtle and demanding undertaking than simply avoiding the submission of cookery articles to political weeklies. Such publications as *The Writers' & Artists' Yearbook* list the basic spheres of interest of hundreds of periodicals and newspapers, but after such listings have been scanned for initial guidance, the freelance writer should then study with care several issues of the publication to which he would like to submit material. He should then aim to research and write up a subject which will fall within the sphere of interest of the publication, but which is unlikely to be covered by the full-time or regular part-time contributors to the publication. Similarly, it is best to avoid initially articles which involve a political or serious economic stance, since these are subjects for which even established staff are chosen carefully.

The aim, then, is to select a subject which is original and about which one may even have special knowledge in the hope that it will land on an editor's desk as a delightful addition to his page rather than a dubious repetition. Sometimes this oblique approach to freelance subject selection can turn into a more permanent proposition if one happens to stumble across a subject which a magazine or newspaper feels it is worth ultimately retaining a correspondent for. A classic example of this is beer, a subject for which at least one national newspaper now retains a correspondent in the manner of the already well-established wine or food correspondent.

In the case of writing short fiction a major market is the supply of romantic short stories to women's magazines. Here, although the choice of subject is in principle already determined, the detailed development of the subject needs to be very accurately tailored to a specific magazine.

Many fiction editors on women's magazines receive a steady supply of short stories from literary agents, so it is virtually useless for the new freelance writer to attempt to place work by these means. The vast majority of literary agents will not agree to place short fiction, or indeed any short pieces, for writers who are not already on their books either as novelists or full-length non-fiction writers.

Presentation

Having thought out a suitable subject, equal care should be expended on the literary style of the potential piece. Here again, range of vocabulary, approach and length, not only of the piece but of paragraphs, can only be judged by a careful study of the publication to which the piece will be submitted. Major points to observe in the presentation of work may be summarised as follows:

1. Work should be typed, using one and a half or double spacing on one side of a sheet of A4 paper only. Always retain a photocopy.
2. Always read your typescript carefully before submitting it and make any corrections, which should be very minor, as clearly as possible.
3. Never submit a manuscript without a covering letter, but keep the letter brief. A covering letter should give the gist of your piece in no more than a sentence or two and draw to the editor's attention any recent or particularly prestigious published work which will help to give a fuller picture of you.
4. Before writing a covering letter, telephone the publication to obtain the name of the person to whom you should submit the work. This is particularly useful when submitting material to newspapers, which tend to be very departmentalised.

5. If your article has any particularly topical connections which give it a limited 'shelf-life', say so in your covering letter and then telephone after several days for a decision. Many articles, rejected by one publication, can quite often be quickly but sensitively revamped and successfully placed with a rival magazine.
6. When submitting articles to illustrated magazines it is often useful to team up with a freelance photographer if, and only if, your article directly benefits from illustrations.
7. Never submit uncaptioned photographs and present captions typed on a separate sheet. Remember that two apposite and technically excellent photographs are better than half a dozen fuzzy snapshots.
8. If your article is rejected accept the editor's decision cheerfully and courteously and never attempt to get him to change his mind by arguing. Rejecting scores of unsolicited articles by telephone is one of the least pleasant editorial jobs and whether you agree with them or not, editors know what they want. Nor should you expect editors to criticise your work constructively; after all, they are running publications, not a school of journalism.

Finally, two rules:

1. Never turn a job down, however small and anonymous that job may be, and always get commissioned work in on time.
2. Spare no effort when checking that your facts are right. The beginner who acquires a reputation for inaccurate reporting or slipshod research may as well give up. If a paper or magazine accepts your article, but holds it over for several months, remember to keep abreast of any new developments in the interim: accuracy applies not only to the time of writing but, more important, to the time of publication.

One full-time writer we approached gave this advice: 'Discipline, discipline, discipline! These are the three key words for any budding writer to remember. Get up early and keep at it. If you're stuck for words get something down regardless – you can always change it later. Work hard at your contacts, the people who will buy or recommend buyers for your work. It's no good writing the finest short story or the best technical description of a new widget if you can't then sell your piece.'

CHAPTER 3.6

Office Skills

Home typing and secretarial work

This kind of work is well suited to those who wish to work from home. Little capital investment is needed apart from a personal computer and a printer.

The choice of a printer is as important as that of the PC itself. Apart from reliability, printer speed and output quality are the two points to look out for in buying a printer. The experts reckon that laser printers combine these qualities most effectively, together with a wide range of graphic capability. Prices have been coming down recently, but allow for £700 to £800. However, if you are only going to do standard typing, printer prices come down by about half. But remember that the more value you can add, the higher the rates you can charge.

No one is going to make a fortune doing typing at home, but the skilled typist may be able to make more money at home than in the average secretarial job, provided she can find sufficient work to do. There are certain pitfalls to be avoided, such as envelope typing, which is notoriously underpaid, but on the whole this is an area in which it is possible to make a reasonable amount of money, and which has the advantage of being flexible enough to fit in with domestic commitments.

We talked to a secretary working at home who gave three pieces of advice to other competent typists/secretaries thinking of working independently: 'Aim your services at the person who does not have sufficient work to employ a secretary (eg local small businesses) or the person with the one-off major job (eg the PhD student with a 500-page thesis). Price your regular work by the hour, and for one-off jobs quote an overall fee. Unless you have an answerphone, be wary of offering to let your clients quote your phone number as a place where messages can be left - you'll be woken up during the night and if you pop out to the shops a desperately urgent call will go unanswered.'

How to find work

Classified advertisements are one source: authors sometimes advertise for people to type their manuscripts, for example. However, you will probably do better to insert your own classified advertisements in selected newspapers or put a note on the local university notice board offering to type manuscripts, theses, etc. Another good place to advertise is the trade press, particularly if you have experience of doing secretarial work in a specialised area. Local advertising in shop windows, local newspapers and magazines might also be effective, as people requiring your services would have the advantage of knowing that you were close at hand.

It is perhaps better, though, to contact potential employers direct. People such as local clergymen, doctors and architects, and various clubs, associations, and even some businessmen often require part-time secretarial services, which can easily be provided from home. For this kind of work, it helps if you can do audio-typing, as you can then collect tapes and take them home rather than having to take shorthand dictation. Do not, however, overlook what some people regard as the best source of all – former employers.

Rates of pay

Pay for home typing is around £8 per hour, or more if you are particularly skilled, if you are typing mathematical formulae or if you are working to a tight brief. Thesis and manuscript typing is sometimes paid according to the number of words typed, with a fixed charge per 100 words, though this is not a sensible arrangement if the quality of the copy from which you have to work varies considerably. For letter typing an hourly charge is usually preferable. Remember to keep an accurate record of the number of hours worked, and include the time that you have to spend collecting and delivering work.

Running your own typing agency

The employment agency field no longer offers the kind of opportunities it once did, as many large firms have moved into the area. However, there is one type of agency, admittedly limited in scope, which is a reasonable proposition for the independent operator. This is the small envelope typing and direct mail agency. You contact firms which do a lot of their business by sending circulars out to people, offering to handle their whole distribution, typing envelopes or labels, inserting circulars into envelopes and handling postage. The administrative work for this kind of business can easily be handled by one person (from his or her own home if convenient) and the actual mechanical work of envelope typing and stuffing can be farmed out to outworkers.

Typesetting

If you are a *very* good typist, one of the most interesting and worthwhile possibilities for freelance work is typesetting. A high degree of skill is needed, and a fairly large investment (particularly for a photosetting machine), but this area offers far greater potential for high earnings and job involvement than straightforward typing.

The job involves preparation of typed matter which will eventually be printed photographically. Most magazines, advertisements and books are now produced in this way rather than by traditional letterpress printing. The best way to get involved in this area would be to gain some initial experience by working for a small typesetting firm, before setting up on your own.

Rates for jobs vary considerably – according to the type of job, the deadline to be met, the quality of your machine, your accuracy, etc. It is best to quote per page rates, and you will need considerable experience to be able to assess and 'price' whole manuscripts! Work can be obtained from publishing firms, design consultants, advertising agents, etc.

CHAPTER 3.7

Playgroups

Playgroup leaders

Playgroups cater for pre-school age children, and are usually run on a fairly informal basis, either by one woman in her own home (possibly with the help of a friend or neighbour) or, for larger groups, by several people using a public hall or similar premises.

No formal training is needed. The criteria for playgroup leaders are laid down by each local social services department. Many local authorities now organise courses for playgroup supervisors, and the National Extension College (18 Brooklands Avenue, Cambridge CB2 2HN) plans a correspondence course to start in 1994.

If you are planning to run a playgroup in your own home, you must be prepared to invest a certain amount of money in sturdy, sound equipment (climbing frame, sandpit, painting equipment, constructional toys, etc). You will need insurance, and you will have to make sure that your home meets the required safety standards, so the Fire Officer will have to inspect your premises. You will also need planning permission, and you are legally obliged to register your playgroup with the local Department of Social Services, which is able to reject planning permission and prohibit that group being organised if it feels that the applicant is not suitable to hold the position.

Most of these requirements also apply to larger, hall-based groups, though you will probably not need to apply for planning permission, since most halls have permission for a variety of community activities which would include playgroups. Larger groups are often run by a committee consisting of the supervisors, at least one parent, the local health visitor, a secretary and a chairman. Staff requirements for a large group (of, say, 25 children) would include a supervisor, one or two paid assistants, and helpers working on a rota basis.

Fees can be calculated by adding together total costs (wages, rent, insurance, a fund for equipment, day-to-day expenses such as postage, repairs, etc) and dividing the total by the number of children who will be attending. If you find that the resulting fees are too high for local mothers to afford, the playgroup can be subsidised by fund-raising activities such as fêtes and bazaars. It will help you to cover your costs if you charge fees in advance, and it is also a good idea to charge an 'absentee' fee of half the normal rate for children who are unable to attend for short periods. For further information, contact the Pre-School Playgroups Association (PPA). They have offices in London (61–63 King's Cross Road, London WC1X 9LL), Glasgow (14 Elliot Place, Glasgow G3 8EP) and Belfast (Boucher Crescent, Boucher Road, Belfast BT12 6HU).

CHAPTER 3.8

Selling

Dealing in antiques

If you know what you are doing – and it must be stressed that this is a big 'if' – you can make money out of buying and selling antiques, to dealers, on a market stall, or at one of the increasing number of 'antique fairs' that are organised in various kinds of public building.

Standard antiques are easily recognised and their values are well known through the existence of various price guides. You are unlikely to get a bargain there, though you may pick up the odd underpriced item. A more promising avenue is to specialise, preferably in an area that is not well charted and where you can use your knowledge and taste to beat the odds: clothes are a case in point. However, if you have an expert knowledge, even of some well-known area like pottery, you can pick up bargains in the sense that you might be able to get a piece that is marked at normal antique shop prices but that you know to be worth far more.

Mail order selling

Many people, particularly women, earn money acting as agents for mail order companies. Anyone over 18 can apply to become an agent, based at home and offering the company's goods as advertised in catalogues which are produced once or twice a year. They receive a commission of 10 or 12½ per cent on sales they make, in return for which they collect and record payments from customers and send regular payments to the mail order company. There may be additional problems of receiving and distributing goods, returning faulty products, dealing with bad debts, etc. These may be considerable if the agent tries to build up a large number of clients, drawn from a wide circle. Many do not do so, preferring to use the catalogues as a source of goods, purchased on credit terms, for friends and family. Few people earn a decent income as an agent, and some who do may experience administrative and other difficulties.

Market stall selling

Although street vending proper tends to be dominated by full-time market sales people with their own barrows and storage lock-ups, there are quite a few vacant sites up and down the country where much more informal market trading goes on. Some of these belong to local authorities; others to private landlords. They have fixed stalls, which are let at weekends on a first come, first served basis. There are limitations on what you can sell – some places, for instance, will not let you sell fresh food or produce because of environmental health regulations – but otherwise the field is wide open. Existing stallholders will usually tell you about the conditions and where to apply for a stall. They can usually be rented on a daily basis at about £25.

Party plan selling

A more elaborate, but also better-paid form of selling is party plan selling, of which the oldest and best-known example is the Tupperware party. The agent in this case recruits hosts or hostesses to give a tea or coffee and biscuits party at which guests are invited to inspect and order the goods brought in for display by the agent. He or she picks up the orders, then delivers the goods to the hostess who is responsible for getting them to the customers and who herself gets a gift for her trouble. The agent's role, in other words, is as much to recruit hosts as to sell the goods. This is a much more demanding form of selling than a mail order agency and is correspondingly better rewarded – commissions run as high as 30 per cent, with bonuses over and above that.

Selling produce

Anyone who has a big enough garden or allotment can make money selling produce: flowers, fruit, vegetables, herbs, honey, home-made jams and chutneys, and eggs.* If you live in or near a main road the easiest way to sell things is simply to put up a stall or barrow at your gate, or else a notice directing people to your house. If you live right off the

---

* Before you start to apply for planning permission, ask a lawyer or the local Citizens' Advice Bureau whether your action would contravene sales legislation or EC regulations on the sale of farm produce.

beaten track you might find it easier to sell to your village store or to one of the 'farm shops' that are to be found now in many villages. In the summer you can make a lot of money from passing trade – tourists and city dwellers on the lookout for country produce.

Two worthwhile investments, when you have made enough money, are a deep freeze and a greenhouse. With a deep freeze, you can freeze surplus fruit and vegetables to sell in the winter, or for people to transfer to their own freezers. This enables you to make a bit more money in the lean winter months. With a greenhouse, you can grow some of the more exotic vegetables such as green peppers and aubergines, produce potted plants, especially for the Christmas trade, and offer bedding plants such as tomatoes for sale to other gardeners.

How much should you charge? A quick scout round the local shops will tell you what the going rate is for the more usual fruit and vegetables. You should, of course, charge more than shop prices for home-made jams, jellies and chutneys.

PART 4:
Freelance Work

Introduction

There are obviously overlaps between working part-time and working as a freelance. A person contributing regular articles to journals and newspapers could be doing so part-time and still be described as a freelance. In general, though, a freelance is regarded as someone who is self-employed full-time, providing a service to a range of different principals as the demand occurs, or as he or she can persuade them to buy the service that is being offered.

Some occupations have a very high freelance content because of the unpredictability of the flow of work. The prime example is the world of films and television. Over a third of the members of BECTU (Broadcasting, Entertainment, Cinematograph Technicians' Union, formerly ACTT), the principal trade union in this sphere, are freelances, employed by a variety of different companies for anything from a day to six months, according to the duration of a particular project. Performing artists, too, tend almost exclusively to be freelances, even though they may have spells when they are attached to a particular orchestra or a repertory company.

In the media and even in certain parts of industry, the tendency to put work out to freelances and other suppliers of *ad hoc* labour is growing rapidly. When trading conditions are uncertain, employers are reluctant to commit themselves to taking on people full-time. It makes more sense to bring them in as and when they are needed or to commission them – even to the point of subcontracting whole jobs to them.

There are also many tasks in many firms which need to be done but where the in-house demand is neither large nor constant enough to justify the employment of a full-time member of staff. It is people in such occupations, which can range from manual jobs like that of the firm's carpenter to services like public relations, who often find themselves at risk when times get hard. Yet, operating as freelances for their own firm, plus other clients, they often have a highly profitable new lease of working life.

How freelances find work

The circumstances just described bring out a number of points about freelance work. It is often very difficult, for instance, simply to decide to 'go freelance', as many redundant executives have found to their cost when they wanted to set up as consultants. You need to have contacts, reliable sources of work and a known track record in your chosen area. Many freelances report, in fact, that their first client was their previous employer or someone whom they got to know through their former workplace.

Even so, freelance work is patchy and unpredictable. The elements of self-marketing and constant self-motivation are vital. Freelance management consultants, for instance, reckon to spend at least 40 per cent of their time hunting for work: identifying opportunities from reports in the business, trade or professional press, and following them up with letters, phone calls or proposals. The same pattern can be seen in other freelance occupations: photographers and entertainers check in with their agents; writers prepare material 'on spec' for book and magazine publishers. It is a fairly insecure life until you get established and clients start ringing you, rather than the other way round. Indeed, many freelances are of the opinion that to make a success of it, you need at least one reliable source of regular work – someone who brings you in for one day a week, for instance.

Characteristics of freelance work

The reason why a lot of practising freelances recommend getting this kind of underlay is not purely financial. There are also psychological factors involved, especially for those who have previously worked alongside others. Freelancing is a lonely way to earn a living. With some kinds of job – writing for instance – you can spend weeks on end without seeing anyone.

It is also unpredictable. There can be long periods, particularly when you first start, when little or no work comes in and your bank balance sinks as low as your spirits. As a self-employed person, you cannot claim unemployment benefit either, even though no work is coming through. On the other hand, you still have to pay your National Insurance stamp.

Periods of inactivity may be broken up by spells when the workload is almost too much. Very few freelances ever turn work away, though. Once you lose a potential customer – even though you may not need him at that juncture – he is very difficult to get back when circumstances change. If, however, you can't do the job because it coincides with something else, it is essential to say so rather than to make promises that cannot be kept. This applies to delivery dates as well.

Costing and pricing

Broadly, the rules set out in Chapter 1.8 apply, but there are additional factors to consider. As we have said, you often have to spend a considerable amount of time just looking for work; it varies, obviously, according to your status and occupation. On the other hand, whether you can reflect this fact in full in your scale of charges depends on our old friends – supply and demand. As against that, you have the advantage, in the case of many types of freelance work, that you are working from home. Usually your equipment costs are low too, though that would not be true of photography. The employer, in engaging you, should consider that it is generally reckoned that the cost of having a person on the staff full-time is twice their annual salary, taking into account NI contributions, holidays, pensions and so forth.

Income tax and freelance work

Freelances are normally taxed under Schedule D. However, as we have pointed out at the end of Chapter 1.12, the Inland Revenue are challenging Schedule D status where a substantial amount of work is done for one particular employer, as that in effect constitutes a master-and-servant relationship. This is a particular danger when people work through an agency and are paid by the agency, not by the client.

CHAPTER 4.2

Management Consultancy

Anybody can call himself a management consultant, though there is a professional organisation, the Institute of Management Consultants (IMC), membership of which is reserved for people who have actually practised in a recognised consultancy firm. Such people should find it relatively easier to get freelance assignments and there is in fact a body called the Richmond Group which consists of some 60 independent management consultants – mostly people who have worked for bigger firms and then set up on their own. The Group embraces a nationwide network of freelance consultants, all of whom, they stress, must have the MIMC qualification.

There are several groups like this, though it is hard to get particulars of any one of them since there is no national organisation of freelance management consultants. However, the way the Richmond Group operates is probably typical: it has an administrator – herself a freelance who works for some 30 hours a week. It runs conferences and issues a handbook. Within the members of the Richmond Group there is a good deal of *ad hoc* networking. Members form project groups to tackle a particular assignment, or bring in colleagues to handle some aspects of a job where a fellow member has special expertise. There is a membership fee, which is quite modest. However, there are some groups where membership fees are a proportion of fee income. Joining such a group can be highly effective, but you have to be sure that the fee represents value for money: is it, for instance, being spent on marketing or on maintaining an office from which the members derive no convincing benefit? Such groups, in the main, consist of qualified consultants.

What happens if you are not qualified? Many redundant managers think that setting up as a consultant is the answer to unemployment, but unless you have very specific expertise to offer and are known in your industry, this is by no means easy. The best way to start is by getting an assignment from your old firm. It is always easier to get more work if you can point to a task you are already doing or which you have completed. Former business contacts are also a possible source of work, but you have to come up with a specific proposal to have any chance of success with your approach: a suggestion for action in some area where you know they have a problem and you have the expertise to solve it.

It is generally considered that the going rate for freelance consultancy is around £30 to £50 an hour. A big firm of consultants would charge three or four times that amount, so the opportunities for freelance work are in approaching smaller clients who could not afford such rates. Local Chambers of Commerce and Enterprise Agencies might provide some leads. Some leading firms of headhunters have occasional assignments for 'interim executives' – medium-term contracts running for three to six months. You do, however, need to have a decent brochure which spells out exactly what your particular expertise is. You also have to reckon with the fact that a lot of your time will be spent on promotion and pitching for jobs. It is reckoned that you need savings equivalent to a year's income to get yourself established as a management consultant.

Good sources of information are *Start and Run a Profitable Consultancy* and *101 Ways to Succeed as an Independent Consultant*, which are full of useful tips; both are published by Kogan Page.

One unofficial piece of advice is to be very careful about describing yourself as a management consultant unless you have actually practised as one. Because of the number of managers on the job market filling in time between jobs by doing some consultancy – or trying to do so – the term has become somewhat synonymous with redundancy. It is better to describe yourself by some other term, such as adviser – with a very specific, one-line description of your particular area of expertise.

CHAPTER 4.3

Media and Communications

Art and design

There are numerous opportunities for freelances in this area if you have talent, creativity, the ability to meet deadlines and a range of contacts in the business. You may be a book designer, illustrator, clothes designer, cartoonist, or furniture or three-dimensional designer. The message is the same: if you are good and people who have used you have liked your work, you will be given a steady stream of work, for which you will be well paid.

You will probably have a design qualification, and you should specialise, but your chosen specialism does not have to be the area in which you qualified. Many designers and illustrators supplement their income by taking on freelance work, and graduate to full self-employment later.

If you are successful as a freelance designer, you should invest in a good, well-lit, well-ventilated studio in which to work. And if demand for your services is very great, think about expansion: is there someone whose work is good who could be taken on as a business partner perhaps, and could you delegate administrative chores to someone?

Editorial work

For proof-reading and copy-editing, experience in a publishing house is a prerequisite. People tend to feel that proof-reading, in particular, only requires a good command of spelling and an eye for detail, but in fact it really requires some knowledge of the way a book is actually put together, and an eye for the kinds of mistake that an inexperienced person would not necessarily pick up. No inexperienced person would be able to obtain freelance editorial work from any publishing firm. However, if you have worked in publishing you may be able to obtain

---

GO FREELANCE!

Train this year as a freelance book editor and proofreader. No overheads, no capital investment. Excellent part-time or full-time opportunities if you have the ambition.

Correspondence courses and seminars from very experienced and respected trainers.

Telephone or write for full details: **Chapterhouse Publishing** (Dept Y), Heath Barton, Pinhoe, Exeter EX4 8QW. Tel: (0392) 69298

---

freelance work through personal contacts. Forget the idea of advertising your services: it will almost certainly not work.

Editorial work is particularly suited to freelancing: most of it can be done more quickly and thoroughly in the quiet of one's own home than in the distracting hubbub of an office atmosphere. It also has the advantage of being time-consuming; once you have obtained a particular piece of work, you will usually find that it guarantees you one to two weeks' employment and so you do not get into the situation, in which some freelances find themselves, of having to spend much of the time collecting and delivering work.

Film-making

This is a notoriously competitive area; for every success, there are 99 (perhaps 999) failures. You will need experience of a range of techniques, including video and slide presentation, and you should work quickly and creatively, fulfilling commissions on time and to the specified budget. Only the fortunate few will *choose* which films to make; the rest will have to be satisfied with industrial, training and promotional films and perhaps commercials. But, remember, these often require great skill and imagination, will provide good experience and may lead to more ambitious and more personally fulfilling projects later.

Freelance journalism

Freelance journalism sounds like an attractive occupation, but it is an extremely difficult one to break into unless you have previously worked as a journalist and have the necessary contacts. Certainly, general journalism can be written off as a dead loss. Freelances writing about politics, literature, humour, sport, etc, do make a great deal of money once they are established, but the number who fall into this category is probably less than two or three dozen in all. The only place where an outsider has a chance is in specialisms, particularly in technical subjects where few professional journalists feel at home. There is, for instance, a great need for freelances in various aspects of information technology and computers.

If you are interested in freelance journalism in spheres such as this – and have the necessary background knowledge – read the main journals to see what sort of topics they cover and how long their articles tend to be. If you see any gaps that you think would be interesting, write to the editor with your suggestions and state your qualifications and background. Going rates at the moment are between £150 and £250 per thousand words.

Photography

As in other fields, in freelance photography you are more likely to succeed by organisation, reliability and perseverance than by sheer talent alone. If you are submitting samples of your work to magazines, journals and newspapers you must expect to have a large proportion of your work rejected, but on the small proportion that *is* accepted you can gradually build up your reputation with your clients.

Don't be misled by camera fanatics – it is important, of course, to have good reliable equipment, but to be a successful professional photographer you don't necessarily need the most expensive, up-to-date gadgets and accessories. Far better to have sound, reliable equipment which you are happy with and you *know* you can take good pictures with, and to take great care with the presentation of your work.

How to get work
Freelance photography embraces such a wide area that it is difficult to cover all the possible avenues of entry to the profession. One fact stands out: there are a great many competent photographers, and so to be successful your pictures will need to have some special quality that makes them stand out, not necessarily in terms of technical proficiency but in terms of ideas. If you are trying to break into the women's magazine field, for example, it is no good taking along a portfolio of photographs which are almost exactly the same as the ones the magazine uses already; they know photographers who can produce these, and you must give them a very good reason for using you, as opposed to people they already know and trust.

Most of the larger magazines commission work, for which the photographer is paid on a fee basis. Standard practice for obtaining commissioned work is the submission of a portfolio, backed up by one or more personal visits, and it is likely that your personality and ideas will carry more weight with the art editor than will your technical expertise, though of course you must be technically competent. Again, it may be worth specialising: in landscape photography, fashion, sport, or a similar area with a readily definable range of potential users of your material.

Submitting work 'on spec'

It is possible to make a living by submitting selections of prints to magazines 'on spec', particularly if you concentrate on small, specialised publications and local magazines and newspapers.

Presentation of your work is very important. Prints should be of the highest quality possible, and should be carefully packed to avoid damage by the Post Office. Your work should be clearly labelled, and to avoid confusion it is a good idea to have a referencing number on each photograph.

You should offer 'single reproduction rights': this means that the print can be resold at a later date, and you retain the copyright.

Wedding photographs, passports, portraits

This area is one of the most attractive to people who want to make extra money from photography on a part-time basis, possibly graduating to full-time freelance work when they have established themselves. Work can be obtained through local advertising and personal contacts, and your local camera club should be able to give help and suggestions.

Payment

Rates of pay vary tremendously, since the work itself is so varied. Fees for commissioned work for the high-circulation magazines can be substantial, but most of this work goes to established photographers.

It is important to remember when dealing with magazines that payment may be delayed by as much as six months, and if you try to push for early payment you may make yourself very unpopular. It is unlikely, in any event, that you will be paid before publication. If you are going to be a full-time freelance photographer, therefore, you shouldn't under-capitalise yourself, as it may be a year or so before you really begin to make enough money to live on.

PR and advertising consultancy

This is an expanding area with good opportunities for the self-employed person who has worked in promotion and marketing and now wants to work independently. But there are problems: how do you compete with large agencies with massive resources? The answer is that, for the most part, you do not: you offer consultancy (often to the agency rather than to the firm) on specific projects, in areas in which you have expertise. You can then allow your enterprise to develop, perhaps employing staff, developing and diversifying your services and challenging the larger organisations. In the short term, cultivate contacts, specialise in a single area, show very personal attention to clients and be satisfied with a steady flow of small projects.

We spoke to a public relations consultant who gave this advice to people thinking of going it alone: 'You have to do two things simultaneously – first the work in hand and second the constant search for new clients. Doing the former will obviously help with the latter, but don't get so tied up in your current work that you neglect to look ahead. If you start getting fairly regular work from a client then suggest you move from billing on a job-by-job basis to an annual contract; this will help your cash flow enormously and such a contract is also of very high value when talking to your bank manager or building society.' One caveat: many firms include a clause in your contract which stops you working with a client for a given period if you leave that company. This reflects the closeness of customers and particular individuals within their agencies. So, check the small print of your contract before trying to bring your three closest contacts among your old company's clients into your newly formed outfit.

Research

The term 'research' covers a broad area. Many researchers for television and radio, for various companies, for advertising agencies and for marketing organisations are not freelance. Some people do part-time market research (for which a telephone and car and an outgoing personality are necessary). Others work in individual research projects, for which particular academic and professional qualifications may be necessary. In general, a researcher should have had varied experience, the capacity to work independently and quickly and to understand a library cataloguing system, and should be able to write reasonably well and to type. Opportunities to work may be erratic, and a range of very different projects may be taken on. There will probably be less opportunity to build relationships with particular clients, and assignments will often be one-off jobs. Rates of pay will also vary considerably.

Repairs and Servicing of Vehicles

Every car owner believes himself to be a mechanic, but to be able to work on a wide range of cars and deal with many different types of problem requires considerable expertise. So, do not set up a car workshop if you do not have the necessary training and experience. Moreover, you will require a good deal of capital – to acquire large premises, and the range of materials and fittings needed to undertake the work. Competition is also severe: there are many large, established garages with a team of mechanics. Can you provide services at competitive prices and with comparable efficiency and speed? Garage mechanics get a bad press, but this does not necessarily make the area an easy one in which to establish a new operation.

Dennis Edmonson, who specialises in car repairs and servicing, emphasises the need for expertise: 'Don't be tempted to take on work you are not sure you can complete to a high standard. Familiarise yourself with all the rules and regulations which surround the transport industry today, and don't get flustered·by the bureaucrats who will constantly be on at you. Be wary of the travellers and agents who will call every week trying to con you into purchasing materials/machinery you don't really need.'

CHAPTER 4.5

Technical Sales

Many smaller manufacturers cannot afford their own sales force and use independent sales agents. These are generally people with previous sales experience who represent several companies with broadly related products, so that they can achieve an economical call pattern.

Sales agents operate on commission, which may range from 2½ per cent on capital equipment to as much as 40 to 50 per cent on 'hard sell' items like home extensions. The usual commissions, though, are around 10 to 15 per cent of sales volume.

Sales agents are paid purely by results, but apart from that their relationships with their principals are not substantially different from those of ordinary employed salespeople. Having agreed a mutually acceptable set of sales targets, agents are responsible for maintaining good customer relations, for providing regular progress reports and journey forecasts, and for feeding back reactions to the principals' products, including ideas for improvements and even for new products.

If you are thinking of becoming a sales agent, you should have a car and at least six months' working capital – that is how long it takes before the level of commissions, usually paid monthly, starts to cover outgoings. Indeed, as with any form of self-employment, preparing a cash flow forecast to make sure that the project is viable, at least on paper, is a wise prerequisite.

Another good move is to join the British Agents Register. For a modest annual subscription members get a variety of services, not the least of which is entry on a computerised list which matches agents, their operating territories and their specialisations with the many inquiries BAR gets from companies seeking representation. Advertisements from potential clients also appear in the BAR monthly newsletter.

CHAPTER 4.6

Direct Selling

Direct selling involves selling products, mostly in the household, garden and cosmetics sphere to friends, neighbours and other contacts. Names like Tupperware and Avon are already familiar, but in recent years they have been joined by an increasing number of direct sales companies, such as Betterware and Kleeneze Homecare. Many companies offer some basic sales training, but for many people the main difficulty is to overcome cultural inhibitions about selling to social contacts.

Essentially selling is done from a catalogue and samples. The Direct Selling Association's Code of conduct specifically advises people to avoid any scheme 'which encourages or permits investment in goods for resale as a way of earning preferential discounts on purchase in advance of customer orders, or as a way of gaining an immediate higher appointment in the organisation'.

The market for what Betterware prefers to call 'home shopping' is large and growing. Members of the Direct Selling Organisation have seen profits and turnover grow rapidly while ordinary retailing has been declining. As the multiples rationalise their shelf display, so niche retailing – considered to be a major growth area – is moving to other channels, such as direct selling. But basic household items are also being supplied direct. This is because, in the words of a *Sunday Times* article: 'Leading supermarket chains would rather sell a high margin prepared dinner than a lowly tin opener.' However, the range of goods supplied by leading direct sales firms is now quite wide and includes many relatively high-priced items.

Finding work is largely up to the individual, with some basic guidance on the principles of how to go about it from existing agents. Betterware reckons that its distributors have a customer base of about 1000 households each. Income is based on the margin between the selling price and the discount to the agent: typically around 40 per cent.

There are two main hazards. One is that there are a number of cowboy direct sales firms, which not only supply shoddy items but also use a variety of high pressure techniques which are nevertheless just inside the border of legality.

The other is that of firms which, while being perfectly reputable, have too limited a range of products. Once everyone you know has bought an all-purpose home widget through you, however good it is, what do you do next?

For more details write to The Direct Selling Association, 29 Floral Street, London WC2B 9DP; 071-497 1234.

APPENDICES

APPENDIX 1

Further Information

Before taking the plunge, it is absolutely essential to get all the help and advice you can, especially if you are planning to invest a lot of money in a business. Ring one of the specialist bodies listed below, go to the public library, do as much background reading as you have time for, consult your bank manager, solicitor and accountant, and talk to any friends who have succeeded in the area in which you are interested.

Employment Department
Telephone freefone 'Enterprise direct' on 0800 222999 to be put through to your nearest Small Firms Centre. The same service is also offered by:

Northern Ireland
Local Enterprise Development Unit
(LEDU)
LEDU House
Upper Galwally
Belfast BT8 4TB
Tel: 0232 491031

Department of Commerce
IDB House
64 Chichester Street
Belfast BT1 4JX
Tel: 0232 233233

Training and Enterprise Councils (in England and Wales) are listed in Yellow Pages under 'Business enterprise agencies'; the central organisation, in case of need, is:

The Employment Department
Training and Enterprise Educational Directorate
Moorfoot
Sheffield SH1 4PQ
Tel: 0742 753275

Local Enterprise Companies (in Scotland) are listed in Yellow Pages under 'Business enterprise agencies', and the central organisations are:

Highlands and Islands Enterprise
Bridge House
20 Bank Street
Inverness IV1 1QR
Tel: 0463 234171
For the highlands and islands of northern Scotland

Scottish Enterprise
120 Bothwell Street
Glasgow G2 7JP
Tel: 041-248 2700
For central and southern areas of Scotland

Advisory, Conciliation and Arbitration Service (ACAS)
Clifton House
83–117 Euston Road
London NW1 2RB
Tel: 071-396 5100
Also regional offices.

Agricultural Development Advisory Service *(advice for farmers)*
Oxford Spires
The Boulevard
Kidlington
Oxon OX5 1NZ
Tel: 0865 842742

Agricultural Mortgage Corporation Ltd
AMC House
Chantry Street
Andover
Hampshire SP10 1DD
Tel: 0264 334344

Alliance of Small Firms & Self-Employed People
33 The Green
Calne
Wiltshire SN11 8DJ
Tel: 0249 817003

Association of British Factors
24–28 Bloomsbury Way
London WC1A 2PX
Tel: 071-831 4268

Association of British Insurers
51–55 Gresham Street
London EC2V 7HQ
Tel: 071-600 3333

Association of British Travel Agents (ABTA)
55 Newman Street
London W1P 3PG
Tel: 071-637 2444

Association of Independent Businesses
1–4 Atwell Road
London SE15 4TW
Tel: 071-277 6337

BBC External Services
(translation/interpretation work)
PO Box 76
Bush House
Strand
London WC2B 4PH

Booksellers Association
Minster House
272 Vauxhall Bridge Road
London SW1V 1BA
Tel: 071-834 5477

The British Agents Register
24 Mount Parade
Harrogate
North Yorkshire HG1 1BP
Tel: 0423 560608

British Franchise Association Ltd
Thames View
Newtown Road
Henley on Thames
Oxfordshire RG9 1HG
Tel: 0491 578049

British Technology Group
101 Newington Causeway
London SE1 6BU
Tel: 071-403 6666

British Venture Capital Association
3 Catherine Place
London SW1E 6DX
Tel: 071-233 5212

Business in the Community
8 Stratton Street
London W1X 5FD
Tel: 071-629 1600
For details of Enterprise Agencies in England and Wales; and

Scottish Business in the Community
Romano House
43 Station Road
Corstorphine
Edinburgh EH12 7AF
Tel: 031-334 9876
For details of Enterprise Trusts in Scotland

Choice Magazine *(retirement planning)*
Apex House
Oundle Road
Peterborough PE2 9NP
Tel: 0733 555123

Confederation of British Industry (CBI)
Smaller Firms Council
Centre Point
103 New Oxford Street
London WC1A 1DU
Tel: 071-379 7400

Cranfield School of Management
Cranfield
Bedford MK43 0AL
Tel: 0234 751122

The Data Protection Registrar
Springfield House
Water Lane
Wilmslow
Cheshire SK9 5AX
Tel: 0625 535777

Department of Employment
Caxton House
Tothill Street
London SW1H 9NF
Tel: 071-273 6969

Department of Trade and Industry
1 Victoria Street
London SW1H 0ET
Tel: 071-215 5000

The Design Council
28 Haymarket
London SW1Y 4SU
Tel: 071-839 8000

The Ethnic Minority Business Development Unit
City of London Polytechnic
Calcutta House
Old Castle Street
London E1 7NT
Tel: 071-283 1030

Federation of Agricultural Cooperatives (UK) Ltd
17 Waterloo Place
Leamington Spa
Warwickshire CV32 5LA
Tel: 0926 450445

Federation of Master Builders
14–15 Great James Street
London WC1N 3DP
Tel: 071-242 7583

Federation of Small Businesses
32 St Anne's Road West
Lytham St Annes
Lancashire FY8 1NY
Tel: 0253 720911

Finance and Leasing Association
18 Upper Grosvenor Street
London W1X 9PB
Tel: 071-491 2783

Institute of Linguists
24a Highbury Grove
London N5 2EA
Tel: 071-359 7445

Institute of Management
Small Firms Information Service
Management House
Cottingham Road
Corby
Northamptonshire NN17 1TT
Tel: 0536 204222

**Institute of Management
Consultants**
32–33 Hatton Garden
London EC1N 8DL
Tel: 071-242 2140

**Institute of Patentees and
Inventors**
Suite 505A
Triumph House
189 Regent Street
London W1R 7WF
Tel: 071-242 7812

Investors in Industry (3i)
91 Waterloo Road
London SE1 8XP
Tel: 071-928 3131

Law Society
Legal Aid Department
113 Chancery Lane
London WC2A 1PL
Tel: 071-242 1222

**London Chamber of Commerce
and Industry**
33 Queen Street
London EC4R 1AP
Tel: 071-248 4444

London Enterprise Agency
4 Snow Hill
London EC1A 2BS
Tel: 071-236 3000

Market Research Society
15 Northburgh Street
London EC1V 0AH
Tel: 071-490 4911

**National Association of
Shopkeepers**
Lynch House
91 Mansfield Road
Nottingham NG1 3FN
Tel: 0602 475046

National Extension College
18 Brooklands Avenue
Cambridge CB2 2HN
Tel: 0223 316644

National Farmers' Union
Agriculture House
Knightsbridge
London SW1X 7NJ
Tel: 071-235 5077

**National Federation of Retail
Newsagents**
Yeoman House
Sekforde Street
London EC1R 0HD
Tel: 071-253 4225

**Northern Consultants
Association**
Unit 1A
Mountjoy Research Centre
Durham DH1 3SW
Tel: 091-386 0800

Office of Fair Trading
Field House
Breams Buildings
London EC4A 1PR
Tel: 071-242 2858

The Patent Office
Cardiff Road
Newport
Gwent NP9 1RH
Tel: 0633 814000
Enquiries only 071-829 6910

Registrar of Companies
Companies Registration Office
Crown Way
Maindy
Cardiff CF4 3UZ
Tel: 0222 388588

**Pre-Retirement Association of
Greater London**
2 Doughty Street
London WC1N 2PH
Tel: 071-404 6664

Rural Development Commission
141 Castle Street
Salisbury
Wiltshire SP1 3TP
Tel: 0722 336255

Small Business Bureau
46 Westminster Palace Gardens
Artillery Row
London SW1P 1RR
Tel: 071-976 7262

Society of Indexers
38 Rochester Road
London NW1 9JJ
Tel: 071-916 7809

Stock Exchange
Old Broad Street
London EC2N 1HP
Tel: 071-588 2355

Translators' Association
Society of Authors
84 Drayton Gardens
London SW10 9SD
Tel: 071-373 6642

West Dean College
West Dean
Chichester
West Sussex PO18 0QZ
Tel: 0243 63301

Women in Enterprise
4 Co-operative Street
Horbury
Wakefield WF4 6DR
No phone. Send SAE.

APPENDIX 2

Select Bibliography

Part 1

Accounting for Non-Accountants, 4th edition, Graham Mott (Kogan Page)
The Allied Dunbar Tax Guide, W I Sinclair (Longman, published annually)
Be Your Own Boss!, David Mc Mullan (Kogan Page)
Croner's Reference Book for the Self-employed and Smaller Business (Croner Publications Ltd)
Directory of Enterprise Agencies (Business in the Community)
Fair Deal: A Shopper's Guide, Office of Fair Trading
Forming a Limited Company, 4th edition, Patricia Clayton (Kogan Page)
Going Freelance, 4th edition, Godfrey Golzen (Kogan Page)
A Guide to Franchising, Martin Mendelsohn (Cassell)
Looking Ahead: A Guide to Retirement, Fred Kemp and Bernard Buttle (Springfield)
Management of Trade Credit, T G Hutson and J Butterworth (Gower Press)
Managing for Results, Peter F Drucker (Pan Books)
Selling to Europe, 2nd edition, Roger Bennett
The Small Business Casebook, Sue Birley (Macmillan Press)
The Small Business Guide, 3rd edition, C Barrow (BBC Publications)
Small Business Guide, S Williams (Penguin)

Many of the pamphlets produced by the Department of Trade and Industry, the Department of Social Security, the Inland Revenue, the Employment Department and the Department of the Environment will also be of value.

Parts 2, 3 and 4

All About Selling, A Williams (McGraw-Hill)
British Rate & Data (monthly)
The Catering Management Handbook 1994, Judy Ridgway and Brian Ridgway (Kogan Page)
How to Run Your Own Restaurant, B Sim and William Gleeson
Money, Health and Your Retirement, E V Eves (Paperback Choice)
Setting up a Workshop (Crafts Council)

278

Writers' & Artists' Yearbook (A & C Black)
Writing for the BBC, Norman Longmate (BBC Publications)

Other useful books from Kogan Page

Buying a Shop, 4th edition, A St John Price
Law for the Small Business, 7th edition, Patricia Clayton
Running Your Own Boarding Kennels, 2nd edition, Sheila Zabawa
Running Your Own Catering Company, 2nd edition, Judy Ridgway
Running Your Own Hairdressing Salon, Christine Harvey and Helen Steadman
Running Your Own Photographic Business, 2nd edition, John Rose and Linda Hankin
Running Your Own Playgroup or Nursery, 2nd edition, Jenny Willison
Running Your Own Pub, 2nd edition, Elven Money
Running Your Own Shop, 2nd edition, Roger Cox
The Small Business Action Kit, 4th edition, John Rosthorn and others
Taking up a Franchise, 10th edition, Colin Barrow and Godfrey Golzen
Understand Your Accounts, 3rd edition, A St John Price
Be Your Own Accountant, Philip McNeill and Sarah J P Howarth
Budgeting for Business, Leon Hopkins

Business Cash Books Made Easy, Max Pullen
Business Plans, Brian Finch
Controlling Costs, John F Gittus
Costing Made Easy, Graham Mott
Pricing for Profit, Gregory Lewis
Taxes on Business, Kevin Armstrong

List of Advertisers

Index